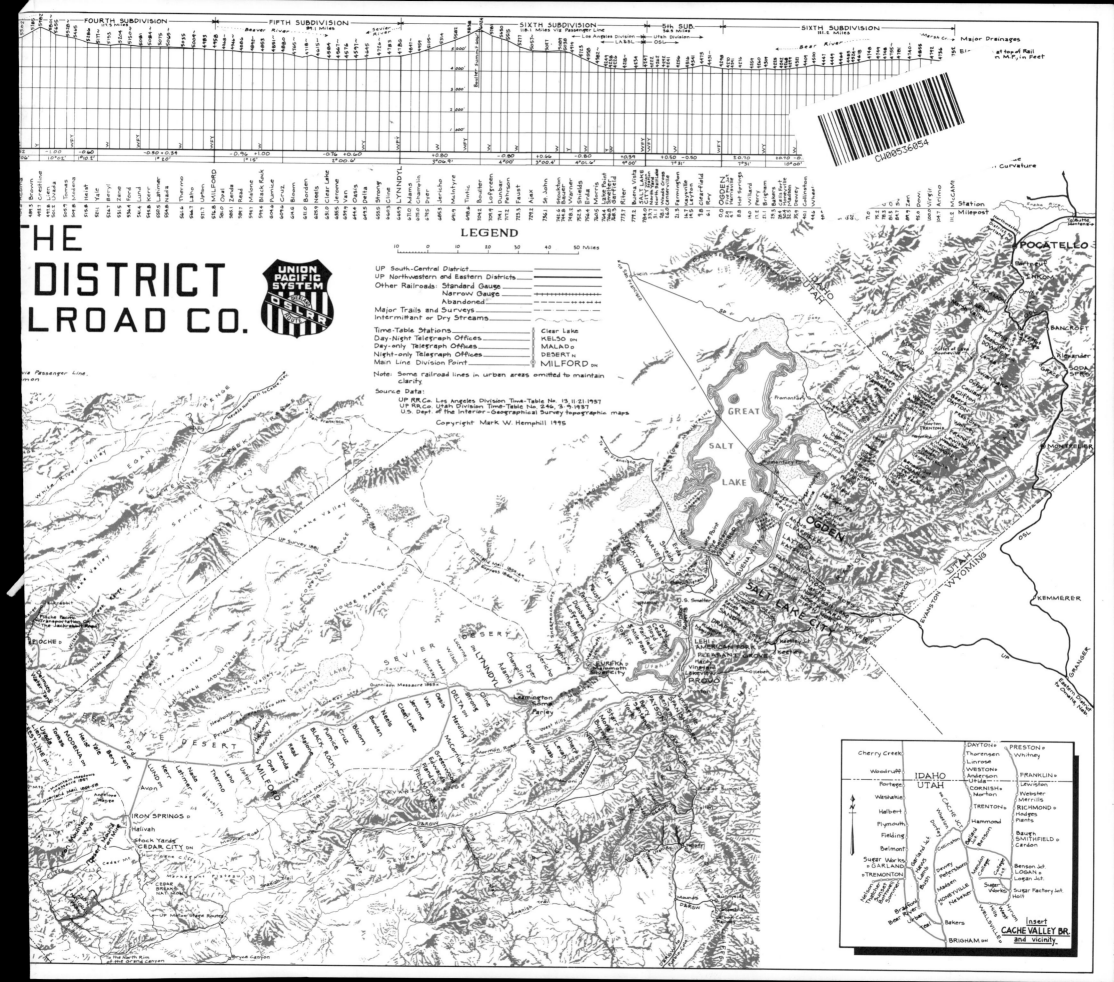

# THE DISTRICT
# [RAI]LROAD CO.

UNION PACIFIC SYSTEM — OVERLAND ROUTE — OSLRR

## LEGEND

| | |
|---|---|
| UP South-Central District | ——————— |
| UP Northwestern and Eastern Districts | ——————— |
| Other Railroads: Standard Gauge | ———+———+——— |
| Narrow Gauge | +++++++++ |
| Abandoned | ++—++—++ |
| Major Trails and Surveys | — — — — |
| Intermittant or Dry Streams | ········· |
| Time-Table Stations | Clear Lake |
| Day-Night Telegraph Offices | KELSO DN |
| Day-only Telegraph Offices | MALAD D |
| Night-only Telegraph Offices | DESERT N |
| Main Line Division Point | MILFORD DN |

Note: Some railroad lines in urban areas omitted to maintain clarity.

Source Data:
UP RR Co. Los Angeles Division Time-Table No. 13, 11-21-1937
UP RR Co. Utah Division Time-Table No. 246, 3-9-1937
U.S. Dept. of the Interior - Geographical Survey topographic maps

Copyright Mark W. Hemphill 1995

Scale: 10  0  10  20  30  40  50 Miles

FOURTH SUBDIVISION · FIFTH SUBDIVISION · SIXTH SUBDIVISION · 5th SUB. · SIXTH SUBDIVISION

Major Drainages — at top of Rail in M.P. in Feet

Insert
## CACHE VALLEY BR.
and vicinity

*I shall always hear their clear, deep exhausts, the cry of their whistles through the night, see the sharp beam
of their headlights piercing ahead and around the curves, through the cuts...the countless stars out on the desert
...the fireman yelling, "Clear order board!"...the wave of an operator's lamp as we passed the open office in a blur
...the caboose marker lights always following.* —Walter Thrall, LA&SL engineer, November 1958

# UNION PACIFIC
## Salt Lake Route

### Mark W. Hemphill

Stoddart

A BOSTON MILLS PRESS BOOK

*For Henry Larson Hemphill and Henry Armond Hemphill*

Canadian Cataloguing in Publication Data

Hemphill, Mark W., 1958–
Union Pacific: Salt Lake Route

ISBN 1-55046-138-9

1. Union Pacific Railroad Company–History
2. Railroads–Pacific States–History.  I. Title

TF25.U5H4 1995     385'.0979     C95–931104–1

Copyright © Mark W. Hemphill, 1995

Quotations from Walter Thrall, Robert Aldag Jr., Tom Baxter, A. C. Kalmbach, and David P. Morgan appear with the permission of *TRAINS Magazine* and Kalmbach Publishing Co.

First Published in 1995 by
The Boston Mills Press
132 Main Street, Erin, Ontario  N0B 1T0
(519) 833-2407   fax: (519) 833-2195

An affiliate of
Stoddart Publishing Co. Limited
34 Lesmill Road, North York, Ontario  M3B 2T6

Layout & Cartography
Mark W. Hemphill

Design & Typesetting
Chris McCorkindale and Sue Breen
McCorkindale Advertising & Design

Copy Editing
Gordon Turner

Printed in China

FRONT JACKET PHOTOGRAPH:
Its four 244 engines churning in sweet unsynchronous harmony, Extra 1604 West rolls its train at a fair pace out of Victorville, California, on October 30, 1950. Stiff white flags, sun visors turned down against the afternoon sun, the smell of hot, oily exhaust, boxcars and reefers begrimed with steam engine soot obediently march by, a yellow caboose dwindles into the distance.... This is the essence of the Union Pacific in southern California's Mojave Desert. *Frank J. Peterson, collection of Alan Miller*

PAGE 1 PHOTOGRAPH:
At dusk on March 18, 1956, the Union Pacific herald on the roof of Salt Lake City Union Station glows bright against a darkening sky. *T. J. Donahue*

PAGE 2 PHOTOGRAPH:
On March 12, 1988, the sun rises through thin winter clouds over the Union Pacific mainline at Basin, California. *Eric Blasko*

PAGE 6 PHOTOGRAPH:
As a smoggy dusk settles over the Pedley Hills on February 29, 1964, train #104, the eastbound *City of Los Angeles,* crosses the Santa Ana River just west of Arlington, California. The San Pedro, Los Angeles & Salt Lake Railroad built this concrete arch bridge in 1904. At the time it was the longest of its type in the world. Its eight 100-foot and two 80-foot spans are still in service today. *Gordon Glattenberg*

BACK JACKET PHOTOGRAPH:
At 7:20 A.M. on March 20, 1985, the sun has begun to light the depths of Meadow Valley Wash. Suddenly the canyon echoes with the noise of Extra 3679 East. It exits Tunnel 8 east of Stine, Nevada, into a brief window of light, then disappears back into the shadows. It has nine loads and 105 empties, mostly grain hoppers from Koppel Bulk Terminal in Long Beach, California. *Eric Blasko*

Boston Mills Press books are available for bulk purchase for sales promotions, premiums, fundraising, and seminars. For details, contact:
Special Sales Department
Stoddart Publishing Co. Limited
34 Lesmill Road, North York, Ontario, Canada  M3B 2T6
Tel: (416) 445-3333   Fax: (416) 445-5967

# TABLE OF CONTENTS

# PREFACE

This story began for me in 1965, when my parents gave me a copy of David F. Myrick's *Railroads of Nevada and Eastern California*, Volume 1. What an amazing, exotic land, the desert! I thought. No clutter of forest and farm and urbanization, just breathtaking vistas, boom towns, and single-track railroads flung far past the frontier. This was a place where possibility hung pregnant in the air. When I first visited the desert in 1980, it was everything I had imagined it to be–even better.

I began this book with the idea that it would be a vehicle for the talents of many photographers, using explanatory captions. I had no intention of writing a history of UP's South-Central District as I believed this had already been done. So I gathered up most of the books ever written about the UP and read them. Soon it became clear that my plan was not going to work: I could not find out enough information to press onwards with this book. I wanted to know about the UP in Utah and in southern California, about the UP's freight traffic and freight trains, about sidings, signals, and switches. Mostly I wanted to know how the UP fits into the broad context of history and geography. I had a lot of questions and I was not finding very many answers.

I thus began the research necessary to answer my questions about the South-Central District. For the history of the South-Central District and its traffic I started fresh with primary sources (written at the time of the event) such as corporate records of the UP, OSL, and LA&SL; periodicals such as *Railway Age, Railway Signaling & Communications, Traffic World, Engineering News, Coal Age, Utah Economic & Business Review,* and *The Mining Congress Journal*; and documents of the Interstate Commerce Commission and the states of Utah, Nevada, and California. For the general history and geography of the region I used many secondary sources, preferably scholarly works. By the time I was finished I had to buy a four-drawer filing cabinet to house the copies I made! I only wish I had the space in this book to present all of this information.

More than any other person Don Strack made this book come together. During my research project Don pointed me in the right directions, gladly answered my questions day and night, and freely shared his years of research on the UP and Utah. Don's enthusiasm for history of all kinds is contagious; it rubs off on me every time we talk. Don is one of few railroad scholars I know concerned not only with the railroad but also with its industrial, geographical, and cultural setting; his ideas have influenced much of this book. I cannot thank him enough for his help.

Mel Patrick provided constant encouragement, which I often needed during many months of research and writing. Mel shares my eagerness for exploring new places, from the abandoned Vulcan Iron Mine at Kelso, California, to the Luxor Hotel in Las Vegas. Mel and Jamie Schmid gave me many insights about railroads and posed many of my research questions. Many of the ideas in this book originated with Mel and Jamie; I only provided the words to flesh out their conceptual frameworks and the documentation to validate their intuition.

I owe David Rector a huge thanks for quickly responding to my requests and furnishing many of the essential documents that I needed throughout the preparation of this book. I could not have completed this book without his help. David Norris answered with exquisite detail my many questions about railroads in the Los Angeles Basin, as did Clifford Prather, and Chard Walker helped with Cajon Pass. James Belmont filled in my gaps on past and current operations in Utah, and Dave Crammer with current operations in California. I owe both Dave Crammer and Jim Belmont a debt of gratitude for taking photographs I needed for this book. Marty Banks answered many questions I had about current operations on the South-Central District. Blair Kooistra and Don Strack put me in touch with several photographers. Eric Blasko, David Norris, David Oroszi, Mel Patrick, Jamie Schmid, Marty Banks, Dave Rector, Don Strack and Tim Zukas all loaned or gave me copies of timetables, books, profiles, and railroad documents I used to write this book.

Alan Burns gave me a copy of Michael Malone's book about Butte, Montana. Barbara Yamamoto at the Port of Los Angeles, Yvonne Evila at the Port of Long Beach, and Bob Senecal at Metropolitan Stevedore updated me about the ports. I am also in debt to the librarians at the University of Illinois at Urbana–Champaign, not just for helping me find things but for having the foresight to accumulate one of the largest collections of railroad books, periodicals, and documents in the world.

David Myrick, Don Strack, Marty Banks, Jim Belmont, Eric Blasko, Rob Leachman, David Norris, Mel Patrick, David Rector, Jamie Schmid, Chard Walker, and Tim Zukas graciously reviewed the manuscript and saved me from numerous embarrassing blunders. I would like to in particular thank David Myrick for sharing with me his encyclopedic knowledge of western railroading, for his stylistic comments, and for instilling in me a passion for desert railroads, and Tim Zukas, whose insistence upon facts in place of speculation and his astonishing grasp of matters both technical and grammatical vastly improved the accuracy and readability of this book. If there are errors in this text, however, they are entirely my responsibility.

I cannot thank enough each of the photographers and owners of photographs represented in this book; without them, this book would not exist. I hope my text has done justice to their outstanding photographs. Their 48 names appear below. Please read these names and remember them. Whether these photographers are represented by one photograph or two dozen, each has preserved for everyone images of the Union Pacific. Each has enriched the historical record immeasurably and each was essential to the success of this book. I want to thank Keith Ardinger, J. P. Barger, Martha Mills, Art Gibson Jr., and especially Alan Miller for allowing me access to their collections. John Denison at Boston Mills Press and Greg McDonnell kept their faith and remained cheerful despite my often glacial progress. My professors at the University of Illinois at Urbana–Champaign, in particular James Barrett, Richard Burkhardt, Orville Vernon Burton, and Evan Melhado, pushed me to refine my level of analysis, and along with Nora Few and Diane Gottheil at the Medical Scholars Program encouraged me to pursue my interest in the history of railroads and railroaders. Lastly, I want to thank my wife, Linda, who retained her sense of humor despite the thousands of hours I devoted to this book and impartially reviewed my work at every step. I do not know words enough to thank all of you.

Mark W. Hemphill, January 1995

| | | | |
|---|---|---|---|
| Keith Ardinger | Kenneth Ardinger | Bruce Barrett | James Belmont |
| Bruce Black | Joe Blackwell | Eric Blasko | Scott Bontz |
| Ron Butts | Dave Crammer | T. J. Donahue | Bob Finan |
| Mel Finzer | Dave Gayer | W. A. Gibson, Sr. | Gordon Glattenberg |
| Ralph Gochnour | Emery Gulash | Doug Harrop | John Hungerford |
| Don Jocelyn | Blair Kooistra | Richard Kundert | Rob Leachman |
| Ralph Lettelier | David Lichtenberg | John Lucas | Fred Matthews |
| Garland McKee | Alan Miller | Wm. (Hank) Mills | Tom Moungovan |
| David Norris | David P. Oroszi | Mel Patrick | Frank J. Peterson |
| Vance Pomerening | David Rector | Jamie Schmid | John E. Shaw, Jr. |
| Mark Simonson | Dennis Smolinski | Scott R. Snell | Dave Stanley |
| J. W. Swanberg | Robert Todten | Chard Walker | Tim Zukas |

ABOVE: *Jamie Schmid*   INSET: *Dave Crammer*

# PART I
# TERRA INCOGNITA

## *The Origins of the South-Central District*

On April 4, 1988, at 6:40 A.M., sunrise and moonset coincide, a pale moon in a cobalt sky over a sunburnt desert. A wan pink suffuses the flat gray of the highest peaks, then suddenly they flare with orange light. The sun boils into the cold blue sky and the mountains' shadows shrink eastward almost as fast as a man can walk. Night's chill drains from the desert; the fragrance of creosote bush permeates the morning air.

Beneath the laminated foothills of the Bird Springs Range west of Sloan, Nevada, a westbound Union Pacific train drones towards Los Angeles; its four locomotives and 94 cars dwindle to insignificance in an infinitude of rock and sand. Here, in a desert where a UP engineer scoffed that there "were not enough people...to fill a good-sized house," two construction crews met on January 30, 1905, to complete a railroad that stretched 805 miles from tidewater at San Pedro, California, through the nearby city of Los Angeles, to the UP connection at Salt Lake City, Utah: the San Pedro, Los Angeles & Salt Lake Railroad. Its name was simplified to the Los Angeles & Salt Lake Railroad on August 25, 1916, because Los Angeles had engulfed San Pedro on August 28, 1909.

For its first 20 years, the LA&SL was an autonomous railroad, its control shared equally by the UP and millionaire mining magnate Senator William Clark. Clark sold his half of the LA&SL to the UP on April 27, 1921. On January 1, 1936, the UP leased the LA&SL (along with UP's other major subsidiaries) so it could streamline its operations and eliminate duplicate office staff. On January 1, 1988, the UP absorbed the LA&SL, and it ceased to exist as a corporate entity. Once, the Salt Lake Route had its own Arrowhead emblem and in 1916 proudly cast it into the concrete spandrels of an overpass in Whittier, California. Now, the LA&SL exists only in history.

UP's system consolidation of 1936 created the Eastern District from the UP proper and the St. Joseph & Grand Island, the Central District from the Oregon Short Line, the Northwestern District from the Oregon-Washington Railroad & Navigation Co., and the Southwestern District from the Los Angeles & Salt Lake. In 1937 the UP combined the Southwestern and Central Districts to form the South-Central District. The South-Central District, as it emerged after World War II, encompassed the entire LA&SL, and the OSL from Salt Lake City, Utah, to McCammon, Idaho.

Each of these three districts has its own character. The Eastern District was, and is, the Overland Route, UP's heart and soul. The commerce of America funnels into its double-track main line across the high plains of Nebraska, over the low mountains of southern Wyoming, and down through the Wasatch Range to Ogden. This is the route that carried one-third of all transcontinental traffic during World War II. Successful superintendence of the Overland was historically the stepping-stone to UP's presidency.

The Northwestern District was, and is, Union Pacific's breadbasket, where five dozen branch lines reached deep into fields and forests, hauling nature's bounty into a great mainline river. Douglas fir, Idaho white pine, and ponderosa pine; wheat, potatoes, and onions; cattle and sheep; potash, copper, silver, zinc, and lead; trade with the Orient; all of these the Northwest has in abundance. Edward Harriman believed the UP would be a weakling among transcontinentals, an also-ran, without this district.

The South-Central District, and in particular its LA&SL component, was, and is, more difficult to characterize. Until the late 1930s, the LA&SL was not fundamental to the UP. Until then, practically no one lived between its endpoint cities. Until then, it had very little traffic. Until then, no one needed the LA&SL. It was never part of the national dream or an early transcontinental scheme. The government did not survey this route for the Pacific Railroad. The public did not clamor for its construction, there being no public along its route. The LA&SL did not replace wagon ruts with ties and rail. If not for Senator William Clark's unrequited thirst for power, it is very likely the LA&SL would not exist. An optimist would call the LA&SL a bet on the future. A realist would call the LA&SL a hopeful expedition into an unpropitious wasteland. A cynic would call the LA&SL a fantastically expensive exercise in ego gratification.

What, then, is the nature of the South-Central District? At its Utah and Idaho end the main line and its parallel branches, all built by the OSL, serve a slender strip of agriculture and heavy industry. This is where Geneva Steel, now the only integrated steel mill west of the Mississippi, and Kennecott Copper's Bingham Canyon Mine, the world's biggest hole in the ground, coexist with dairy farms and placid towns. At its California end the railroad burrows through a hundred miles of city and suburbs before ending at the ocean docks of the ports of Los Angeles and Long Beach. This is where containers dance endlessly between ships and double-stack trains, where mountains of Utah and Colorado coal pour into the holds of Orient-bound bulk carriers.

To focus on either end, however, is to miss the point. The South-Central District is dominated by the desert, a desert larger than all of England, and, excepting Las Vegas, a city created by idiosyncrasy, a desert with fewer people than attend a typical state university. This is a desert of little towns, separated from each other by long journeys down empty highways. Many of these dots on a map are just a handful of mobile homes for a section gang, a few weather-beaten ranch hands, and the man who drives the county road grader. This is terra incognita—the unknown land.

Out in the desert the Union Pacific is sometimes man's only work as far as the eye can see. Out there, the railroad crosses featureless plains past dry lakes, and clambers up bleak mountains on long, exhausting grades. Out there, the railroad is nothing but rails, ties, ballast, signals, and sometimes a train. Out there, where the railroad came first and civilization has never followed, trains dwindle into thin watery lines in a landscape as vast as time.

Out in the desert, each new day is not much different than the last. The sun burns through an empty sky above a silent panorama, where there are no trees to rustle in the breeze, no brooks to trickle. Each evening ends like the evening before, with the sun's blazing disc extinguished behind a saw-toothed horizon, a violet sky suffused with scarlet, saffron and teal, and a mind-boggling panoply of stars. And every night the headlights of long trains flicker through the dark mountains and across the starlit deserts, through basins of creosote bush, Joshua trees, and sagebrush, through ranges of Pleistocene gravel, congealed lava and uplifted seabed...in 1995 as in 1905.

# SENATOR CLARK OF MONTANA

*Senator Copper of Tonopah Ditch*
*Made a clean billion in minin' and sich.*
*Hiked for New York, where his money he blew,*
*Buildin' a palace on Fift' Avenoo.*
*'How,' says the Senator, 'kin I look proudest?*
*Build me a house that'll holler the loudest.*
*None of your slab-sided, plain mossyleums!*
*Gimme the treasures of art an' museums!*
*Build it new-fangled, scalloped and angled,*
*Fine, like a weddin' cake, garnished with pills.*
*Gents, do your duty. Trot out your beauty.*
*Gimme my money's worth—I'll pay the bills.'*
  —Poet Wallace Irwin, 1911

The story of the San Pedro, Los Angeles & Salt Lake Railroad begins as the story of one man's fierce ambition. The man is William Andrews Clark, Copper King. Clark was born to poverty, on a Pennsylvania farm in 1839. His meager beginnings fueled an unquenchable hunger for wealth, power, and respect. By age 33 Clark had grubstaked himself to modest wealth through gold panning, freight hauling, and money lending in Montana Territory. That year, 1872, Clark visited the moribund gold camp of Butte. Prospectors had found veins shot through with silver in the Butte hill, but the ore was intractable to every known refining technique. Perhaps Clark was convinced he could do better; perhaps Clark just saw mines he could buy cheap and bank for a better day. In any event, he picked up four claims and decamped for New York, where he quickly absorbed the sciences of geology and ore reduction at Columbia University's School of Mines. Butte's dusky slopes concealed an incredible treasure of copper and silver. By 1890 Clark was a multimillionaire, by 1900 he was worth $50 million, and when he died in 1925 he was worth $200 million—easily two or three billion in today's dollars.

But what to do with the money? Clark had three goals: wealth, power, and respect. Wealth he had. His power, however, was circumscribed by archrival Marcus Daly, Butte's other Copper King. As for respect, well, Butte's miners respected Clark, but unlike Daly, Clark didn't care. Clark lusted not for the idle chatter of Helena's drawing rooms and the boisterous bonhomie of Butte's saloons, but for acceptance by New York City's sophisticated elite. Clark fancied himself a cultured Francophile, but New York saw Clark as just another uncouth, newly rich, pretentious, mining magnate.

Clark was not daunted. He decided he would become one of Montana's U.S. senators. "Senator Clark" —that had a nice ring to it. New York, he believed, would have to respect him if he was Montana's millionaire senator.

Marcus Daly naturally took exception to Clark's plans. In 1888 the Democratic Party nominated Clark to be Montana Territory's nonvoting delegate to Congress. Daly rigged a massive election fraud, causing Clark to lose. After Montana achieved statehood in 1889, Clark and Daly each tried to seize control of the statehouse, for whoever controlled the legislature would also get to pick Montana's first senators. (U.S. senators were not chosen by popular election until adoption of the 17th Amendment to the Constitution in 1913.) Neither Clark nor Daly could wrest control of the legislature from the other, so *two* legislatures met simultaneously and elected *four* senators. Clark's Democratic legislature elected Clark and another Democrat; Daly's Republican legislature elected two Republicans. The Republican-controlled U.S. Senate naturally sat the two Daly Republicans and sent Clark packing. In 1893 Clark tried again, but as fast as he bought Montana's legislators Daly bought them back. The legislature deadlocked and the governor sent another Republican to the U.S. Senate.

In 1899 Clark tried for senator a third time. This time he got serious. Clark's lieutenants paid private visits to Montana's legislators. The deal was simple: a vote for Clark in return for $10,000 (or more) in that legislator's pocket. A legislator could buy a ranch and retire with that much money. Soon evidence of Clark's spending spree spilled out. When one legislator dramatically spread $30,000 in crisp new bills before the legislature and publicly accused Clark of trying to bribe him, Daly's men were sure Clark was finished. Not so. Clark cranked up his money machine, buying judges, juries, and witnesses; wives, friends, and families of legislators; reporters, editors, and entire newspapers; mobs, miners, and bystanders; and anyone else who looked remotely useful. Some key legislators got as much as $50,000. On the morning of January 28, 1899, while infuriated hecklers in the statehouse gallery shouted out the amount of each legislator's bribe, Montana's legislators elected Clark to the U.S. Senate. Clark had spent about $400,000 on bribes, and about a million dollars on the whole election! It was a corruption so naked that even Clark's fellow millionaires in the U.S. Senate could not avert their gaze; they voted to void the election four months after Clark took his seat.

This debacle would have permanently humiliated any other man. Not Clark! The next year things changed. Marcus Daly, now old, tired, and ill, sold his fabulous Anaconda Mine to John D. Rockefeller and H. H. Rogers, the men who controlled Standard Oil. Although the Daly machine tried to carry on, Clark's newspapers easily terrified Montanans with the specter of a Rockefeller Copper Trust that would force them into poverty and servitude. Montana's voters swept Clark's legislative ticket into office in the general election of 1900. Clark's legislators promptly elected their master to the Senate. Clark took his seat in Washington in 1901 with enormous vindication.

It might seem surprising that Clark did not bother to run for re-election six years later, but he had never had any interest in politics except as it gained him power, prestige, and public adulation. Senator Clark had already shifted his sights to an occupation of even greater power: he would become a railroad baron. On August 21, 1900, it was announced that Clark had purchased an interest in a minor California railroad, the Los Angeles Terminal Railway, and that he would build an 805-mile transcontinental railroad linking Los Angeles and Salt Lake City.

On the one hand, Clark's decision to build the San Pedro, Los Angeles & Salt Lake Railroad seemed logical. By 1900 only two principal cities in the western U.S. were not directly connected by rail–Los Angeles and Salt Lake City. Also, Clark had extensive real-estate and sugar-beet holdings in southern California. Perhaps Clark was as prescient about southern California as he had been about Butte.

On the other hand, Clark's line ran straight through a forbidding and uninhabited desert, and it was highly improbable that his railroad, once built, would stimulate settlement or industry in this desert. Not that this was any mystery. *Railway Age* disparaged Clark's plan as "geographically a tempting proposition, if the difficult and unproductive character of the country to be crossed is ignored." For this reason other railroads had looked over and passed up opportunities to build this line, long before Clark had ever thought of it. The UP had more than once run a survey to southern California, and once even began to lay a track from Utah towards California, but it had never been able to muster up lasting enthusiasm for the route. Moreover, it was now 1900, not 1860, and Clark's adventure would not take place in a railroad vacuum (except out in the desert). In 1900 Utah was a Union Pacific state, California was a Southern Pacific state, and by early 1901 both railroads were the property of Edward Henry Harriman, who brooked no bandits in his realm. Clark acted, Harriman reacted, and in the grand tradition of Western railroading, a right-of-way brawl was on.

When Clark's construction crews arrived in the strategic canyons of Clover Creek and Meadow Valley Wash, Harriman's forces were there to meet them. Heated arguments, threats, and fist fights between the rival crews ensued. The battle continued in courthouses from Carson City, Nevada, to Washington, D.C., where attorneys for the two titans pored through the dusty charters and water-stained survey logs of forgotten paper railroads, cited arcane precedents, and argued boring trivialities with the zeal of revolutionaries. In the end, Clark realized he could not beat Harriman, and ceded 50 percent of his SPLA&SL to Harriman on July 9, 1902.

Construction resumed with the railroad under joint control, and on January 30, 1905, the rails from Los Angeles met the rails from Salt Lake City on an empty plain 307 miles east of Los Angeles. In May 1905 Clark hosted a special train from Salt Lake City to Los Angeles and back. In each city he attended banquets where he was idolized by western politicians, newspapermen, and businessmen. It was Senator Clark's Olympic moment. He had vaulted into the pantheon of railroad gods.

As might be guessed, Senator Clark had no more patience for the trials and tribulations of the SPLA&SL than he did for the problems of his Montana constituents, and almost as soon as the banquets were over he delegated his management role in the SPLA&SL to his brother, J. Ross Clark. Senator Clark built the 198-mile Las Vegas & Tonopah Railroad without Harriman's involvement in 1905-07, but got burned when the Nevada mining camps it served crashed in the Panic of 1907.

In his later years Clark collected expensive French paintings, built a 131-room mansion in New York City (its boilers consumed 17 tons of coal a day), tried to marry his daughters into aristocracy, and titillated the newspapers when he married a Butte girl 40 years his junior. At age 82, Clark decided he had had enough of railroading. On April 27, 1921, he sold his half of the LA&SL's stock to the UP for $2.5 million cash and traded his LA&SL bonds to the UP for a like value of UP and SP bonds.

New York's upper crust never did respect Senator Clark. His death in 1925 gave New York's newspapers an excuse to sneer one last time. *Railway Age*, which wrote obituaries for all railroad officials great and small, did not even notice. William Andrews Clark had built a railroad, but he had never been a railroad man.

Butte, Montana, in the age of the Copper Kings was a city of fabulous wealth and hopeless squalor, industrial muscle and frightful pollution, selfless heroism and naked corruption. Butte was the epitome of Gilded Age America—progress at any cost. By 1969, Butte's glory was gone, its once-fabulous mines an aging open-pit operation, and UP's *Butte Special*, trains 35 and 36, was an anachronism. As dusk approaches on May 10, 1969 (100 years after the driving of the last spike at Promontory), #35 rolls quietly through the shadows behind UP's Salt Lake City Diesel Shop. Behind its single E9A are a baggage, one-of-a-kind sleeper-buffet *American View*, two coaches, and a club-lounge which will be cut off in Pocatello. Out of Salt Lake City at 7:30 P.M., #35 will arrive Butte the next morning at 7:30. *The Butte Special* ceased running when Amtrak took over on May 1, 1971. *Bruce Black*

AT LEFT: Although the Union Pacific and Central Pacific met at Promontory, they soon removed their junction to Ogden, where it has remained ever since. On August 27, 1960, mechanics at UP's grimy Ogden roundhouse look over cow-and-calf 1877-1877B, a combination built for LA&SL helper service and now assigned to heavy switching in the Wasatch Front industrial belt.
*W. A. Gibson, Sr., collection of W. A. Gibson, Jr.*

## TOWARDS THE FRONTIER

*When the last spike is driven...we will say "done."*
—Omaha Telegraph, May 10, 1869

There is a general impression in books that transcontinental railroads begin at the last outpost of civilization. A band plays a stirring march, the politicians work the crowd, railroad officials force a smile through their dark beards, and then the sons of Ireland step forward and begin driving spikes. They lay track past the livery stable, and leave town and civilization behind, embarking upon an epic steel journey into a savage wilderness. Soon the track gang dwindles into a little cloud of dust and disappear over the western horizon.

Meanwhile, on the other side of the continent, another gang lays rail in the opposite direction. Steadily the two gangs narrow the gap between their ends of track. The men swing their mauls in ceaseless robotic motion, mile after mile, clank, bang, until one day, out in the middle of the wilderness, they meet. There is a huge celebration. The new railroad is done.

You could call this the Promontory parable. Yet no transcontinental railroad quite fits this picture. Most were built in fits and jerks, laying rails in a frenzy one year, out of bucks the next. The depression years of 1873–1878, 1883–1885, and 1893–1897 stalled most railroad construction. Most transcontinentals incorporated one or more extant railroads into their route. And most were not actually completed until some time after their golden-spike ceremony. The Northern Pacific, for example, drove its "last spike" at Gold Creek, Montana, on September 3, 1883, but did not get around to completing its line over the Cascades to Tacoma, Washington, until July 1887.

Clark's San Pedro, Los Angeles & Salt Lake was similar. More than half of Clark's completed railroad consisted of other railroads, some

of which dated back 36 years to the completion of the nation's first transcontinental railroad in 1869. In California, the SPLA&SL took over Clark's little Los Angeles Terminal Railway, and trackage rights on the Southern Pacific and Santa Fe carried the SPLA&SL 100 miles from Riverside over Cajon Pass to Daggett. In Utah, the Salt Lake Route absorbed a welter of UP branch lines. Once these had been Mormon railroads: built by church members, owned by church members, and operated for the greater good of the Mormon church, the Mormon people, and the Mormon state of Deseret.

### THE STATE OF DESERET

Chased from Illinois by violence and persecution culminating in the murder of leader Joseph Smith, the Mormons arrived in Utah's Great Salt Lake Desert on July 24, 1847. They traveled to this empty, isolated place to build a new civilization free from religious oppression. They rapidly colonized the arable land north and south of their headquarters in Salt Lake City, and built colonies as far afield as San Bernardino, California. They dammed the waters of the Wasatch Range and channeled them into communal ditches to irrigate the fields they plowed. They platted orderly towns in the valleys, planted trees to shade their well-kept homes, and erected schools, mills, and temples. In just a few seasons the Church of Jesus Christ of Latter-Day Saints built an agricultural theocracy in the wilderness, unique in American history in its size and success. They named it the State of Deseret. If not for gold, Deseret might have become a nation. Instead, Utah became a center of commerce for the entire West.

Gold was discovered in California on January 24, 1848. The next year an army of gold-crazed "forty-niners" rushed through Utah. Soon there was talk of building a railroad from the Mississippi River through Utah to San Francisco. This pleased the nation's Mormon-

haters. A railroad, they thought, would end Utah's isolation, and shorn of isolation the Mormon apostasy would surely perish. They were completely wrong.

The Mormons had turned a good profit supplying the forty-niners with food, hay, and animals. This cash infusion was very welcome in their first difficult years. The Mormon leaders decided that as grocers to the miners their people could succeed and at the same time remain true to their church and its teachings. The railroad, they decided, was inevitable; besides, it would bring even more economic opportunity and greatly ease the emigration of new Mormon converts to Utah. Confident in the strength of their church and state, the Mormons welcomed the railroad to Deseret. The Utah Territorial Legislature, a body of Mormon elders, appealed to Congress in 1852 for the construction of the Pacific Railroad, and when the Union Pacific Railroad Co. was organized on October 29, 1863, church president Brigham Young bought some of the first UP shares sold and was named one of UP's first directors (a position he held until 1866). At Young's direction, the Mormon Church contracted to build the Union Pacific grade from the Wyoming–Utah line to Promontory.

### THE UTAH CENTRAL RAILROAD

At 2:30 P.M. on March 8, 1869, the UP track arrived in Ogden. Nearly 1,500 Mormons watched the track-layers enter town. Brigham Young was not there. He and four other prominent Mormons met that day to organize the Utah Central Railroad, which would span the 37-mile gap between Ogden and Salt Lake City. Young, an eminently practical and farseeing leader, had determined that if the UP would not come to Salt Lake City, then Salt Lake City would go to the UP. Young also looked to the long term. He saw that just as the Union Pacific Railroad had tied together the Union and the Pacific, Mormon railroads would tie together the Mormon people, distribute the fruits of their fields, develop Utah's mineral bonanzas, and make the Mormon kingdom prosperous.

Brigham Young determined that Utah's railroads should be Mormon-owned railroads, but he also saw that an alliance with the Union Pacific might help shield the Mormons from their persecutors. Young therefore solicited the UP's financial backing for the Utah Central. Besides, the UP had paid the Mormons only half of what it owed them on their grading contracts on the UP main line, and the UP could not pay up. Despite the hoopla that surrounded the completion of the transcontinental railroad, in 1869 there was very little traffic over the line. Brigham Young sent Joseph A. Young and Bishop John Sharp to Boston to wrangle with the UP board over its $1.14-million debt. Bitter negotiations culminated in a grudging down payment: the UP transferred $600,000 worth of surplus track materials and rolling stock to the Utah Central in return for a like amount of Utah Central bonds.

Grading on the Utah Central began on May 17, 1869, just seven days after the last spike was driven at Promontory. The Mormons quickly completed their railroad, and service between Salt Lake City and Ogden began on January 12, 1870. Mormon men freely gave their labor to grade the Utah Central roadbed, cut its ties, and spike down its rails. Some of these workmen were given credit towards the cost of their emigration to Utah (which had been advanced by the church), or towards their tithes to the church, or towards food and supplies from the Mormon cooperatives. Nevertheless, the Utah Central's construction was little different than the men of a Mormon ward coming together to build a temple.

UP rails, though essential to the success of the Utah Central, were not the same as UP cash. Brigham Young had seriously overextended himself on the UP grading contracts and the construction of the Utah Central. The church brethren looked to Young for payment of their bills, not to the UP. Young's efforts to induce church members to buy Utah Central bonds or take bonds in lieu of payment were unsuccessful, and the UP insisted it had no more cash. In December 1870 Young offered his Utah Central stock to Collis P. Huntington of the Central Pacific, who was sufficiently interested to talk terms with Young. The UP board woke up; they were about to lose control of Utah to their principal rival. In February 1871 they scraped up enough cash to mollify Young and fend off Huntington, and in April 1872 Young sold 5,000 of his 7,600 Utah Central shares (there were 15,000 total) to the UP.

Thus was UP's policy towards Utah established. From this point forward, the UP viewed Utah as its private preserve. Nevertheless, when the Mormons came calling in the future, the UP found them money for their railroads only after considerable agony, and usually it took the threat of a competitor to roust the UP into writing a check. The UP, however, never paid off Young's grading bill; when Brigham Young died in 1877 his books still showed $130,000 owing.

## THE UTAH SOUTHERN RAILROAD

The Mormons' second railroad, the Utah Southern Railroad, was incorporated on January 17, 1871. This line was to run south from Salt Lake City to Payson, 65 miles, and perhaps onward to St. George, Utah. It would connect the Mormon farming towns that dotted the fertile, watered soil of Utah Valley with Salt Lake City, and it would shorten the haul to the many mining camps which had sprouted high above the Salt Lake and Utah Valleys in the Wasatch Range and the Oquirrh and Tintic Mountains. The Union Pacific backed the Utah Southern by purchasing $500,000 of its stock and the majority of its first issue of construction bonds, paying for the bonds with 20 miles' worth of leftover rail and miscellaneous rolling stock. (Such backing was not unique to the Mormon roads; through this stratagem a big road could protect its flanks and increase its traffic, and if all came to naught, the rails could always be repossessed.) More money came from church tithes. Grading began at Salt Lake City on May 2, 1871. As soon as the rails promised by the UP arrived, track-laying proceeded at about a third of a mile per day, reaching Sandy, 10 miles to the south, on September 23. A quarry a few miles east of Sandy was producing the granite blocks used in the construction of the church's temple in Salt Lake City. The quarry, along with two silver smelters built at Sandy shortly after the railroad arrived, gave the Utah Southern an immediate source of traffic.

The Utah Southern reached Draper in December 1871, where construction halted because of cold weather, and because it ran out of both money and rail. That winter Bishop Sharp coaxed from the UP enough cash and surplus iron rail to build another 20 miles of track by reminding the UP that the Collis P. Huntington and the Central Pacific might still be a good customer for Utah Southern bonds. On the strength of this backing construction resumed in spring 1872. The Utah Southern achieved Point of the Mountain by August 1872, and Lehi, 31 miles from Salt Lake City, by October.

At Lehi, construction stalled again for lack of cash. The UP, for the moment, was tapped out. In light of the money shortage that followed the Panic of 1873, it appeared to Young and Sharp that it would be a while before the UP would be in a position to provide more capital. With nothing to lose, the Utah Southern's directors visited the church elders of the 13 major towns along the route south of Lehi and convinced them to trade the labor of their church members on the grade for some 3,700 shares of Utah Southern stock. The church in each town held the stock for its members. The free labor was enough to extend the Utah Southern from Lehi to Provo, where it arrived on November 25, 1873. Construction ceased until late October 1874, when Bishop Sharp got more cash from the UP. The Utah Southern reached Spanish Fork on December 23, 1874, and Payson on January 23, 1875. Since there was enough rail on hand to lay six more miles of track, Sharp decided they might as well push on to York, where the Utah Southern arrived on February 16, 1875. York, 73 miles south of Salt Lake City, was not a town (not even a dot on the map), but that was as far as the rails could reach. And despite Bishop Sharp's entreaties for more iron or cash, this time the UP could not be budged.

was replaced by Ogden's current depot, a beautiful Italian Renaissance structure. During April 1971, one of the last runs of the *City of Los Angeles* waits to depart for Los Angeles. *Keith Ardinger*

ABOVE RIGHT: The first depot at Ogden, Utah, was small, wood-framed, and painted "a violent shade of red." Ogden's second depot, built in 1889, was a multi-turreted, masonry monstrosity, its gloomy interior more appropriate for a gothic novel than the meeting place of the nation's first transcontinental railroads. Gutted by fire on February 13, 1923, it

BELOW: Salt Lake City Union Station was completed in 1909 for the OSL and the SPLA&SL. Murals in its vaulted waiting room display the two greatest events in Utah's history: the arrival of the Mormons on July 24, 1847, and the driving of the golden spike on May 10, 1869. *Dennis A. Smolinski*

AT LEFT: Mormon farmers built this railroad, the Utah Southern, in 1872–75. Then, these were valleys of farms. Now, these are valleys of copper-smelting, steel-making, and rocket-building. Railroads irrevocably changed Utah from agricultural theocracy to industrial technocracy. On February 24, 1978, Extra 75 West coasts past U. S. Steel's Geneva Works on UP's Provo Subdivision. The Provo switch crew has traded coil-steel empties for coil-steel loads in the Geneva yard. The crew will follow Extra 75 West to Provo. *Doug Harrop*

## THE UTAH NORTHERN RAILROAD

The Mormon farming towns in northern Utah's Bear River and Cache Valleys were as much in need of rail service as the towns to the south of Salt Lake City. Although mining activity in this area was meager, there was a heavy overland wagon trade between Corinne, a town 25 miles north of Ogden on the Central Pacific, and the new gold and silver camps of Montana Territory. The wagons carried food and manufactured goods north and ore south.

Corinne, the only Gentile (non-Mormon) town in Utah, was a perennial irritation to the Mormon leadership. A railroad that served northern Utah would not only serve the church and help its northern members prosper, it would divert the Montana trade away from Corinne and its obnoxious Gentiles. Accordingly John W. Young, another of Brigham's sons, and Joseph Richardson, an eastern businessman, incorporated the Utah Northern Railroad on August 23, 1871. They planned to build their line north from Ogden up the Bear River Valley through Brigham City to Collinston, where it would turn east and climb over a ridge to enter the Cache Valley at Mendon. After crossing the Cache Valley to Logan, the principal town in the valley, the line would turn north and end at Soda Springs, Idaho, about 125 miles north of Ogden. Later they could extend the Utah Northern into Montana Territory.

Richardson agreed to furnish the necessary rail and rolling stock in exchange for Utah Northern stock and bonds. The Mormon men of the northern Utah communities agreed to build the grade, cut the ties from the neighboring forests, and lay the track, all in exchange

for Utah Northern stock. That fall, the Mormons began work on the grade, "with frequent interruptions while the farmers left to harvest their crops," commented historian Clarence Reeder, Jr. To stretch his limited cash as far as possible, Young chose to start work not at Ogden but at a point on the Central Pacific three miles south of Brigham City (which the CP named Utah Northern RR Junction), and build from there to Logan. Work commenced on August 26, 1871. Young figured that once the Utah Northern began earning money he could extend it south from the junction to Ogden. To save even more cash, Young chose to build the Utah Northern as a narrow-gauge.

The following spring the Mormons laid 23 miles of track from Utah Northern RR Junction to Hampton's, a stage station where the toll road to Montana crossed the Bear River. Freight and passenger service began operating to Hampton's on June 13, 1872. Most of the summer of 1872 was consumed building the grade over Collinston Divide, a 500-foot-high ridge between the Great Salt Lake and Cache Valleys, and the first train did not reach Logan until January 31, 1873.

At first Corinne's Gentiles had scoffed at the Utah Northern, but they soon they realized the Mormons were serious. Corinne businessmen incorporated a competing railroad, the Utah, Idaho & Montana, on April 13, 1872. But without cash or volunteer Mormon labor, the company could accomplish nothing of substance. In desperation, Corinne businessmen appealed to the Utah Northern for a branch line, which they hoped would keep for Corinne a measure of the Montana trade. In return for $3,000 in cash and goods, and free depot land, John W. Young agreed to build a 4.1-mile

branch from a junction 4.5 miles north of Brigham City, and on June 12, 1873, the first Utah Northern train entered Corinne.

During 1873 and 1874 the Utah Northern built both north and south from its middle. The northern section was the most important because it would enable the Utah Northern to take the lucrative Montana traffic away from Corinne. In 1873, as in 1872, Mormon farmers were the engine of construction, and grading was again interrupted now and then when the farmers had to tend their fields. The end-of-track reached Smithfield by November 17, 1873, paused for the winter, then resumed northward progress in March 1874 and entered Franklin, Idaho Territory, on May 2. In the meantime the railroad built south to Ogden, which it reached on February 5, 1874.

Despite having reached into Idaho, the Utah Northern could not deprive Corinne of its Montana trade. The road through aptly named Marsh Valley north of Franklin was too soggy for the teamsters, and the cost of transloading goods from standard to narrow-gauge cars at Ogden soaked up most of the hoped-for advantage of rail over wagon transportation. There was so little business on the Corinne Branch that the Utah Northern quit running there on January 1, 1876, and the branch was later pulled up. Nor were the Utah Northern's local revenues enough to pay its way, due to grasshopper infestations that destroyed Cache Valley crops (and reportedly because of the frugality of the Mormons–Wells Fargo agents claimed that "one Gentile makes as much business as a hundred Mormons"). The Utah Northern was trapped by the classic conundrum of western railroading: the traffic of its destination would pay the cost of its construction, but until it reached its destination it had no traffic, and without traffic it could not pay for its construction. The Panic of 1873 eliminated any hope of floating more bonds. John W. Young and Joseph Richardson could push their 78-mile line no farther.

In the early 1870s, Montana's mines prospered despite their distance from the nearest railheads. The Northern Pacific, the only other line that had made much progress towards Montana Territory, had seemingly expired on the banks of the Missouri River at Bismarck, Dakota Territory. Jay Gould and Sidney Dillon, the men who then controlled the Union Pacific, observed two facts: (1) if they could build a railroad to Montana's mining districts it would make them lots of money, and (2) the Utah Northern would be the cheapest way to do this.

Between 1874 and 1878 a complicated series of transactions took place: the Utah Northern Railroad was reorganized as the Utah & Northern Railway (on April 30, 1878); the debts of the road were erased, leaving its creditors with little or nothing; Gould and Dillon bought the Mormon-owned stock for 10 cents on the dollar; Richardson did a little better on his stock, realizing 40 cents on the dollar; and Gould then sold his Utah Northern stock to the UP for about a 50 percent profit. With this accomplished, the UP drove the Utah & Northern toward Montana at a somewhat faster pace. Grading began at Franklin in October 1877. The Utah & Northern reached Pocatello, Idaho, in August 1878; Dillon, Montana, in 1880; and Butte on December 15, 1881.

Capital had proven more powerful than community; the UP built 357 miles, many through rough terrain, in about the same amount of time it took Mormon farmers to build 60 miles in easy terrain. As for Corinne, it soon dwindled from a rowdy Gentile trading town to a sleepy Mormon farming town.

## THE UTAH WESTERN RAILROAD

Prospecting in the Great Basin was a lonely pursuit during the 1850s. Although several gold and silver discoveries were made, most prospectors moved on, sure these veins were teasers compared to the fortunes in gold nuggets they presumed lay scattered on the ground in California's Mother Lode. In 1859, when gold miners at Virginia City, Nevada, realized that "the damned blue stuff" they were throwing away was actually extremely rich silver ore, they reconsidered, and during the 1860s and 1870s the Great Basin was heavily prospected. Each valley, it was hoped, contained the next Virginia City.

One camp that showed great promise was Pioche, in southeastern Nevada. Located in early 1864, when Indians showed its rich silver outcrops to a Mormon missionary, the camp's first boom in 1870-72 attracted the Salt Lake, Sevier Valley & Pioche Railroad. This narrow-gauge, incorporated on May 3, 1872, planned to build west from Salt Lake City around the northern end of the Oquirrh Mountains, past the mining camps of Tooele, Stockton, Ophir, and Mercur, then south through the Sevier Valley, the Escalante Desert, and Clover Creek Canyon to Pioche, about 300 miles distant. Officers were elected, stock was subscribed, and a ground-breaking ceremony was held at Salt Lake City on April 14, 1873. Some grading was completed that summer. Then the officers fell to squabbling, and the company failed with hardly a rail laid.

The SLSV&P's general superintendent was able to interest John W. Young of the Utah Northern in the road, pointing out to Young that the SLSV&P could serve the Mormons' struggling iron works at Iron City, 25 miles southwest of Cedar City, and transport iron ore to Young's proposed iron works in Salt Lake City. This would further the cause of Mormon self-reliance, and thereby greatly enhance John W. Young's sometimes troubled relations with the Mormon Church. Excited, Young reorganized the SLSV&P as the Utah Western Railroad on June 15, 1874. Unlike the SLSV&P, the Utah Western was primarily a Mormon affair. Track-laying commenced on November 12 and progressed 21 miles to Clinton's Landing (near present-day Lake Point) by February 7, 1875. Early the next spring, construction resumed, and by March 31 the end-of-track

reached Half-Way House, 4.5 miles past Lake Point, when Young's cash ran out.

Young tried to play the Central Pacific against the UP in October 1875 to get more money. The UP, now wise to the ways of the Mormon railroads, correctly calculated that Huntington had no need for the line and called Young's bluff. Construction ceased. In spring 1876 Young scared up more cash, which was enough to complete 14 miles of grading from Half-Way House to within a mile of Stockton. The grade halted near the portal of a proposed 800-foot tunnel, which would be needed to take the Utah Western through the Stockton Bar, a gravel ridge just north of Stockton. This grade could not be railed until the following summer because Young had trouble selling the bonds to pay for the work. The end-of-track reached the tunnel site, prophetically named Terminus, on September 10, 1877. It was a railroad to nowhere; not only did the 37.2-mile Utah Western stop short of Stockton, it missed the town of Tooele by 3 miles, to the disgust of Tooele's residents, because Young decided Tooele was too far above the valley floor to justify the detour.

By 1875 the rich surface ores in Pioche were mined out, and 90 percent of its population of 6,000 quickly left. The chloride-silver lodes at Ophir devolved into complex sulfide ores that baffled the smeltermen. Activity there virtually ceased. The placer-gold deposits at Mercur petered out as well. Ore traffic on the Utah Western evaporated. Although the Utah Western had a substantial summer

business carrying excursionists from Salt Lake City to the Great Salt Lake resort at Black Rock, its revenues fell far short of paying its operating expenses and interest on the bonds. Brigham Young helped out his son by paying $24,500 in interest charges due in July 1877, but it was not enough. The Utah Western defaulted on its interest payments on January 1, 1878, and entered receivership.

AT LEFT: When the Utah Western laid rails past the northern fringe of the Oquirrh Mountains in 1874–75, there was nothing there but mud flats. In 1906 Utah Copper Co. and American Smelting & Refining Co. built a huge copper-refining complex at Garfield and nearby Magna. By April 1971 autos had long since rendered the depot superfluous; while the Tooele Local switches at Garfield, workmen dismantle the depot. *Keith Ardinger*

BELOW: The Wellsville Mountains soar 5,000 feet above Brigham City, Utah, separating the Cache and Bear River Valleys. To circumvent this barrier the Utah Northern ran north along the Bear River from Brigham City to the end of the range, then crossed a low ridge to enter the Cache Valley. The power for the Malad Local lays over at the former OSL depot at Brigham City on August 3, 1993. *James Belmont*

The major bondholders purchased the company at a foreclosure sale on November 3, 1880, paying $36,000. It was reorganized as the Utah & Nevada Railroad on February 15, 1881.

Utah's railroad situation changed dramatically on July 21, 1881, when the Denver & Rio Grande incorporated the Denver & Rio Grande Western Railway as its agent for an aggressive expansion into Utah. The D&RGW's plans were grandiose. They included a connection with the Central Pacific at Ogden, a line from Ogden to southern California, an extensive network in western and southern Utah, and even a line that paralleled the CP to San Francisco. Fearing that the D&RGW would buy the Utah & Nevada and use it as a springboard for an invasion of western Utah and all of Nevada, the UP reluctantly bought the little line on August 20, 1881. UP president Sidney Dillon commented to the ubiquitous Bishop Sharp that he "would have preferred not to have bought the road, but it was absolutely necessary in self-defense." Another Mormon line had been brought into the Union Pacific camp. John W. Young, forever unlucky, tried his hand at other railroads destined to failure, then spent the last years of his life as an elevator operator in New York City.

## THE UTAH SOUTHERN RAILROAD EXTENSION

In the financial meltdown that befell the United States after the banking house of Jay Cooke failed on September 18, 1873 (when Cooke attempted to float Northern Pacific bonds that no one would buy), the overcapitalized Union Pacific sank fast, and its board members ran for the lifeboats. Into the void stepped Jay Gould. At age 37 Gould was a Wall Street wizard with a fearsome reputation. He was laughed at by few, hated by many, and respected by nearly all. He also knew railroading perhaps better than anyone until Edward Harriman. "No man," said historian Maury Klein, "did more to shape the railroad map of America or the structure of the industry than Jay Gould." Early in 1874 Gould quietly took control of the Union Pacific. Under his leadership the UP was pulled from the wreckage of the Crédit Mobilier debacle and recast as a western powerhouse. Jay Gould believed that mining, not agriculture, was the future of the West, and that no road was better positioned to take advantage of mining than the Union Pacific. And for a time he would be proven right.

In spring 1874, Bishop John Sharp made another of his by now regular trips to New York and Boston to plead the case for the Utah Southern. Gould and Sharp evidently liked what they saw in each other, and in December 1874 Sharp took a seat on UP's board of directors, which he held until his death in December 1891. Sharp also got the rails he needed to build the Utah Southern a little farther.

In the mid-1870s Jay Gould began to toy with the idea of extending the Union Pacific to California in order to flank the Central Pacific. (Others had the same idea. The San Diego & Utah Southern Railroad was incorporated in 1876 to build from San Diego to a connection with the Utah Southern. Way ahead of its time, it soon faded out of existence.) UP president Sidney Dillon inspected the Utah Central and Utah Southern in July 1875, and implied that he and Gould were interested in pushing the Southern south to the head of navigation on the Colorado River at Callville (near what is now Hoover Dam). To be safe, Gould purchased controlling stock in the Utah Central and Utah Southern in June 1875, and John Sharp was installed as their president and general superintendent.

In 1878 the rich Horn Silver Mine at Frisco, Utah, 160 miles southwest of end-of-track at York, captured Gould's attention.

Discovered in September 1875, in 1879 the Horn Silver was sold to Jay Cooke for $5 million, by which time it had already produced $1 million in silver. Gould, Sharp, and Sidney Dillon all purchased large amounts of stock in the Horn Silver, Frisco's best property. A geologist who inspected the Horn Silver the next year estimated it had at least $15 million of ore "in sight." Another property at Frisco was estimated to contain five million tons of lead-silver ore. With these breathless predictions in hand, in June 1878 the UP revved up the Utah Southern, deciding to extend it 16 miles from York to Nephi, and perhaps farther when money permitted. By December the UP considered this too limited, and the Utah Southern announced plans to build all the way to Frisco as soon as winter was over.

Back on December 29, 1874, Sharp and his associates had incorporated the Utah Southern Railroad Extension Company, which was supposed to build about 200 miles southwest from the legal terminus of the Utah Southern at Payson to the Utah–Nevada border. Nothing was done except some survey work and the company was allowed to die. On January 11, 1879, the name was dusted off and given to a second Utah Southern Railroad Extension Company. Its charter called for a 120-mile line from Chicken Creek to Milford, a 17-mile branch from Milford to Frisco, and possibly an extension to Pioche, Nevada. The Utah Southern would fill the 32-mile gap between York and Chicken Creek.

Promptly that spring, on March 1, 1879, the Utah Southern began work at York, and under the aegis of Bishop Sharp the road was opened for business to Chicken Creek on June 13. "At that time," noted historian Clarence Reeder, Jr., "the rather undignified name of Chicken Creek was changed to Juab." The track crews kept going on the Utah Southern Railroad Extension grade, stopping for the winter on December 19 at the town of Deseret (now Oasis), 60 miles south of Juab. The next spring work resumed, and the track crews rapidly laid rails through the Sevier Desert to Milford, then turned west and climbed 2,300 feet to Frisco, on the slopes of the San Francisco Mountains. The Utah Southern carried its first carload of ore out of Frisco on June 24, 1880, the day after the road's completion.

## CONSOLIDATION

Since the Utah Central Railroad, Utah Southern Railroad, and Utah Southern Railroad Extension operated as one, it made sense to consolidate them. On July 1, 1881, they were merged into the new Utah Central Railway Company. Bishop Sharp and two other Mormons were on the board, but for all purposes this was a UP subsidiary. The Mormon railroad experiment was over. So ended Brigham Young's dream of a nation where the Mormon people would be free of domination of railroads and eastern capital. Confirming Young's fears, the UP played its transportation monopoly for all it was worth and habitually gouged Utah's citizens on coal rates during the 1870s.

The Mormon railroads were unusual for the communal commitment the church and its members made to their construction and finance. For their volunteer labor the Mormon farmers received stock certificates whose value was ultimately ephemeral, yet if they had waited for others to build their railroads they probably would have waited for a decade.

The Mormons expected their railroads to bring greater prosperity to church and community. Their railroads fulfilled the promise. The transportation economies afforded by the Mormon railroads and the Union Pacific made possible the profitable mining and refining of Utah's refractory and often mediocre silver and lead ores, and for many years the Great Salt Lake Valley was the smelting capital of the world. An influx of smelter workers created urban populations that made it possible for Mormon farmers to diversify. While Great Plains grain farmers and Southern cotton farmers suffered through perennial poverty, Mormon farmers prospered with dairy cows, orchards, and vegetable farms. And Salt Lake City, the Mormon capital, permanently secured its role as the commercial capital of the intermountain West.

# TOWARD CALIFORNIA

*This has long been a favorite route for imaginary lines...*
—*Railway Age,* August 31, 1900

Just as the arrival of the Union Pacific in Utah in 1869 ended the Mormons' isolation, the arrival of the Denver & Rio Grande Western in Utah in 1881 ended UP's domination. Both railroads expanded frantically in Utah, each seeking to head the other off at the pass. Their engineers surveyed a bewildering number of lines, schemed to capture the crucial mountain passages and canyons, and began to think about ways to build to California. The contest soon exhausted both contenders.

## THE SALT LAKE & WESTERN RAILWAY

The Tintic District slowly grew to prominence in the early 1870s. The district, which spread through several hollows on the west side of the Tintic Mountains, was just 20 miles west of the Utah Southern at Payson, and 40 miles from the Utah & Nevada at Terminus, but money was tight and neither line was extended to the district. Three different railroads, the Lehi & Tintic Railroad, the Utah Midland Railway, and the Salt Lake, Bingham & Tintic Railroad, were incorporated in 1872-73 to serve the district, but in those panic years none of these companies could obtain financing and no track was built.

In 1881 UP's 12-year grasp on transcontinental rail traffic was nearing its end. To the north, the Northern Pacific, resurrected from the dead, marched west through Montana. To the south, the Atlantic & Pacific, Texas & Pacific, and Southern Pacific maneuvered for position. In UP's own back yard, the Chicago, Burlington & Quincy, the Denver & Rio Grande, and the Denver & Rio Grande Western were building a route that would flank the UP all the way from Chicago to Ogden. Once the Rio Grande met the Central Pacific at Ogden, the CP would be able to dictate rates to the UP. Jay Gould's position was murky. He suddenly sold his UP stock, took control of the Missouri Pacific System and the Texas & Pacific, and announced he would take the T&P to California.

Dillon moved quickly to defend UP's position from these numerous threats. The Oregon Short Line, a UP affiliate, began building northwest towards Oregon to intercept the Northern Pacific. On May 30, 1881, Dillon incorporated a new line, the Salt Lake & Western Railway, to parallel the Central Pacific from Utah to San Francisco. Grading crews started work at Lehi, Utah, the next day. The SL&W's proposed route more or less followed the Pony Express Trail of 1860–61. It left the Utah Southern a mile north of Lehi, ran through a gap between the Oquirrh and Tintic Mountains at Five Mile Pass, crossed the bleak wastes of northwestern Utah, then entered Nevada. It touched the Nevada mining towns of Cherry Creek, Eureka, and Austin, and its capital, Carson City, then crossed the Sierra Nevada south of Lake Tahoe. Since the route passed close by the Tintic District, in October 1881 Dillon decided to include a branch to Silver City, then the district's major camp.

This bold plan to parallel the CP, which could have only been one of Jay Gould's more elaborate ruses, was laid to rest when Gould, Dillon, and the CP's Huntington negotiated a peace treaty in November 1881. For a time the UP contemplated building the Salt Lake & Western to Los Angeles instead of San Francisco (via Nevada's Railroad Valley, which despite its name never hosted a railroad), via a connection with the Southern Pacific at Mojave, California. The proposed line appeared on UP maps of 1882, then was dropped.

Since the 53.8 miles of SL&W grade from Lehi Junction to Mammoth Smelters (later called Tintic) were virtually complete by this time, and Denver & Rio Grande subsidiary Tintic Range Railway was at work on its own branch from Springville to Eureka, the UP went ahead and laid track on the finished grade the next spring, reaching Tintic on June 24, 1882. The SL&W then laid rails on a 3.8-mile extension from Ironton (about three miles north of Tintic) to Silver City, reaching that busy mining town on August 9, 1882. A 3.2-mile branch was completed from Silver City Junction to Eureka on September 9, 1889; a 3-mile extension from Silver City up Ruby Hollow to the Northern Spy Mine was completed in February 1892; and a 1.8-mile branch was completed from Mammoth Junction to Mammoth Mill in December 1893, its last mile joint with Rio Grande's Tintic Range Railway. The last major addition in the district to the UP system was the New East Tintic Railway, an independent line purchased by the OSL in 1900. Incorporated by a mine owner on May 20, 1896, and completed the next year, the Shay-powered New East Tintic ran 2 miles from Mammoth to several mines and mills high in Mammoth Hollow.

## THE OREGON SHORT LINE & UTAH NORTHERN RAILWAY

The Union Pacific's number one problem, until it went bankrupt in 1893, was that its railroad cost about twice as much to build as did its competitors' railroads. Much of this had to do with the cost of iron (for rails, spikes, and so forth), which became cheaper as the U.S. became industrialized, dropping from $40.62 a ton in 1869, to $21.50 a ton in 1879, to $17.75 a ton in 1889. Almost everything was cheaper in 1879 than it was in 1869. In addition, the Crédit Mobilier, the company that built the UP, had grossly overcharged the UP for its services. While other railroads nimbly snatched up opportunities, by the 1880s the UP started to stagger like a wounded mastodon, trying to fend off territorial incursions and rebuild its main line while burdened with an enormous debt.

In 1881 the Texas & Pacific, Atlantic & Pacific, and California Central (a Santa Fe affiliate) were all surveying lines to San Francisco through southern Utah. The D&RGW had made public its intent to build into southwestern Utah, and possibly onward to southern California. These lines would outflank the UP, so Bishop Sharp hastily announced that the Utah Central would build from Milford south to a connection with the California Central near present-day Lund, and extend a branch to Cedar City and the nearby iron-ore deposits.

The threats soon disappeared. The Denver & Rio Grande Western finished its narrow-gauge main line to Ogden on May 19, 1883, but the effort bankrupted its Colorado parent. The T&P bogged down in west Texas, and the Santa Fe exhausted its resources pushing the A&P to Needles, California.

As for the Union Pacific, it could afford to build nothing in 1883. Competition from the NP in Montana, the Rio Grande in Colorado and Utah, and everyone else on the Great Plains forced the UP to slash its rates. Perversely, this did not result in increased traffic. Droughts, insect plagues, and brutal winters on the western plains had devastated farmers and ranchers. The miners had dug up all the ore they knew how to refine, and the technology to mill complex ores was not yet at hand. Overcapitalized and fraudulently promoted, Utah and Colorado mining stocks plummeted, and their boom towns emptied out as fast as they had filled up. The Frisco District began to decline inexorably in 1883. Ore traffic from the great Horn Silver Mine surged in 1883-84 as it gutted its reserves. Once these were gone there was nothing left to mine, and the Horn Silver

closed in February 1885. The Utah Central, drawn deep into an otherwise hopeless wasteland, lost much of its traffic, and its revenues dropped by half from 1882 to 1885.

In 1883 the U.S. went into a massive economic funk. Gould saw this coming and unloaded his UP stock while it was still valuable. In May 1884 UP's stock crashed. Sidney Dillon resigned on June 11, 1884. A new leader untainted by corruption emerged to manage the UP back to prosperity: Charles Francis Adams. Unlike Gould, Adams had no passion for gold and silver, and believed the UP's problems had been exacerbated by foolish lines to mining camps. The UP's sad experience with its Denver, South Park & Pacific caused Adams to grump that "the chief source of revenue of the road was in carrying men and material into Colorado to dig holes in the ground called mines, and until it was discovered that there was nothing in those mines the business was immense."

In 1885 the economy improved, which allowed Adams to do something about the Northern Pacific's competition. Since the narrow-gauge Utah & Northern could not compete with the standard-gauge NP, the U&N widened its main line from Pocatello, Idaho (where it met the OSL), to Butte all on one day, July 24, 1887. A new standard-gauge line from Ogden to McCammon opened on October 1, 1890, which included a low-grade line from Dewey, Utah, through the Bear River Gorge to Oxford, Idaho, 48.6 miles, replacing 12 miles of steep track over Collinston Divide. An 8.6-mile connection from Cache Junction to Mendon provided access to the old main line, which became the Cache Valley Branch and was standard-gauged on October 26. The old main line between Preston and Oxford was abandoned.

The UP was encumbered with 58 affiliated corporations as of 1888. To ease Adams's headaches, several consolidations were effected. The Utah Central, Utah & Northern, Utah & Nevada, Salt Lake & Western, Nevada Pacific, Ogden & Syracuse, Idaho Central, and Oregon Short Line were merged into a new company, the Oregon Short Line & Utah Northern Railway. Incorporated on July 27, 1889, the OSL&UN reached from Frisco, Utah, to Butte, Montana, and from Granger, Wyoming, to Huntington, Oregon. The Ogden & Syracuse Railway, incorporated on February 8, 1887, had built a 5.85-mile line from Syracuse Junction (later renamed Clearfield) to Syracuse. It opened for business on July 5, 1887, to haul salt harvested from the Great Salt Lake at Syracuse for use in the chlorination of silver and copper ores. The Nevada Pacific Railway was UP's next tentative feeler towards California.

## THE NEVADA PACIFIC RAILWAY

During the mid-1880s Bishop Sharp fretted about UP's unprotected southern flank. In March 1887 he talked Adams into running a survey from Milford to a junction with the Atlantic & Pacific Railway (the Santa Fe) at Barstow. The surveyor found the route feasible, but warned Adams that beyond Pioche the countryside had little mining, settlement, agriculture, or other potential for revenue. Since the line would cost at least $12 million to build, and UP's rivals were at the time in no position to build anything similar, Adams concluded that "we have, therefore, sufficient time to look about us."

Soon Adams was forced to look. The D&RG and D&RGW sprang to life, standard-gauged, shortened, and bettered their main lines, sprouted new branches, and began talking about southern California. In California, a ridiculously small line called the San Pedro, Los Angeles & Utah Railway hunted for money to build eastward. Another tiny company, the California Short Line Railway, was try-

ing to build a railroad in the Sanpete Valley. The D&RGW, reorganized as the Rio Grande Western, was laying track south from Thistle into the Sanpete Valley, a valley which led right to southern California. Was Gould hatching schemes? Adams wondered. Sharp got his answer. The UP would go to Los Angeles.

Sharp sent two survey parties into the field in 1888. They soon established a route from Milford to Daggett, California, a Santa Fe station 8 miles east of Barstow. Since Nevada law required railroads operating in Nevada to be incorporated in Nevada, on May 13, 1889, the UP incorporated the Nevada Pacific Railway to build from a place called Summit, on the Utah–Nevada state line, through Pioche to Nevada's western border, with branches from Pioche (145 miles from Milford) southwesterly through Bristol to Ash Meadows, Nevada, about 200 miles, and from Pioche north to Steptoe, Nevada,

about 100 miles. The Utah Central would fill the gap from Milford to the Nevada line. Bishop Sharp, indefatigable as always, took charge of the work, announcing in October 1889 that the UP would build the line to Pioche immediately, and to Daggett as soon as possible, because the UP "could not afford a 200-mile stub-end track ending up in the desert" (which of course was exactly what the line to Frisco already was). To clean up loose ends in Utah, in April 1890 Adams purchased an option on the San Pete Valley Railway, a narrow-gauge coal hauler that had occupied the grade of the defunct California Short Line.

As soon as the snow was gone in 1890, two thousand workmen were set to work along the survey from Milford through the Escalante Desert to Uvada, from Uvada down Clover Creek Canyon to its junction with the Meadow Valley Wash, thence up the wash

ABOVE: The Utah Northern's Mormon graders avoided Bear River Canyon and laid their narrow-gauge over Collinston Divide, a low point in the mountains 4 miles to the south, accepting 2.2 percent grades because they could not afford any better. In 1890 the OSL&UN replaced the climb over Collinston Divide with a new water-level route through the canyon, work which included two large timber trestles and 210-foot Tunnel 15. Steel trestles replaced the wood trestles in 1901. On a pleasant autumn day in October 1971, Extra 472 East squeals through the 10° curves at milepost 45 in the Bear River Gorge, just west of Wheelon, Utah. Behind the five units are covered hoppers loaded with Idaho fertilizer en route to California. A large irrigation ditch and the penstock to Cutler Dam's powerhouse have reduced the rushing currents of the Bear River here to a series of idyllic pools.
*Keith Ardinger*

ABOVE: On October 8, 1950, UP train #4, the *Utahn*, runs up the eastward track towards Summit, California. At Yermo, the fireman will climb down into PA 604's nose and change the number boards to read "4" instead of "604." As tenant on Santa Fe's railroad, the UP follows Santa Fe's rules, such as using engine numbers instead of train numbers, even on first-class trains.
*Frank J. Peterson (collection of Alan Miller)*

to Pioche. *Engineering News* reported on March 22, 1890, "The first 75 or 80 miles of the road from Milford presents no difficulties whatever, it is nearly as level as a floor." This was not the case in Clover Creek Canyon, where tight bends required nearly 100 creek crossings and six tunnels, more tunnels than were necessary for the entire original UP main line. By September 1890 the 145-mile grade to Pioche was largely complete. Early in October the track gangs arrived. Sharp's crews had laid 7.75 miles of track south of Milford when suddenly Adams ordered Sharp to cease work.

Once again, the UP was in deep money trouble. In spite of himself Adams had made no progress towards reducing UP's huge debt, but instead had spent UP's revenue on new lines, and to purchase controlling stock in the Oregon Railway & Navigation Co. before the Northern Pacific could do the same. As long as revenues were strong in the boom years of the late 1880s, Adams could juggle UP's debt by taking out new loans to pay off old loans. But when the economy turned sour in the summer of 1890, Adams got caught with $7 million in floating debt he could not refinance. The UP's stock collapsed again. In despair, Adams resigned on November 20.

Jay Gould had sold UP stock high in 1883. Now he could buy it low. He had enough UP stock by November 1890 to put Sidney Dillon back in charge. The change in leaders made no difference; the UP was doomed. In February 1891 the last of the Nevada Pacific construction crews were laid off, and the idle rail that poked 7.75 miles south from Milford was taken up in December 1892. The grade through Clover Creek Canyon was deeded over to Lincoln County, Nevada, in 1893 when the OSL&UN refused to pay taxes owed. Crushed by the worst depression the U.S. had ever seen, the UP could no longer cover its expenses, and on October 13, 1893, it went bankrupt.

Gould, Dillon, and Sharp were not there to witness the Union Pacific's humiliation. Dillon died on June 9, 1892, Gould on December 2, 1892. Bishop John Sharp, who next to Brigham Young had done more for Utah's railroads than any other man, died in December 1891, the month after the UP gave up on his dream of a railroad from Utah to California.

# SENATOR CLARK MEETS CITIZEN HARRIMAN

*At last account the two forces were using every endeavor each to outwit the other.* —*Railway Age*, April 19, 1901

For nearly a decade the derelict grade of the Nevada Pacific yielded its bare earth to wind, snow, and encroaching sagebrush. Its trestles bleached to white, and its six tunnels provided a cool refuge for bats and cattle during the heat of the day. One day, two rival crews materialized on the grade and battled for its possession like linemen scrambling for a fumbled football. To the dozen Mormon families who grew hay and tended livestock in the Clover Valley, it must have seemed as if an asylum had suddenly emptied out its entire stock of lunatics, armed them with shovels, and sent them into the wilderness to do battle.

The cause of this commotion was William Andrews Clark. He intended to build his railroad through Clover Creek Canyon. Edward Henry Harriman intended to stop him. Clark's springboard was the Los Angeles Terminal Railway, a small operation which hauled freight and excursionists between Los Angeles and the seaport of San Pedro, and occasionally dreamed of building a main line to Salt Lake City.

## THE LOS ANGELES TERMINAL RAILWAY

Los Angeles was swept by a real estate frenzy in the late 1880s. In part the boom was sparked by a fare war between the SP and the Santa Fe. Tickets from the Midwest to Los Angeles dropped from $125 to $25, and even as low as $5. Several entrepreneurs began building railroads to connect the new city with its multitude of new satellite towns. Seven little railroad companies, and their byzantine corporate history, ultimately became part of the San Pedro, Los Angeles & Salt Lake.

The Los Angeles & Pasadena Railroad was incorporated on June 27, 1884, to build a railroad of about 8 miles from downtown Los Angeles to Pasadena by way of Arroyo Seco, but never accomplished anything. The Los Angeles & Glendale Railway was incorporated on January 13, 1887, to build a 6.5-mile narrow-gauge line from its station on Downey Avenue in Los Angeles (this station was on the east bank of the Los Angeles River near the present-day intersection of Pasadena Avenue and North Broadway) to Glendale. The line opened for business in March 1888. The Pasadena Railway was incorporated on March 3, 1887, to build a standard-gauge line from Raymond to Altadena, 7.25 miles. It opened for business on January 31, 1888. The Los Angeles & Raymond Railway was incorporated on September 14, 1887, to build a line from Hoff and Chestnut Streets in Los Angeles (a few blocks from the Downey Avenue station) to Raymond, about 7 miles, but like the Los Angeles & Pasadena, it built no track.

BELOW: On July 23, 1950, the engineer of UP Extra 1414 West, the DLS (Day Live Stock), talks with trackmen at Summit while the brakemen set up retainers. Helper 1360 will follow the 1414 West down the westward track to San Bernardino. Out of place on this hot summer day in southern California is the massive snowplow on the 1414.
*Chard Walker*

During the spring of 1888 Los Angeles sobered up from its real-estate binge. The Pasadena Railway became financially embarrassed. The Los Angeles, Pasadena & Glendale Railway, a sister corporation to the Los Angeles & Glendale, was incorporated on March 30, 1889, to take its place. Between March and July 1889, the LAP&G built 1.8 miles of narrow-gauge from Glendale to Verdugo Park, an amusement park the line was promoting. The LAP&G leased the Pasadena Railway on November 6, 1889, and acquired both the Los Angeles & Pasadena and the Los Angeles & Raymond to give it rights to the route from Los Angeles to Pasadena. To fill this gap, the LAP&G laid a third rail on the Los Angeles & Glendale's narrow-gauge track from Downey Avenue to a junction 0.76 miles to the north at Well and Humboldt Streets, and constructed 6.4 miles of standard-gauge to reach the Pasadena Railway at Raymond. This connection was placed in operation in March 1890. The LAP&G's owners also incorporated the Los Angeles Terminal Railway Company (first) on August 29, 1890, and commenced but did not complete work on 1.7 miles of track between LAP&G's Downey Avenue Station and the site of what would later become the Salt Lake Route's

First Street Station in Los Angeles. In sum, the LAP&G and LA&G in 1890 operated 12.9 miles of standard-gauge from Downey Avenue in Los Angeles to Pasadena and Altadena, and 7.5 miles of narrow-gauge from Downey Avenue to Glendale and Verdugo Park, using for their little empire four locomotives, seven passenger cars, three "baggage, etc.," and four freight cars.

On January 2, 1891, several St. Louis businessmen led by Richard C. Kerens incorporated the Los Angeles Terminal Railway (second), merging into it the Los Angeles Terminal Railway (first), the Los Angeles & Glendale, and the Los Angeles, Pasadena & Glendale, assuming the lease on the Pasadena Railway. They purchased the Pasadena Railway at a sheriff's sale for $70,000, and merged it into the Los Angeles Terminal on September 2, 1892. They quickly converted the narrow-gauge to Glendale to standard-gauge, and restarted construction on the 28.8-mile San Pedro Extension. It was rapidly completed, on November 7, 1891. The line ran south from Downey Avenue to a new station at First Street in Los Angeles, then south to Long Beach, where it turned west and followed the shoreline to San Pedro Bay. The line crossed over the Los Angeles River's estuary to reach Rattlesnake Island (renamed Terminal Island),

and ended at East San Pedro. There the Los Angeles Terminal built a wharf and began to compete with the SP. It was widely believed that the UP was backing the Los Angeles Terminal, and though this was untrue, the Terminal encouraged the rumors in hopes that some transcontinental such as the UP would purchase the property and give its promoters a quick and juicy profit.

BELOW: The narrow-gauge Los Angeles & Glendale ran through empty country in 1887 to connect its namesake towns. Within a short period these towns agglomerated into a metropolis separated only by lines on maps. When UP 0-6-0 4439 hauled an excursion into Glendale on June 9, 1956, it ran not through orange groves but down Glendale Avenue, past citizens waiting for the bus in front of the Thrifty Drug Store. Officially, UP's California Division was all-diesel by 1951, yet four 0-6-0's were assigned to the Harbor Belt Line at the Ports of Los Angeles and Long Beach for some time after this date, and the 4439 ran on the Harbor Belt Line until 1957, just two years from the end of all regular UP steam operation. *Gordon Glattenberg*

Since 1872, when the SP consented to route its main line through Los Angeles in exchange for a large subsidy from the citizens of Los Angeles, the SP had dominated southern California transportation. With the completion of the Los Angeles Terminal, this dominance began to slip through Collis P. Huntington's fingers. In 1890 the federal government decided to build a deepwater port at Los Angeles. The obvious choice was San Pedro Bay. Although this would benefit the SP's San Pedro Branch, it would equally benefit the Terminal. Historian Richard Barsness explains: "For a corporation accustomed to having its own way, the situation was clearly intolerable, and the Southern Pacific fought back with all the aggressiveness, vigor, and cunning it could muster–which under Collis P. Huntington was considerable."

The SP began work on a big iron wharf at Santa Monica, alleged that San Pedro Bay was unusable because of a rocky bottom, and promoted its own "Port Los Angeles" as the place where the government should spend its money. Huntington chose the location of his new wharf cleverly. It backed up to a 180-foot-high bluff, and his agents purchased all the land around the site, which denied access to his wharf to any other railroad. Ultimately Huntington's deception was exposed, and on March 1, 1897, the government decided that San Pedro would be the place for the deepwater port. Work finally began in April 1899 on the breakwater that would make the Ports of Los Angeles and Long Beach into one of the greatest ports in the United States. The citizens of Los Angeles were delighted, for at last they would have a deepwater port with competitive rail access. The SP's monopoly had been broken.

ABOVE: West of Crestline the Nevada Pacific grade spiraled down Clover Creek Canyon, scraping the sides of the pinnacles, crossing the creek about 100 times, and tunneling through the canyon's corners six times when the corners were too tight to be turned. With some relocations of both track and creek, the creek is now crossed "only" 36 times, but most of the curves remain and still deny speed to UP's trains. At 8:15 A.M. on April 30, 1985, Extra 3763 East lugs its APL double-stacks upgrade through Islen, Nevada, the howl of five units and the screech of flanges echoing from the canyon's walls. *Tim Zukas*

AT RIGHT: Before the SPLA&SL arrived, Caliente, Nevada, was only a wide spot in Meadow Valley Wash, home to a few ranchers who grew hay in the bottom of the wash and grazed cattle in the rugged mountains on every side. At the base of the steep climb up Clover Creek Canyon to Crestline, and a day's run in either direction from Milford and Las Vegas, Caliente was the logical place for a division point and helper terminal. On May 28, 1967, a GP30 and two SD24's have trudged into town with a long eastbound empty coal drag, and wait on the siding while the brakeman walks toward the depot to talk to the operator. An open cab door, coupled with forward progress, generates a slight breeze, meager relief in the blazing heat of the Nevada summer.
*Wm. (Hank) Mills (collection of Martha Mills)*

In 1896 an unknown stockbroker named Edward Henry Harriman demanded, and received, a seat on the executive committee of the reorganized Union Pacific Railroad. By 1898 Harriman chaired that committee. He now controlled the West's most important railroad. Soon he would be one of the most important and powerful men in railroading.

The Union Pacific before 1893 did not have a firm grip on its subsidiaries, and in the bankruptcy of 1893 they wandered off like sheep from an overturned stock car. Immediately after Harriman took control of the Union Pacific in May 1898, he took stock of the lost waifs. Here were the Oregon Short Line and the Oregon Railway & Navigation Co., robust and teeming with traffic. Harriman herded them back into UP's corral. There was the Union Pacific, Denver & Gulf, feeble and lame. Harriman culled one useful line from this mixed-gauge hodgepodge; the rest became the Colorado & Southern.

Cut apart in 1893, the Oregon Short Line & Utah Northern and UP soon began to argue about rate divisions, which set the OSL&UN to thinking about ways to make itself less dependent upon the UP. Perhaps it could reclaim the abandoned grade from Milford to Pioche and extend itself to California. Since the OSL&UN did not have the money to finance this adventure, in 1895 it gave a corporation called the Utah & California Railroad the right to lay rails on the empty grade. Lincoln County, Nevada, offered to give the U&C the grade from Uvada to Pioche free of charge if it would lay track within three years. But in 1896 the president of the U&C died, as did its plans.

As the economy improved in the late 1890s, the OSL&UN, reorganized on March 15, 1897, as the Oregon Short Line Railroad, rekindled its idea of building to California. On August 20, 1898, prominent Mormon businessman David Eccles and other men previously involved in the Utah & California incorporated the Utah & Pacific Railroad to lay track on the old grade from Milford to the Nevada state line. Five days prior, OSL Vice President and General Superintendent W. H. Bancroft assigned to the Utah & Pacific the rights to the grade. The OSL sold to the Utah & Pacific, at a low price, the necessary ties and 52-pound iron rail. In return, the Utah & Pacific gave the OSL a five-year, fixed-price purchase option.

Work on the Utah & Pacific began at once and continued through the winter and the following spring. On June 30 its track gangs reached Uvada, 74.5 miles from Milford, and just east of the Nevada state line. From track's end the U&P men could walk to Crestline, look at the grade where it twisted into Clover Creek Canyon, and imagine a railroad to California.

## THE UTAH, NEVADA & CALIFORNIA RAILROAD

The summer of 1899 it was noticed that a survey party headed up by a J. H. Long was driving stakes upon the old Nevada Pacific grade in Clover Creek Canyon. Long's instrument boxes were marked "Southern Pacific Company," but who his actual employer was nobody knew. The OSL, aware that its five-year right to build track through Clover Creek Canyon had expired, renewed its rights by incorporating the Utah, Nevada & California Railroad (of Nevada) on February 2, 1899, and filed maps of its proposed alignment with the Federal Land Office in Carson City. The maps called for the UN&C to build from Nevada's eastern border to Vanderbilt, California, where the UN&C would connect with the California Eastern, a short line that connected with the Santa Fe at Blake

(now Goffs). A branch of 30 miles from Clover Valley Junction (now Caliente) to Pioche was included. These maps were returned to the UN&C for corrections but for some reason the OSL never bothered to make them, rendering its right to the old grade questionable. Curiously, the OSL made no effort to buy back the old Nevada Pacific grade from Lincoln County, Nevada, which was now a wagon road.

Harriman purchased sufficient stock in the OSL by September 1898 to bring it and the Oregon Railway & Navigation Company back into the UP fold. In 1899 Harriman sent surveyors out to look at the proposed line to California, and engineer Samuel Felton inspected the Los Angeles Terminal Railway as a possible connection. Richard C. Kerens, president of the Terminal, had already approached the UP about either buying the Terminal, or perhaps joining forces to build a new transcontinental from Los Angeles to Salt Lake City. Harriman was courteous to Kerens, but was deeply involved in more pressing matters, such as rebuilding the Union Pacific. Nor was Harriman anxious to pick a fight with Collis P. Huntington, which an invasion of California would surely spark. Although W. H. Bancroft warned Harriman on May 25, 1899, that Senator Clark might be interested in Kerens's ideas, Harriman demurred from precipitate action.

In 1900 all of the western railroads were busy. *The Salt Lake Tribune* noted that "there is not an idle grading contractor in sight ...something like 8,000 men and 3,000 teams are at work or wanted for railroad construction within a radius of 500 miles from Salt Lake." Soon the West would get much busier.

In June 1900 the Santa Fe's chairman announced that his company, in consortium with the Southern Pacific, planned to build a railroad to Salt Lake City from some point between Needles and Mojave. He would not say, however, if the line was to connect in southwestern Utah with the UP, the Rio Grande, or neither. The story could have been false, and intended to force someone's hand. But whose?

On August 13, 1900, Collis P. Huntington of the Southern Pacific suddenly died. The emperor had no heir, and his railroads were Harriman's to take. As soon as Huntington's stock became available, Harriman was there, cash in hand, and by February 1, 1901, Harriman had control of the SP.

ABOVE: On October 30, 1950, UP train #4, the eastbound *Utahn*, runs up the eastward track between Cajon and Pine Lodge, California. In the distance, four new Santa Fe F7's take their train down the westward track toward the little town of Cajon, their dynamic brakes in maximum amperage and their train's retainers turned up to hold the train at the 15 mph speed limit. The California Southern, a Santa Fe ally, opened its line over Cajon Pass on November 15, 1885. The Santa Fe began running trains to Los Angeles over its own or its allies' rails on May 31, 1887, ending the SP's iron grip on southern California transportation.
*Frank J. Peterson (collection of Alan Miller)*

The announcement on August 21, 1900, that the Los Angeles Terminal would build a railroad to Salt Lake City caused little stir. Although *Railway Age* gave front-page space to the story on August 31, this was mostly to question how a 27-mile road could possibly undertake "an enterprise of such magnitude," and supposed that "some great eastern company" was the backer. *Railway Age* hoped that agreements would be effected with the UP between Uvada and Salt Lake City to avoid duplication of the UP, and on the Santa Fe from San Bernardino to Barstow, "which, if possible, would be a very good thing for the Terminal enterprise, as the question of getting over the range, which the Santa Fe climbs through the Cajon Pass, is a serious one."

Buried in the same issue was more speculation. "The mission of the [Terminal]...has always been a mystery," said *Railway Age*, but it was "commonly reported that it was to form part of an extension of the Union Pacific." It quoted unnamed sources who claimed that "ex-Senator W. A. Clark of Montana has become a heavy stockholder and all the needed capital is said to have been provided." The Terminal insisted that its line would not stop until it got to Salt Lake

City, where it would connect with all transcontinental lines that were "there, or might ever get there...including the Burlington."

On October 26 *Railway Age* reported that Clark was negotiating with the UP to use its track from Uvada to Salt Lake City, and guessed that the instigator of the project was "as far east as Lake Michigan" that is, its instigator was James J. Hill and his Chicago, Burlington & Quincy.

On November 30, 1900, Clark and his friends organized the Los Angeles & Salt Lake Railroad at Salt Lake City (its articles of incorporation were filed on March 20, 1901), and announced that the LA&SL would absorb the Los Angeles Terminal Railway (executed on March 5, 1901). The next day the corporation changed its name to the San Pedro, Los Angeles & Salt Lake Railroad, to emphasize its connection with Orient trade. Conceivably the line could have been called the Salt Lake & Los Angeles; however, another railroad by that name had been in existence since September 1891, running from Salt Lake City to the Saltair Resort 17 miles west of the city. Later this became the Salt Lake, Garfield & Western.

The Burlington simultaneously announced that it would build from Cheyenne, Wyoming, to Salt Lake City to connect with the SPLA&SL. Also encouraged, the RGW announced late in December

that it had reactivated its on-again, off-again plans for a shortcut between its main line at Green River, Utah, and its Marysvale Branch in central Utah, and would extend the Marysvale Branch south and west until it connected either with the SPLA&SL or with the Santa Fe at Barstow. And the Santa Fe now denied it had ever planned to build a line from Los Angeles to Salt Lake City.

Clark's men went to work. In Utah, Clark's attorney, Charles O. Whittemore (who also happened to be the U.S. Attorney for Utah), discovered that in 1896 the OSL&UN had given the Utah & California the right to build upon its abandoned grade from Milford to Pioche, and never taken it back! The U&C had filed maps with the government Land Office in Carson City, Nevada, which gave it the right to remove the land from the public domain. Whittemore thus resurrected the U&C, reorganized it in Clark's interests, amended its articles and had them filed, but had these facts suppressed, "and no one knew what was being done."

Harriman reacted immediately. Clark had no foothold in Utah. The best approach to Salt Lake City was around the western flank of the Oquirrh Mountains, where the Nevada & Pacific had stalled at Terminus in 1877. Harriman moved to seal off this approach. In December 1900 the OSL announced that it had begun to survey an all-new main line, called the Leamington Cut-off, which left the former Nevada & Pacific at Garfield, crossed the former Salt Lake & Western near Tintic, and ended at Leamington Hill Spur (later Lynndyl), where it connected with the former Utah Southern Railroad Extension. This cut-off would be virtually useless unless it became part of a main line to Los Angeles, but at this stage, Harriman had not yet made a substantial financial commitment to that main line.

AT LEFT: On April 14, 1974, UP Extra 6935 West meets a Santa Fe eastbound at West Tower in Barstow, while a second Santa Fe eastbound, made up mostly of perishable traffic, zigzags into Barstow Yard for classification. At left Santa Fe's main line to the San Francisco Bay area swings north and crosses the Mojave River. At right Santa Fe's First District to Los Angeles curves around B Hill. When the Santa Fe built a large hump yard at Barstow in 1974-75, it straightened its First District tracks to eliminate the sharp curve at B Hill and moved the junction to San Francisco, 3 miles to the west.
*Gordon Glattenberg (collection of Keith Ardinger)*

AT RIGHT: The SPLA&SL went a few miles past Daggett to Otis to build a division point. In 1908 Otis became Yermo, a Spanish word that translates as desert or deserted. On July 17, 1971, a westbound waits for a fresh crew at Yermo's stucco-over-masonry depot, built in 1922. The depot housed a cafeteria until the mid-1960s; the house specialty was a prime-rib dinner every Sunday for $3.50. The depot was the work of Los Angeles architects John and Donald Parkinson. Here they attempted to update the aging Mission style with elements from the new Spanish Eclectic style. It was not their best effort, and on subsequent LA&SL depots they reverted to pure Mission style. The UP replaced it in 1981 with a bland steel bungalow. *Gordon Glattenberg*

## Contest for a Right-of-Way

*For some time past the railway world has been following with interest the reports of the conflict between the Oregon Short Line and the W. A. Clark people for right of way below Uvada. The matter has assumed quite an interesting phase, and the situation is, to say the least, exciting.*
— *Railway Age,* April 19, 1901

Early in 1901 Whittemore had the Nevada legislature rewrite Nevada's laws to give out-of-state corporations such as the Utah & California the right to build railroads in Nevada. The bill whipped through the legislature and was signed by the governor on March 11. On March 4 Whittemore met with the Lincoln County Commissioners, and bought the OSL&UN grade from the state line to Clover Valley Junction (Caliente) and Pioche for $5,083! On April 19 the Utah & California quitclaimed its title to the OSL&UN grade to the SPLA&SL.

The OSL claimed that it had the sole right to build through Clover Creek Canyon, on the basis of its Utah, Nevada & California maps filed in 1899. A hearing was held at the Land Office in Carson City and a decision was reached in six days. The OSL was thunderstruck; not only did the Land Office give the rights to Clover Creek to Clark's Utah & California, but it also declared that the OSL had no rights to the grade.

"Quick as a flash" the OSL rushed six gangs and outfit trains to Uvada, according to *Railway Age*'s correspondent. Arriving there on April 7, the gangs rapidly recreated the grade to the Nevada state line. There they were met by Whittemore and all the graders he could hire from nearby farms and mines. Whittemore, waving a shovel, forbade them from trespassing on the right-of-way inside Nevada, but OSL Superintendent J. H. Young, also waving a shovel, pushed his 150 laborers ahead, "and as Mr. Whittemore had no

actual court injunction or anything with which he could legally bar the way of the invaders, the Short Line was enabled to push on unmolested." The next day the OSL's Bancroft returned from a meeting with Harriman in New York, and announced that Harriman had instructed him to push the OSL onward to California, probably to a junction with the SP near Beaumont. Harriman also purchased all the outstanding securities in the Utah & Pacific on April 4, 1901, giving Eccles a nice profit. "Obviously this time," dryly commented historian David Myrick, "no loose pieces were going to be allowed to get away."

The OSL crews rapidly built track into the canyon from Uvada, figuring that what they took by force the lawyers could make legal later. Clark's men attempted to hold the grade, and blocked the OSL with trees, boulders, and barbed-wire fences, but were understandably reluctant to wreak real damage, such as blowing up the six tunnels. Harriman's men easily removed the obstacles. The OSL also appealed the decision of the Land Office in Carson City to the Secretary of the Interior in Washington, D.C. On April 24, that worthy official found that the maps filed by the Oregon Short Line & Utah Northern back in 1890 took precedence, even though the five-year period in which the OSL had to build track or relinquish its rights had long since expired. This gave Harriman's men the right to the *route* from the state line to Clover Valley Junction and Pioche, but it did not give them the rights to the *grade*. And Clark, though he owned the grade, could not legally build track upon it! Both railroads insisted they would build their line no matter what the other did. *Railway Age* sighed lugubriously: "...and so the good, or bad, old days of parallel railway building are now being repeated in the wilds of eastern Nevada."

On April 26 the OSL men tried to sweep the Clark men from the canyon in one great push. After a rather heated day, a truce was reached that backed the Clark forces several miles down Clover

Creek Canyon, where it was agreed they could remain until the courts reached a decision. The very next day, the OSL got that decision. The U.S. Circuit Court at Carson City issued a temporary injunction that restrained Clark's men from interfering with the OSL's construction forces between Uvada and Clover Valley Junction. On May 1 the U.S. Marshal served the papers and Clark's forces reluctantly abandoned their barricades in Clover Creek Canyon.

Harriman's attorneys also tried to rescind Lincoln County's sale of the grade to Clark on the grounds that the title was not clear. On May 5 an overflow crowd listened to Whittemore and the OSL attorneys argue the case before the Lincoln County Commissioners. The evening went poorly for Harriman. Late that night the commissioners decided that Clark held firm title to the grade from Clover Valley Junction to Pioche, and gave Clark the first right to buy the grade from Uvada to the Junction once the title was made clear.

In southern California, the SP did its part to harass Clark. Noting that Clark's survey paralleled its main line along First Street through the city of Pomona, on April 13, 1901, the SP abruptly built a spur across the SPLA&SL right-of-way. The citizens of Pomona took it upon themselves to immediately and enthusiastically tear up the spur, and the city marshal clapped the SP foreman and track gang into jail. The city quickly passed an ordinance permitting the SPLA&SL to occupy First Street, and on June 15 the Superior Court in Los Angeles validated the ordinance, ending the SP's blockade.

On July 31, 1901, the Utah, Nevada & California, the OSL's agent in Nevada, laid its track into Calientes (the new name for Clover Valley Junction; later the "s" was dropped). For the moment, Clark was stymied in Clover Creek, but Meadow Valley Wash was still open. Back in 1890 the OSL&UN had not graded in the wash, nor had it filed a detailed map of its route through the wash. Thus, whoever took possession first would have the best right. In July, Clark awarded a contract to build 60 miles of railroad from Calientes south through Meadow Valley Wash. Three hundred men were soon at work, and by October they had completed 25 miles. The OSL rushed its own survey party into the wash, and began staking out a grade parallel to the SPLA&SL grade.

Clark also put three survey parties to work in Utah in the same area where the OSL was surveying the Leamington Cut-off. One party worked out a line over Boulter Summit, and the other two ran stakes from Salt Lake City through Stockton and the Rush Valley. More Salt Lake Route surveyors looked for the best route into Los Angeles. One crew ran lines through Cajon Pass north of San Bernardino, and the other through Morongo Pass north of Palm Springs. Clark was happy to note in May that "so far we are paying cash for the work." In July, Senator Thomas Kearns of Utah, one of the SPLA&SL's incorporators and like Clark a mining millionaire, announced that 60 miles of grade were under construction in Nevada and 20 miles of the Los Angeles Terminal had so far been rebuilt to main line standards.

By August 9, 1901, the OSL's Utah, Nevada & California track was complete to Calientes, and its crews began grading a line down Meadow Valley Wash parallel to the SPLA&SL's line. The OSL's surveyors hustled through the wash and got their map filed with the Land Office ahead of Clark's surveyors. Whittemore promptly asserted that the UN&C map was of dubious validity, and that the UN&C was interfering with the SPLA&SL's rightful occupancy of the wash. On August 9 the U.S. Circuit Court at Carson City agreed, and granted the SPLA&SL a temporary restraining order which prevented the UN&C from entering upon the SPLA&SL grade, all the way from Calientes to the California state line.

A hearing for a final order was set for September 19 in Carson City, but it was obvious that Clark and Harriman had reached an impasse at Calientes. Clark's SPLA&SL could build no further east, and Harriman's UN&C could build no further west. Their attorneys arranged a truce in November. The two railroads agreed to jointly survey parallel lines through Meadow Valley Wash that did not cross or interfere, and agreed to negotiate a joint-use or trackage-rights agreement for the SPLA&SL on the UN&C in Clover Creek Canyon at a later date. Since the surveys would take time to complete, and there was no longer any reason for panic, in November both railroads laid off their grading crews in Nevada.

By this time the Salt Lake men had settled on Cajon Pass, and the OSL men had decided to run their line to the SP at Banning, having incorporated the Utah, Nevada & California Railroad (of California) on June 3, 1901, for this purpose. Construction on the first 30 miles of the SPLA&SL from Los Angeles to Pomona began in late September 1901, and in December the Salt Lake Route awarded a contract for a 41-stall roundhouse in Los Angeles. The OSL's surveys on the Leamington Cut-off were wrapped up that winter; early in March 1902 the grading crews of David Eccles's Utah Construction Company got to work. First, they installed a third rail for standard-gauge construction trains on the former Utah Western/ Utah & Nevada between Salt Lake City and what is now Garfield. On March 20, with this work complete, they widened about 2.4 miles of the narrow-gauge roadbed to standard-gauge dimensions between the west bank of the Jordan River and Buena Vista, and another 4.9 miles east of Garfield. Elsewhere on the cut-off they began work on a new grade.

The next summer both roads diligently advanced their respective lines in Utah and California. The OSL began to lay track on the Leamington Cut-off in early July, and grading was virtually complete by September except for the big cut through the Stockton Bar (where the Utah Western had proposed to bore a tunnel). The last narrow-gauge train ran on November 15, 1902, ending all narrow-gauge operation on the UP in Utah. By October the SPLA&SL had laid track from Hobart Junction, just south of Los Angeles, to Pomona, and its grading between Pomona and Riverside was well advanced.

In Lincoln County, Nevada, it was very quiet in 1902. People there figured it was 1890 all over again, and the railroad construction crews would never be seen again. In fact, on July 9, 1902, Clark and Harriman had signed an agreement to merge their interests, but did not make this deal public until the following summer. There were hints, however, that a deal had been struck. In mid-August Clark could not resist letting leak that he had agreed with the OSL to use its track for a distance of 40 to 50 miles, "thus terminating all our litigation."

In November the OSL told *Railway Age* that all of its track south of Sandy, Utah, and west of Salt Lake City would be sold to the SPLA&SL by January 1, 1903. Because of difficulties in agreeing upon a value for these properties and in drawing up a joint-owner-ship agreement, this date came and went. Clark and Harriman did not formally announce the deal until April 1903, and it took until June to iron out the last details. Four agreements were signed to close the deal, on June 2, 3, 7, and 15, 1903. Formal transfer of the properties involved took place at midnight, July 7, 1903. The fundamentals of these agreements were as follows:

1. Clark and Kerens sold to the SPLA&SL the Los Angeles Terminal Railway, the Los Angeles Terminal Land Company (which owned about 2,700 acres on and around Terminal Island), and the Empire Construction Company, the company they owned which was actually building the SPLA&SL. For the Los Angeles Terminal and the Land Company Clark and Kerens received $2,500,000; for the Construction Company and its work on the SPLA&SL they received $4,265,472.08.

2. The OSL sold to the SPLA&SL all of its lines in Utah and Nevada south and west of Salt Lake City, 511.95 route-miles in total, including the properties of the New East Tintic Railway, the Utah & Pacific Railway, and the Utah, Nevada & California Railroad. The points of division were set at the south end of yard limits at Sandy on the Provo line, about 13.9 miles south (railroad west) of the Salt Lake City depot, and the west bank of the Jordan River on the Leamington Cut-off, about 1.2 miles west of the Salt Lake City depot. For this and 17 locomotives, 13 passenger cars, 209 freight cars, 27 road-service cars, and other material, the SPLA&SL paid $10,777,993.23.

3. The OSL leased to the SPLA&SL joint-use rights from these two division points to the north yard limits of Salt Lake City, for 99 years.

4. The SPLA&SL agreed to exclusively route its traffic to the OSL and Union Pacific at Salt Lake City, so far as could be legally done, and to the SP in California.

5. Both roads agreed to not invade the other's territory.

6. The SP gave trackage rights to the SPLA&SL from Riverside to San Bernardino, California, in an agreement dated June 18, 1903, and Harriman induced the Santa Fe to grant the SPLA&SL rights between Colton, San Bernardino, and Daggett, California, on April 26, 1905.

7. Clark and Harriman agreed to jointly construct and own the SPLA&SL; to this end the SPLA&SL issued $25,000,000 in stock, divided the stock equally between Clark and the OSL, and placed it in a joint trusteeship.

8. The SPLA&SL issued $50 million in 4 percent bonds equally to Clark and the OSL.

9. Clark and the OSL each got an equal number of representatives on the SPLA&SL's board of directors, and agreed to manage by common assent.

10. All lawsuits were settled out of court.

It is impossible to determine whether it was Clark or Harriman who got the better financial deal at the time because records of the predecessor companies are hopelessly confused (though a bonanza in oil still undiscovered beneath Terminal Island would make this one of the best buys in railroad history). But the political ramifications were already clear. Clark, the irresistible force, had recognized that Harriman could flummox him forever. Historian Nelson Trottman concluded that Harriman "adopted a course which finally compelled the San Pedro Company, if it wished to escape failure as a business enterprise, to amalgamate with the Union Pacific."

Harriman, the immovable object, had an empire to run and could not afford the aggravation. During this time Harriman was rebuilding the SP, CP, UP, OSL, and OR&N; sparring with James J. Hill for control of the Chicago, Burlington & Quincy, the Northern Pacific, and the Pacific Northwest; fending off Wall Street speculators who were trying to take over the SP; skirmishing with the Santa Fe in Arizona; managing the Illinois Central and a dozen steamship, street railway, and interurban lines; and helping to rebuild the Kansas City Southern. By co-opting Clark, Harriman deterred James J. Hill, who was thinking of pushing the Burlington west to connect with Clark in Salt Lake City, and finished off David H. Moffat, who was trying to build the Denver, Northwestern & Pacific across Colorado and Utah to a connection with Clark in Salt Lake City. By closing the Ogden and Salt Lake City gateways to George Gould's Rio Grande, Harriman gave Gould little choice but to build the Western Pacific to San Francisco.

Clark got what he really wanted, a reputation as a railroad builder. Harriman kept what he already had, control of California. Harriman also got a useful route, delivered a powerful warning to other would-be interlopers, and permanently plugged a hole in his borders.

Most important of all the terms of the agreement was the traffic arrangement. By agreeing to route all traffic to the OSL at Salt Lake City and the SP at Los Angeles, Clark had irrevocably welded the San Pedro, Los Angeles & Salt Lake to the Union Pacific System. Superficially, because the SPLA&SL name survived, it gave the appearance that Clark had prevailed. He had not. Harriman had won. And now that the titans had played their games to completion, the work of building the San Pedro, Los Angeles & Salt Lake could begin.

*There has been no disagreement between Mr. Harriman and myself, and our relations have been of the most harmonious character.*

—W. A. Clark, June 1905

## HOW TO BUILD A TWENTIETH-CENTURY RAILROAD

*In comparison with him, the Vanderbilts, the Goulds, the Garretts, the Huntingtons represent the parochial period in our railroad history. They consolidated small railroads into kingdoms, Harriman is federating their kingdoms into empires.*

—Burton J. Hendricks, journalist, October 1909

Harriman had been forced into building a railroad to Los Angeles. Nevertheless, he made the best of it by building the SPLA&SL from the beginning to permanent standards, that is, to Harriman standards. The Leamington Cut-off and Caliente to Daggett were built properly from the beginning. The dirt-track railroad from Leamington to Uvada, and the hasty track from Uvada to Caliente, still had to be brought up to snuff.

While the lawyers were still haggling over the peace treaty, work continued in Utah and California. The SPLA&SL opened its main line to Ontario, California, on March 7, 1903, and commenced work on a 1,000-foot, eight-arch concrete bridge over the Santa Ana River at Arlington. The $200,000 bridge took the rest of the year to build, and the first train did not run from Los Angeles to Riverside until March 12, 1904.

Track-laying on the 116.69-mile Leamington Cut-off proceeded from both ends and in both directions from Tintic, the line opening for business on July 1, 1903. The remainder of the narrow-gauge was then abandoned, 31.11 miles in total, as was a 2.42-mile branch from Saltair Junction to a beach resort at Saltair, Utah, built by the Utah & Nevada in February 1888. Also abandoned were 10.04 miles of the former Salt Lake & Western from Boulter to old Tintic, plus 1.86 miles of the Eureka Branch, which were overlapped by the cut-off. A new junction with the Eureka Branch was made at new Tintic.

The cut-off adhered to the standards the UP established when it rebuilt its main line, using a maximum grade of 0.8 percent and maximum curvature of 4°. The Utah Southern route, by comparison, was heavily curved in Sevier and Leamington Canyons, and crossed three summits between Salt Lake City and Lynndyl with ruling grades of 1.0 to 1.5 percent. The cut-off was also 16 miles shorter than the original line.

The SPLA&SL did not build its own track over Cajon Pass, but instead received trackage rights on the SP and Santa Fe between Riverside and Daggett, California. At first look it seems odd that the Santa Fe would willingly give a competitor this benefit; however, it was then under Harriman's thrall. In 1904 Harriman and his associates had bought $30 million in Santa Fe stock, 14 percent of its entire issue, and so empowered, two UP men were elected to the Santa Fe's board in February 1905, two months before the trackage rights agreement was signed. Nelson Trottman found that the Santa Fe "operated in complete harmony" with the UP and SP during this period.

When Clark and Harriman reached their agreement, 302 miles remained to be built between Daggett and Calientes. Work began to fill the gap even before the final agreements were signed. By May 22, twenty carloads of rail were en route to Calientes, and the survey had been finalized between Calientes and Daggett. In August 1903, David Eccles's Utah Construction Co. commenced work at Caliente. By November, 700 of his men were at work on the grade at Calientes, and track-laying down the wash started that month. Work began at Daggett in August 1903. By January 1, 1904, the ends-of-track were 16 miles west of Calientes and 24 miles east of Daggett.

By May 1904 the track reached 85 miles west of Calientes; Eccles's forces were building a large fill at Moapa and grading between Moapa and Las Vegas. By August the gap between the two grading forces was down from 302 miles to 70 miles, and it was hoped that the rails would meet by December 1. By November the gap between

ABOVE: At Las Vegas Rancho, where a creek trickled across the desert floor, some 30 people eked out a living in 1900, tending cattle and running a roadhouse for wandering prospectors. The place was flat, it had water, and it was the right distance between Otis (Yermo) and Caliente, so Clark built a division point here. On May 5, 1963, train #116, the *City of Las Vegas,* has been wyed for its return trip to Los Angeles, and awaits its cargo of lucky winners and skillful losers. When its engine crew arrives, they will change the number boards of E9A 911 to read 115. This was UP's third and final depot in Las Vegas. Built in 1939, it was demolished in 1971 with the end of passenger service on the LA&SL. *Gordon Glattenberg*

the rails was down to 75 miles. Work began that month on roundhouses at Las Vegas and Caliente—after being called Clover Valley Junction, Clover Junction, Culverwell, and Calientes, the new railroad town of Caliente now had its permanent name.

Since the Utah Central, Utah & Pacific and Utah, Nevada & California between Leamington and Caliente were too poorly built for a main-line railroad, certainly a Harriman railroad, several contracts were let to David Eccles for their complete reconstruction, bringing the SPLA&SL up to Harriman standards in most respects except maximum gradient and curvature. The first contract, let to the Utah Construction Co. in November 1904, called for it to build forty-five 3,000-foot sidings spaced 5 miles apart, to widen the grade from Milford to Uvada to 18 feet on fills and 20 feet in cuts, to replace the old 52-pound rail with new 75-pound rail, to

replace the decayed and broken ties, to install tie plates (there were none), and to ballast the track with waste material from the big cut at Stockton. The old grade built by Bishop Sharp's crews was all of 7 to 10 feet across, hardly wide enough for the ties; the existing sidings were sometimes as far apart as 20 miles and were usually only 1,200 to 1,800 feet long. The second contract, let on December 1, called for a 10.8-mile relocation from Modena east to Yale to reduce the 1.0 percent westward ruling grade to 0.6 percent. Contracts for two more relocations, one nine miles in length at Black Rock, and one about six miles in length where the line crossed the Sevier River just north of Delta, were let to Eccles later that month.

In addition, the contractors strengthened, replaced or rebuilt 25 bridges, and equipped them with ballasted decks; established telegraph offices at maximum intervals of 30 miles; built 17 new section houses; installed coaling facilities at Tintic, Lynn Junction (Lynndyl), Milford, Stockton, and Modena; installed oil fuel facilities at Las Vegas, Otis (later renamed Yermo), and other points; erected over one dozen 70,000-gallon water tanks; constructed a brick engine house at Tintic; and built new terminals, including roundhouses, turntables, shops, and employee housing, at Lynndyl, Milford, Caliente, Las Vegas, and Otis, and a helper terminal at Kelso. Imposing depots of Mission-style architecture were built at the important towns of Riverside, Pomona, and Ontario, California, and simple masonry depots at smaller California towns. Inexpensive wood-frame depots sufficed out in the desert. For its depot, Las Vegas received only a surplus coach.

## THE LAST SPIKE

On January 30, 1905, the two track gangs approached each other on a featureless plain 307 miles east of Los Angeles (accounts differ as to the exact location), and joined the rails together. Disappointed that no official golden spike celebration of Promontory proportions was planned, the wife of SPLA&SL general manager R. E. Wells had a tiny gold spike made up. After the last steel spike was driven, chief engineer E. G. Tilton pushed the miniature spike into the last tie with his thumb. A cheer went up from the workmen, and a construction locomotive rolled over the last rails.

The railroad was not finished, however. Incomplete cuts and fills between Dry Lake and Garnet were bypassed with a five-mile temporary track, and a 12-mile temporary track from Arden to Erie bypassed more unfinished rock cuts and 304-foot Tunnel 2. In addition, ballasting was incomplete, and engine and water facilities were still half built. The first through train to Los Angeles left Salt Lake City on February 9, but it was not until May 1 that the line officially opened for through business. The bypass at Arden remained in use until May 26, 1905.

Terminal improvements at each end were required for the new main line. In 1905, the SPLA&SL and OSL built the 3.6-mile Poplar Grove Line from Buena Vista to a connection with the former Utah Southern nine blocks south of the Salt Lake City depot, to allow SPLA&SL passenger trains to enter and leave the depot without a reverse move. This was called the Passenger Line to distinguish it from the original Freight Line; it opened on December 1, 1905. In 1905 the OSL and SPLA&SL also began building a large union terminal in Salt Lake City to replace the OSL's cramped facilities. In Los Angeles, the SPLA&SL built a 1.47-mile line from Butte Street Junction to a connection with the SP main line at Washington and Alameda Streets, to handle interchange traffic.

On October 9, 1905, a special car carrying 23 elderly Mormons invited by Senator Clark left Salt Lake City for San Bernardino and Los Angeles. They were surviving members of an expedition that had left Salt Lake City on March 24, 1851, and made an exhausting overland journey through the desert to San Bernardino to establish a new Mormon colony. In 1858 they abandoned their homes, orchards, and farms at San Bernardino, on the instructions of Brigham Young, and trudged *back* across the desert to Salt Lake City to help defend Utah from a possible attack by the U.S. Army. By wagon their journey had taken many arduous weeks; by rail it was a few pleasant days.

It has been claimed that the SPLA&SL recreated old trails with steel rails. These were minor, short-lived trails, not important trade routes. The Old Spanish Trail, which ran in a looping path from Santa Fe, New Mexico, through southern Utah, thence southwest to Los Angeles, had fallen into disuse over 50 years prior. The Mormon Road ran from Salt Lake City to Los Angeles, using portions of the Old Spanish Trail, but most of its route was far removed from the SPLA&SL, and as a through trail it fell into disuse after the Union Pacific and Central Pacific met at Promontory in 1869.

From beginning to end it had taken 35 years to connect Salt Lake City and Los Angeles by rail. It took 18 months to fill the 302-mile gap from Caliente to Daggett, a rate of about one-half mile a day. While this was not anything like the pace set by the Central Pacific and Union Pacific in the last months of their dash to Promontory, the Salt Lake Route had been built to much higher standards on a better alignment, whereas the CP and UP had to be almost completely realigned at a later date.

ABOVE: Late on the evening of September 15, 1959, on one of its last runs as an independent schedule, train #107 makes its station stop at Salt Lake City. In a few minutes the crossing watchman will raise his stop sign and the *Challenger's* massed E9's will rumble out of the depot on the overnight run to Los Angeles.

UP's stately Salt Lake City Union Station was shared by the OSL and the SPLA&SL, the two UP lines that served the city. Completed in 1909, it used Second Empire architecture, a formal style created during France's Second Empire (the reign of Emperor Napoleon III). The style was very fashionable for American houses from 1855 to 1885, and for public buildings during General Grant's presidency, 1869–77. By the time the UP embraced Second Empire, it had been out of date for 20 years. Railroads, being cautious by nature, were seldom on the cutting edge of architecture, usually taking up a style only after everyone else had dropped it and moved on to something new. *Fred Matthews*

## THE PRICE OF THE ROUTE

*...dawn offered a spectacle you could hardly equal.*
— Lou Martin, SPLA&SL fireman, January 1, 1910

Every transcontinental railroad has its definitive mountain passage, the place where its builders faced their most vexing geographic problem. Sometimes a pass, sometimes a canyon, this place is the railroad's pinnacle of scenic wonder and the wellspring of eternal despair for the operating and engineering departments. For the Southern Pacific this place is Donner Pass; for the UP it is Sherman Hill; and for the Salt Lake Route it is Meadow Valley Wash and Clover Creek Canyon.

These canyons are truly the cornerstone of the entire railroad. They route it through the labyrinthine mountains that wrinkle the map north of the Grand Canyon of the Colorado River, lifting the railroad from 2,000 feet above sea level in the southern Nevada deserts to 5,000 feet above sea level in Utah's Escalante Desert. Clark and Harriman had searched for an alternative to these canyons without success before and after they collided at Caliente. "There was never any question as to the route," said SPLA&SL assistant chief engineer H. M. McCartney in 1911. "The Meadow Valley had no competitors. It ran in the right direction, cut through three mountain ranges, and afforded the same grades which were necessary on any of the other routes."

Like the SP on Donner Pass and the UP on Sherman Hill, the Salt Lake Route has paid a steep price to occupy Meadow Valley Wash and Clover Creek Canyon. Five thousand square miles of Nevada and Utah drains into these two canyons. On January 1, 1910, a flood flushed the Salt Lake Route from the canyons. Between Guelph and Barclay the flood severely damaged 71 miles of the SPLA&SL main line. Twenty-six miles of roadbed completely disappeared. *Railway Age* decided it was "the worst railway washout ever known."

Historically, the wash was known more for its *lack* of water. Ranchers who had lived in the valley since 1876 had noted that in most years there was no running water in 100 of the 113 miles of Meadow Valley Wash and Clover Creek Canyon. In 1901, when the OSL reoccupied the grade, it found that the channel crossings and embankments it had built in 1890 were undisturbed by flooding. The engineers' cedar survey stakes still stood in the channel where they had been hammered in 11 years before!

In most of Clover Creek Canyon and Meadow Valley Wash the SPLA&SL found plenty of room to build its main line, which crossed the channel over a hundred times to minimize curvature and grading. Heavy rock work was necessary in only 20 of the 113 miles, most

of them in Clover Creek Canyon. The SPLA&SL accepted the OSL&UN's 1890 survey almost in its entirety and completed its main line with little concern for the possibility of high water. Many of the pile trestles had barely a foot of clearance between the bottom of their stringers and the channel's dry, sandy surface.

On March 24, 1906, spring freshets caused damage between Hoya and Minto, closing the line for 22 days. Then, between February 22 and March 5, 1907, two consecutive floods brought the highest water yet seen in the canyon. These floods and another on March 19 destroyed several trestles and undermined several miles of track. The railroad was closed from February 22 to April 7, 1907, when a temporary track reestablished service at a cost of $872,293. The creek was not as dull as it had first appeared, so the SPLA&SL raised its grade in the wash until all was at least 4 feet above the new high-water line, armored 34 miles of exposed embankments with heavy riprap, and installed eight steel through trusses in place of pile trestles at critical channel crossings. Extensive channel relocations involving the excavation of 220,000 cubic yards of rock and sand allowed the SPLA&SL to eliminate 18 of 104 channel crossings. Local wits gleefully noted that the engineers had relocated the creek, not the railroad, though small line relocations were made at mileposts 429, 441.5, and 448 (totaling 2.0 miles of new line which replaced 1.94 miles of old). Over 1,000 men were engaged in the work, which was completed in autumn 1909 at a cost of $769,572, whereupon the SPLA&SL announced, "Today the railroad runs through the cañon, forever safe from the ravages of storm. The roadbed is laid to last for all time...."

Reportedly, an engineer on this work ignored the advice of an elderly Indian and local residents that the true high-water line in

the canyon was considerably higher than the elevation of the raised roadbed. More to the point, consulting bridge engineer H. G. Tyrrell and the SPLA&SL's chief engineer both informed SPLA&SL management in 1907 that the line should be rebuilt on higher ground and the pile trestles eliminated to avoid a repeat occurrence, but were overruled in the interests of economy. Some sources indicate that Clark and Harriman disagreed in this matter, Clark opting for economy and Harriman for security, but this has not been confirmed.

The year 1908 was dry and there was no flooding. In December 1909, however, an unusually large storm deposited heavy snow in a broad swath stretching from the California line into central Utah. By December 28 the accumulation measured 18 inches in the wash, and more in the mountains above. By itself this snowfall would have melted slowly, and caused no great problem. But on the last day of the year an extremely powerful Pacific storm entered southern Nevada, deluging the mountains with warm rain. In hours the snow pack turned to water, and being unable to soak into the frozen ground, three million acres of runoff all at once funneled into Clover Creek Canyon and Meadow Valley Wash.

The first day of 1910 dawned on a rising, thundering flood that filled the wash from wall to wall. Floating atop the brown, churning water were chunks of ice, trees, logs, and brush. The debris rapidly collected behind the low pile trestles. Very quickly this pressure overwhelmed the first trestle and it collapsed with a vicious crackling sound. The raging waters propelled its shattered timbers downstream to rip out the next in an instant. The flood peeled the heavy riprap from the embankments; exposed to the current, the earthen roadbed dissolved as if made of sugar. Five times as much water raced down

the canyon as in 1907. In the narrow portions of the wash, the flood filled the canyon 15 feet deep and 12 feet above the rails.

An eastbound passenger train that left Caliente the night of December 31 was trapped by the flood at Eccles. Fortunately the train was safe on a rocky shelf above the water; after spending a frightening night in the dark canyon the passengers were rescued the following day in wagons. The train did not reach Salt Lake City until May 17, 1910, 138 days after it left Los Angeles, some sort of a record. A westbound freight train that left Caliente just after midnight on January 1 made it 12 miles before it could proceed no farther, and as the track behind it had also washed out, it could not retreat. Soon the flood undermined the track it stood on. One by one, 37 of its 42 cars toppled over into the river, some sinking, some floating downstream to be dashed against rocks. Its locomotive, heavy Consolidation 3657, rolled over into the water with an enormous splash and disappeared. It was not recovered for another year. The crew made their way on foot back to Caliente. Not so lucky was a

trackwalker, who drowned, as did 36 horses in a stock-car.

When the flood abated, the SPLA&SL's engineers picked their way through the canyon on foot. They were appalled by the destruction. In steep places the flood had scoured the stream bed 5 to 15 feet down to bedrock, and in level places it had deposited silt and raised the bed 5 to 8 feet. One-ton rocks were lifted onto the roadbed. Rails were later discovered buried under 9 feet of sand and silt. Many rails disappeared altogether, and ties were seen floating hundreds of miles downstream in the Colorado River. Twenty-three miles of main line and 6 miles of siding were completely gone. Of the 86 trestles that crossed the channel, the flood totally destroyed 36 and partially destroyed the rest. Of the eight steel bridges installed in 1907-08, one was overturned and partially buried, and two were undermined. At Caliente the flood smashed through a dike, ripped a 110-foot hole in the back wall of the brick roundhouse, and filled the roundhouse pits and turntable pit with sand.

Two photographs at left: The headlines of the *Clark County Review* on January 8, 1910, told the story of the devastation that had befallen the Salt Lake Route and the farmers who grew hay and melons downstream of Moapa. Years later, pieces of the original SPLA&SL occasionally resurface when spring runoff rearranges the creek bed. In 1985 some old track reappeared at Elgin, Nevada, 75 years after it was swept from its grade by the great flood of 1910. Two years later it was again buried in sediment. *Eric Blasko*

Above: On May 28, 1967, Extra 405 East thunders through the steel truss at the tenth crossing of Meadow Valley Wash, milepost 433.47 just west of Kyle. The truss, which dates to the 1907–08 line reconstruction, was lifted onto new piers after the 1910 flood. The 1907 line was considerably lower at this location. It passed through the fill west of this bridge at about the same elevation as the base of the two code-line poles in the right background—almost down at stream level. *Wm. (Hank) Mills (collection of Martha Mills)*

The SPLA&SL's officers in Los Angeles and UP's officers in Omaha were stunned, concluding that a railroad in Meadow Valley Wash would never be safe from catastrophes. Believing it pointless to pour more money into the wash, they shut down the railroad and told their engineers to find a new line which bypassed Meadow Valley Wash and Clover Creek Canyon. By February 1910, however, it became apparent that alternatives to Meadow Valley Wash were too steep, too expensive to build, and just as vulnerable to flooding. They kept looking for an alternative to Clover Creek, however. On March 1 construction crews were dispatched to the wash to build a temporary line and put the main line back into service. By driving over five miles of temporary pile trestles, the crews stitched the main line together in 107 days, saving months over what it would have taken to fill the gaps with earth. Through train service resumed on June 15. The flood of January 1 had closed the SPLA&SL main line for six and a half months, probably a record for a twentieth-century transcontinental main line.

Having given up the search for an alternative to Meadow Valley Wash, the engineers went into the wash to figure out how to build a new flood-resistant railroad. They determined the best solution to be a "High Line" located up on the canyon wall, 8 to 12 feet above the flood's high-water line. The SPLA&SL continued to toy with an alternative line over Miller Pass that would bypass Clover Creek Canyon between Caliente and Crestline, so at first the High Line was planned only for Meadow Valley Wash below Caliente. That fall the SPLA&SL determined that the Miller Pass alternative was too expensive, so it extended the High Line project up Clover Creek Canyon to Minto, with minor revisions as far east as Barclay.

Work began on the High Line in August 1910 and was completed in April 1912. The engineers were able to reuse 6.20 miles of old grade in Meadow Valley Wash and 1.93 miles in Clover Creek Canyon, in disconnected pieces. They abandoned 10.40 miles east of Caliente and 59.39 miles west of Caliente, constructing 72.19 miles of new line. This lengthened the railroad by 2.40 miles. Unlike most post-1900 relocations the High Line added many curves to the railroad. The work required 10 new tunnels totaling 5,901 feet in length, 24 new steel bridges, and a large quantity of heavy rock work to create a ledge for the new grade on the canyon wall.

Crossings of the main channel west of Caliente were reduced in number from 86 to 24; all were now made on steel bridges instead of the pile trestles which had proven incapable of resisting flood damage. The steel bridges totaled over 5,000 tons of steel and were 4,715 feet in length (including the eight steel bridges installed in 1907). The engineers paid particular attention to making bridge piers and abutments resistant to undermining; they were sunk at least 12 feet into the streambed to bedrock or hard gravel, and skewed where necessary so they would not hinder the creek's flow

at flood stage. The engineers used pile trestles across tributaries only. Concrete retaining walls, of which the largest was 400 feet long and 18 to 20 feet high, were installed at several critical points; elsewhere many miles of heavy riprap were installed to armor the grade.

The total cost of the High Line, less salvaged material, was $4,007,306. The temporary line cost an additional $658,407. Not including lost revenue, etc., this one flood cost the SPLA&SL about a third as much as it had cost to build the whole railroad from scratch in 1903-05! And of the money spent in 1903 to

build the line, and the money it took to rebuild the line after the floods of 1906, 1907, and 1908? The flood of 1910 flushed every penny into the Gulf of Colorado.

*And what will the Meadow valley creek do? Will it repeat its tactics of 1910 and make one final effort for supremacy, or will it sulk along as it has for the thirty years from 1876 to 1906?*

–H. M. McCartney, 1911

# EXPANDING THE SYSTEM

*Branch lines went almost literally everywhere, because, except for horse-drawn wagons, no other means of getting freight to or from the railroad existed.* —Albro Martin, historian, 1990

The settlement of the West can be seen in four distinct periods, albeit with some overlap. In the first period people went west in search of free wealth–gold and silver mines. In the second period people went west in search of free land–watered bottomlands for farming, open range for grazing, and forests for logging. In the third period people went to the West's new cities in search of freedom–from cold weather, the dust bowl, and the ills of eastern cities. In the fourth period the government and its employees went west in search of free space–clear skies and empty land for military bases.

The South-Central District's branch lines were constructed in similar fashion, again with some overlap. First, the Salt Lake Route built branches to the Great Basin's easy wealth, gold and silver bonanzas. Second, the LA&SL and the OSL looked to agriculture for local business, once irrigation projects enriched previously arid valleys. Third, they built branches to the quarries and refineries that produced gypsum, cement, and iron ore, the mundane stuff that builds cities. And fourth, they built branches to military bases and government projects.

Typically, branches on the South-Central District were short and inexpensive. This was dull, but it was good business. This is not to say that the SPLA&SL never contemplated any long extensions. In 1906 it drew up plans for an extension south to San Diego and a branch from Tintic about 125 miles west to Utah's Deep Creek mining district, and the same year the OSL thought about building a cut-off from Malad northwest to Mountain Home, Idaho, about

200 miles. A few years later the SPLA&SL looked at building a line from Pioche north to the copper mines at Ely, Nevada, about 110 miles.

## THE FRISCO BRANCH

In May 1904 Samuel Newhouse, owner of the mining properties at his namesake town, paid the SPLA&SL to build a six-mile extension of the Frisco Branch from Frisco, Utah, over the San Francisco Mountains to Newhouse. It was completed on August 30, 1904. The SPLA&SL also built the Newhouse, Copper Gulch & Sevier Lake Railroad, a three-mile industrial railroad between the mill at Newhouse and Newhouse's Cactus Mine. Newhouse's mines gave out in the mid-1920s and his railroad shut down in 1927. The LA&SL applied for authority to abandon the entire 22.37-mile branch from Milford to Newhouse on September 24, 1934. At that time Frisco consisted of two families, two houses, the LA&SL depot, and a great deal of debris. At Newhouse, the depot was the last building extant. The ICC granted permission to abandon the 6.22 miles from Frisco to Newhouse on April 21, 1937, but waited until 1943 to give the LA&SL permission to abandon the remainder. In its life the district had produced some $90 to $100 million in lead, silver, zinc, copper, and gold ore.

## THE LAS VEGAS & TONOPAH RAILROAD

Nevada's last big mining boom began with the discovery of silver at Tonopah on May 19, 1900, gold at Goldfield in 1902, and more gold in the Bullfrog Hills above Rhyolite and Beatty in 1904. Goldfield's mines were so rich that a *pound* of ore was often worth $2 to $20, i.e. several days' wages. Late in 1904 Clark sent the

SPLA&SL's engineers to survey a branch from Las Vegas to Goldfield, but when Clark approached Harriman to get his approval for the SPLA&SL to build the branch, Harriman demurred, suspecting the boom would be short-lived. Undeterred, Clark and his brother incorporated the Las Vegas & Tonopah Railroad on September 22, 1905.

Rival Tonopah & Tidewater had already begun work at Las Vegas; Clark chased them out of town by refusing to make a connection, delaying shipments, and charging outrageous rates. Clark's men took over at Las Vegas in October 1905. Floods in Meadow Valley Wash in 1906, summer heat, and shortages of ties and rails slowed progress. The first LV&T train arrived in Rhyolite, 124 miles from Las Vegas, on December 14, 1906, and in Goldfield, 73 miles farther, on October 26, 1907. The boom, however, had ended nine days earlier, with a run on Goldfield's largest bank. The Panic of 1907 had commenced, and the hyperinflated Nevada mining camps crashed hard from their giddy heights.

The LV&T made a modest profit in 1908, then lost money every year thereafter. In March 1918 the USRA diverted the LV&T's traffic to the Tonopah & Tidewater, and on November 1, 1918, operations ceased. Clark scrapped the 13-year-old LV&T in 1919. As usual Harriman had been right.

## THE PIOCHE AND PRINCE BRANCHES

Although Pioche, Nevada, was one of the richest silver camps in the West, and remarkably long-lived, it had no rail connection with the outside world until 1908, forty-four years after its discovery. Pioche's first boom began in 1870. There was not enough water at Pioche to mill its ore, so in 1872 local interests incorporated the Nevada Central (unrelated to the other railroad of that name in northern Nevada) to haul ore 20 miles to mills at Bullionville.

They completed the isolated narrow-gauge line (which was sometimes called the Pioche & Bullionville) in June 1873, and ran it for four years until the mines encountered water 1,200 feet below the surface and could no longer operate profitably. The Pioche & Bullionville was pulled up in 1884.

In 1890 the OSL&UN graded a line into Pioche. But the UP ran out of money, and no rails were laid. About the same time, new ore bodies were discovered north of town at Royal City, which brought about a minor revival of Pioche. The Pioche Pacific Transportation Co. (known locally as the Jackrabbit Road) was incorporated in 1889 to haul this ore to a smelter at Pioche. Using some of the P&B's derelict equipment and rail, and some of its grade, the narrow-gauge Pioche Pacific was completed in 1891. It ran off and on until 1948, when it was replaced by trucks.

In 1901, with the OSL and the SPLA&SL battling over the old grade in Clover Creek Canyon, it looked as if Pioche would soon have its railroad. But not until June 23, 1905, six months after the main line was finished, did the SPLA&SL even announce that it would build the branch, and still nothing happened for another year, until the Caliente & Pioche Railroad, an SPLA&SL subsidiary incorporated on June 8, 1906, began work. Progress was unhurried; the 32-mile branch did not open for business until January 1, 1908. Title to the $481,000 branch was transferred to the SPLA&SL on March 8, 1909. Maximum grade was 2 miles of 3.20 percent where it climbed into Pioche, and curves were as tight as 10° in Condor Canyon between Panaca and Delmues.

AT LEFT: Pioche's mines had almost as many lives as a cat, but it seems they have finally run dry. A tidy business in lead and zinc ore once came down the Pioche Branch to Caliente, destined to Bauer, Utah, for concentrating, but on July 3, 1967, GP9 162 had only one boxcar in tow in the alkaline flats north of Panaca, Nevada.
*Gordon Glattenberg*

BELOW: The urban Glendale and Pasadena Branches were in total contrast to the Pioche Branch. On October 11, 1975, a transfer from SP's Taylor Yard runs east on the Glendale Branch at Spring Street in Los Angeles, double track at this location because it is joint with SP's main line. At right is the Pasadena Branch. Visible at left is Santa Fe's Second District bridge over the Los Angeles River, now gone.
*David J. Norris*

New discoveries at nearby Caselton revived Pioche a third time in 1911. The Prince Consolidated Railroad was incorporated in 1911 to build 8.71 miles of standard-gauge from Pioche to the Prince Consolidated Mine at Caselton. It was completed on June 12, 1912, and operated until 1927 when the mines ran out of ore. The railroad was reactivated in 1933 when new ore bodies were found. The LA&SL purchased the 8.62-mile line on May 27, 1940, rehabilitated it, added 2.49 miles of track, and named it the Prince Branch, just in time for World War II to send lead and zinc values soaring, reviving Pioche yet again. In 1958 exhaustion of these ore bodies ended Pioche's last boom.

Pioche produced more than $50 million of lead-zinc-silver ore between 1923 and 1957, most of it hauled by the LA&SL to the Combined Metals Reduction Co. concentrator at Bauer, Utah. After 1957, a small amount of outbound ore, perlite, and fertilizer made from pyrite mill tailings moved down the branch to Caliente, and some Utah iron-titanium ore moved up the branch to a pilot smelter, but eventually this traffic declined to practically nothing. The UP abandoned the Pioche and Prince Branches in August 1984.

### THE CACHE VALLEY'S SUGAR BEET BRANCHES

In the 1890s farmers in Utah's Cache Valley began growing sugar beets for the factories at Ogden and Lehi. To minimize rail transportation costs, in 1901 the Logan Sugar Co., a David Eccles company, built a sugar factory with a 350-ton daily sliced-beet capacity about 1.5 miles south of Logan. The OSL reached the new factory via a short spur from East Logan Junction built the same year. By 1906, the factory, now part of the Amalgamated Sugar Co., had doubled in size. To supply more beets, and to serve the farming towns of the southern Cache Valley, the OSL opened the 14.53-mile Wellsville Branch on September 12, 1906, between Mendon and East Logan Junction (incorporating the Logan Sugar Plant Spur). Most trains between Mendon and Logan used the Wellsville Branch because it served more of the towns in the valley.

The OSL completed another beet line, the 8.13-mile Ballard Cut-off, between Benson Junction and Logan Junction (later Ballard Junction) on October 31, 1912. Generally the OSL used it only during the fall beet rush. Because of congestion at the Logan Sugar Factory, on September 30, 1916 the OSL completed a 1.89-mile cut-off between Sugar Factory Junction and East Logan Junction. This became the through route to Logan.

After the closure of the obsolete Logan factory in 1926, the OSL had some excess track in Cache Valley. In 1932 the OSL abandoned 2.78 miles in the middle of the Cache Valley Branch between Mendon and College. To sort out all the pieces, (1) East Logan Junction was renamed (new) Logan Junction; (2) (old) Logan Junction was renamed College Junction; (3) the portion of the (old) Cache Valley Branch between College Junction and College was renamed the College Branch; (4) the portion of the Wellsville Branch from Sugar Factory Junction to Logan Junction (through the Logan Sugar Factory) was renamed the Logan Sugar Factory Branch; and (5) the (new) Cache Valley Branch was reassembled using the original Cache Valley Branch from Cache Junction to Mendon, the Wellsville Branch from Mendon to Sugar Factory Junction, the cut-off from Sugar Factory Junction to Logan Junction, and the original Cache Valley Branch from Logan Junction to the end of the branch at Preston, Idaho.

Better roads killed the Cache Valley beet branches in the 1940s. The ICC granted OSL permission to abandon the Ballard Cut-off between Ballard Junction and Benson, 2.95 miles, in 1942 (the

remainder was renamed the Benson Branch), and all of the College Branch between College Junction and College, 2.98 miles, in November 1947. The Logan Sugar Factory Branch between Logan Junction and the Logan River bridge, 1.57 miles, was abandoned in 1949; the 0.9-mile remainder is in service today as the Sugar Factory Spur. Finally, the remainder of the Benson Branch from Benson to Benson Junction, 5.2 miles, was abandoned in 1954, bringing Cache Valley to its current state.

### THE MALAD BRANCH AND BEAR RIVER VALLEY BEET BRANCHES

Farmers in Utah's Bear River Valley also began growing sugar beets for the factories in Ogden and Lehi in the 1890s. The valley was well suited to this crop, so in 1901 the Utah Sugar Co. asked the OSL to build a branch to haul beets from the valley. The OSL incorporated the Malad Valley Railroad on November 25, 1902. The next spring Utah Construction Co. began work at a connection with the Central Pacific at Corinne, completing a 14.57-mile line from Corinne to Garland on June 16, 1903. To reach this branch, the OSL built the 4.09-mile Brigham City Cut-off between Brigham City and the CP at Corinne Junction, 1.8 miles east of Corinne, between October and November 26, 1902. The CP and OSL signed a trackage-rights agreement for the short stretch from Corinne Junction to Corinne on July 26, 1903 (which was former UP trackage built in 1869). As soon as the branch opened on July 1, 1903, the OSL began hauling machinery and construction materials to the site of Utah Sugar Co.'s (Utah-Idaho Sugar Co. after 1907) new 600-ton sugar factory at Garland.

To enlarge the beet-growing area in the Bear River Valley, the Utah Sugar Co. built a 7.04-mile spur from Tremonton west to Thatcher in 1904. The OSL operated it as the Thatcher Branch, and purchased it from successor Utah-Idaho Sugar Co. in September 1922. Later it was extended 1.24 miles to Nelson. To the north, the OSL extended the Malad Valley Railroad 31.83 miles from Garland to Malad, Idaho, opening the line on December 22, 1905. The Malad Valley Railroad was leased by the OSL until October 31, 1910, when it was conveyed to the OSL as the Malad Branch.

In 1918 the OSL completed the 10.6-mile Bear River Branch from Garland south to Bear River City to transport sugar beets. On the other side of the river, the OSL built the 4.9-mile Urban Branch from Bakers to Urban in 1916 to haul beets to a new 500-ton sugar factory at Brigham City. This branch incorporated the 1.1-mile, 1909-built Opco Spur from Bakers to Opco (short for Ogden Portland Cement Co.).

The SP began operating over the Lucin Cut-off in July 1903, but retained its original CP line via Promontory until the U.S. Navy requisitioned the rails in 1942. Operations on the Promontory line ceased on July 30, 1942. The navy sold 4.82 miles from Dathol to Corinne to Utah-Idaho Sugar Co.; the OSL continued to use 1.9 miles of trackage rights between Corinne and Corinne Junction until November 14, 1947, when it purchased the track from Utah-Idaho Sugar. The SP used 17.81 miles of OSL trackage rights from a point near Ogden to Corinne Junction from 1905 until 1947, when it quit running to Corinne.

Because of declining beet traffic, in 1942 the ICC gave the OSL permission to abandon the Bear River Branch from Bradford to Bear River, 0.74 miles, and the Thatcher Branch from Thatcher to Nelson, 1.24 miles. The Thatcher Branch was trimmed 0.61 miles back to Sunset in 1945, and the remainder disappeared in the late 1960s. The Urban Branch was torn up in 1947. The remainder of the Bear River Branch, 8.5 miles, was abandoned in 1964.

### THE ST. THOMAS (MEAD LAKE) BRANCH

The SPLA&SL built the St. Thomas Branch to haul cantaloupes, vegetables, and hay grown in southeastern Nevada's Muddy River and Virgin River valleys, as well as gypsum rock. Work began on the 21.3-mile branch from Moapa south (railroad west) to St. Thomas in May 1911. Most of it was light valley work with one mile of medium-heavy mountain work in the Muddy River narrows. The branch was opened for traffic in May 1912. Passenger traffic was light; an open gasoline-powered motor car "with accommodations for eight passengers and a small quantity of light baggage" was put into service in December 1912. Although it was reported at various times that the SPLA&SL was planning to extend the branch up the Virgin River to St. George, Utah, the branch instead got shorter when Boulder Dam's pool began to cover its end. In 1938 the LA&SL abandoned 2.26 miles from Silica to St. Thomas, and in 1939 another 2.20 miles from Nepac to Silica. Nepac and the branch were both renamed Mead Lake. In recent years traffic on the branch has been silica sand and gypsum. The maximum grade is a brief 2.0 percent ramp from Moapa down to the valley, and maximum curvature is 10°.

### THE CRESTMORE SPUR AND RIALTO BRANCH

To supply riprap for breakwater additions at San Pedro, in 1905-06 the SPLA&SL built a spur from Bly Junction east (railroad west) and north to Bly Quarry, California, 2.9 miles. The 5.44-mile Crestmore Spur was built in 1911-12 from Henshaw, on the Bly Quarry Spur, to Riverside Portland Cement Co.'s new plant at Crestmore.

On December 1, 1917, the LA&SL acquired the Riverside, Rialto & Pacific Railroad from William Henshaw, an owner of Riverside Portland Cement, for $465,000. Incorporated on January 11, 1915, the Riverside, Rialto & Pacific owned a 9.57-mile electrified short-line from Riverside Junction through Crestmore to Rialto. It was originally called the Crescent City Railway. The Pacific Electric had leased the Crescent City on September 1, 1911, to give its interurbans a shortcut between Los Angeles and Riverside; this lease continued after the LA&SL purchased the RR&P. The LA&SL ran freight on the line, which it called the Rialto Branch, under PE's rules.

Crestmore to Rialto, 5.19 miles, was abandoned in 1941 after the PE ceased its Los Angeles–Riverside service on June 9, 1940. The Bly Quarry Spur from Henshaw to Bly Quarry was abandoned in 1942 after the quarry closed. Riverside Junction to Crestmore, 2.0 miles, was abandoned in 1948, leaving a short stub at Riverside Junction that was later abandoned. The 6.89-mile Crestmore Branch (now called the Crestmore Industrial Lead) still serves the Riverside Cement Co. plant. The branch twists into the low Jurupa Mountains on a grade of up to 2.0 percent with many curves as tight as 12°.

### THE DELTA AND HINCKLEY BRANCHES

In 1912 the Delta Land & Water Company began work on an irrigation project in the Sevier Desert west of Delta, Utah. To haul away the expected harvests of grain, hay, and sugar beets, the company graded a branch from Delta northwest to Lucerne, 12.82 miles, beginning in January 1914. In May 1914 the SPLA&SL began laying track on the line, which had a maximum grade of 0.5 percent and few curves, none sharper than 6°. The Delta Branch opened for business on October 1.

Encouraged by high sugar prices during World War I, the Delta Beet Sugar Co. built a 1,000-ton sugar factory in Delta in 1917. To expand the sugar-beet farming area, in April 1918 the LA&SL completed the Hinckley Branch, 3.35 miles, from Moody (on the Delta Branch) south to Hinckley. Sugar-beet blight, drought, and falling sugar prices caused the Delta Sugar Factory to close after 1924. Beet farming with disease-resistant plants resumed in the late 1930s, though now the beets were shipped to factories at Spanish Fork, West Jordan, and Gunnison. It was too late for the Delta and Hinckley Branches, as the LA&SL had received permission to abandon them on October 20, 1932. At that time Lucerne's population was zero, Hinckley's 700. Traffic on the branches had fallen to 1,962 tons in 1931. A portion of the Delta Branch, from Delta to Wilson, 8.2 miles, remained in place until 1934. At Delta, 0.76 miles and the wye remained to serve a grain elevator.

### THE FILLMORE BRANCH

In order to haul grain, alfalfa, sugar-beets, produce, and lumber from Utah's upper Pahvant Valley to market, the ICC approved the LA&SL's construction of a 32.2-mile branch from Delta southeast (railroad west) to Fillmore on July 1, 1922. The Sevier River Land & Water Co. was then developing irrigation in the area. The branch, which cost about $700,000, was placed in operation on January 15, 1923. Once it left Delta, it had just three curves; the ruling grade was 0.90 percent as the branch approached Fillmore, the largest town on the branch at 1,600. Stations were built there and at Harding, McCormick, and Greenwood. Passenger service was reduced to a motor car on June 10, 1929, and downgraded to bus service in 1930. The LA&SL first tried to abandon this branch in 1942. After a bridge was damaged by flooding in 1983, the UP

ABOVE: On June 23, 1993, a 26-car Malad Local motors up the Malad Branch at milepost 22, just south of the former siding of Belmont, Utah. At present there is but one siding in the 30 miles between Garland, Utah and Malad, Idaho, at Nucor, Utah, where the local will exchange its gondolas loaded with scrap for a similar number of gondolas loaded with new steel. Directly across pastoral Bear River Valley is the Ogden to Pocatello, Idaho, main line. The low ridge in the near background is Collinston Divide, over which the Utah Northern ran in 1872 to reach the Cache Valley. The Ogden, Logan & Idaho (later the Utah Idaho Central) reused the old U&N grade over the divide for its interurban line from Ogden to Preston, Idaho, in 1915, twenty-five years after the grade was abandoned by the OSL&UN.
*James Belmont*

was able to abandon it in 1984. The branch's last customer, which shipped pumice, switched to trucks, and bought the Fillmore depot for its office.

### THE SANTA ANA (ANAHEIM) BRANCH

In September 1916 the LA&SL announced plans to build a branch of about 25 miles from Pico, California, southeast (railroad west) to the citrus towns of Whittier, Fullerton, Anaheim, and Santa Ana. Work began on the branch, which invaded territory served by the Santa Fe, SP, and Pacific Electric, early in 1917. On January 1, 1918, the USRA took control of the nation's railroads; in April it ordered work discontinued on almost all railroad expansion and improvement projects, which included the Santa Ana Branch. The first 2.3 miles from Whittier Junction (just east of Pico) southeast to Whittier was by then complete and in service.

In September 1920, after the war, the LA&SL reapplied to complete the Santa Ana Branch, as well as another branch from La Habra east and south to Tustin, 21.8 miles. After listening to the SP, Santa Fe, and PE, the ICC turned down the Tustin Branch and approved 17.49 miles from Whittier to Anaheim, but not to Santa Ana. Work resumed in May 1922 and the LA&SL placed the renamed 20.0-mile Anaheim Branch in operation on May 2, 1923. Mission-style stations at Fullerton, La Habra, and Anaheim joined a prewar station at Whittier.

The LA&SL abandoned the Anaheim Branch between mileposts 5.18, Colima Junction, and 10.51, Fullerton Junction, in 1962, and began using trackage rights over Pacific Electric's (SP's) La Habra Branch between these points on March 20, 1962. In turn the PE (SP) received rights over the Anaheim Branch from Fullerton Junction to Anaheim. In 1993 the branch was cut back to the Santa Fe crossing at Basta, milepost 15.5. Maximum grade is 1.10 percent from Basta to Fullerton Junction; curves are very sharp.

### THE CEDAR CITY AND IRON MOUNTAIN BRANCHES

The iron-ore deposits just west of Cedar City were an early target for railroads. In 1874 the Utah Western declared it would build there. The Utah Southern and the Rio Grande said the same in 1881. In 1890 the OSL&UN surveyed the line. In January 1899 the Utah & Pacific announced it would build a branch from Cedar Junction (Lund) to Cedar City. But no one built a line to the iron-ore deposits,

NEAR RIGHT: By the mid-1950s, smog was a plague on all the houses in the Los Angeles Basin, but the citizens could not blame UP's steam engines, because they were all gone, except for 0-6-0 4439, still working the Harbor Belt Line five years after its main line brethren had departed California. Under brown skies on June 9, 1956, the 4439 runs down the Anaheim Branch at Whittier with a three-car excursion train. The 1916 Baldwin product was then in its fortieth year of service. The Whittier depot has been demolished.
*Gordon Glattenberg*

FAR RIGHT: A mile above sea level on a sunny day, March 17, 1971, five SD24's switch the ore tracks at Iron Springs, Utah. Snow lingers on the 5,000-foot-high Hurricane Cliffs above Cedar City. Cecil B. DeMille's epic *Union Pacific* was filmed at Iron Springs in 1938; the depot received signboards proclaiming it to be "Cheyenne."
*Kenneth Ardinger*

because iron and steel produced back east, and at Colorado Fuel & Iron at Pueblo, Colorado, were more than sufficient for the West's needs.

In 1922 Columbia Steel Corporation began building a blast furnace at Ironton, just south of Provo. Columbia formed two railroad subsidiaries to reach its coal and iron-ore mines, named for the Utah counties in which they would operate: the Carbon County Railway and the Iron County Railway. The Iron County applied to the ICC in August 1922 to build its line from the LA&SL at Lund to the iron-ore deposits. Unwilling to let an originating carrier grab a share of the ore revenue, the LA&SL protested that it had already planned to build this line to haul tourists to Cedar City, where they would transfer to buses to visit Zion Canyon, Cedar Breaks, Bryce Canyon, and the north rim of the Grand Canyon. Despite the fact that the LA&SL had bused these tourists between Lund and Cedar City for over five years, and had shown no interest in the branch until the Iron County Railway appeared, on October 18, 1922, the ICC gave the nod to the LA&SL, approving its 32.5-mile Cedar City Branch from Lund to Cedar City, and its 4.19-mile Desert Mound Spur from Iron Springs to Desert Mound.

The $800,000 Cedar City Branch and Desert Mound Spur opened for business on July 2, 1923. Depots were built at Iron Springs (pop. 10) and Cedar City (pop. 2,550). Columbia Iron Mining Co. and Utah Iron Ore Corp. began shipping ore from Desert Mound to Columbia's blast furnace, which went into production on May 1, 1924. Both the LA&SL and D&RGW served Ironton, the LA&SL via a 1.87-mile spur from Provo built in 1923–24. To reach more iron ore, the ICC granted the LA&SL authority on November 8, 1934, to extend the Desert Mound Spur 11.31 miles southwest to Iron Mountain. The $320,000 extension was placed in operation on

August 15, 1935, at which time it was combined with the Desert Mound Spur to form the 14.46-mile Iron Mountain Branch.

The LA&SL also hauled crops from irrigated land at Cedar City and timber from the Sevier National Forest Reserve above Cedar City, but the real attraction, other than iron ore, was tourism. LA&SL subsidiary Utah Parks Co., incorporated on March 29, 1923, built beautiful, expensive hotels, pavilions, and guest cabins at the parks, and a hotel in Cedar City. Despite UP's efforts the park concessions usually lost money, and after several unsuccessful attempts to sell them the UP donated its concessions to the National Park Service in 1972.

The first 20 miles of the Cedar City Branch are perfectly straight. The branch rises slowly as it runs southeast (railroad west) across the Escalante Desert, then more rapidly up a 1.90-percent grade into Cedar City. For many years it terminated in a balloon loop where the passenger trains turned. The Iron Mountain Branch ascends over 1,000 feet, with a ruling grade of 2.50-percent for 4 miles. Its maximum curvature is 8°. The Cedar City was the last true branch built on the LA&SL; branches built after this date have all been single-purpose industrial spurs. Both it and the Iron Mountain Branch are in operation today; most of the Ironton Spur came out in 1977.

### THE BOULDER CITY (BMI) BRANCH

To supply water and power to California and provide flood control on the lower Colorado River, in 1928 the U.S. government approved the construction of Boulder Dam (officially renamed Hoover Dam in 1947) in the Black Canyon of the Colorado River, near Las Vegas. At 587 feet from streambed to tip top, it was then the biggest dam in the world. In 1931 the LA&SL built the 22.69-mile Boulder City

Branch from Boulder Junction southeast (railroad west) to Boulder City, at a cost of $840,000, to haul construction materials to the site. Maximum grade on the branch was 1.35 percent, and maximum curvature 6°. The government built its own railroad from Boulder City 10.0 miles down to the dam site, and the construction company built a temporary line upriver to several aggregate quarries. The dam and its powerhouse were completed in 1935, by which time the LA&SL had hauled to Boulder City one million tons of cement, three million board-feet of lumber, 70,000 tons of steel, pipe, valves, electrical equipment, etc., and 250,000 tons of construction equipment, a godsend for the LA&SL during the Depression.

Modern wars require huge quantities of magnesium to make flares, incendiaries, and tracer bullets. Magnesium refining requires equally huge quantities of electricity and water, both of which were available in abundance at Boulder Dam when World War II began. In 1941 Basic Magnesium Inc. (BMI) began building the nation's largest (112 million pounds annual capacity) magnesium refinery at

Henderson, reached via a short spur from Royson on the Boulder City Branch. The $130 million refinery, paid for by the U.S. government, employed 13,000 in its construction, 2.5 times the peak workforce at Boulder Dam. It took 9,700 men and women to run the plant, more than Las Vegas's entire prewar population. The ore came from Gabbs, Nevada, 300 miles away, first by rail and later by truck. The plant began operation in August 1942, and made 39 percent of the world's magnesium in 1943, but as war ended so did the need for its magnesium; production ceased in November 1944. Much of the plant has since been converted to process various other minerals and chemicals.

The Boulder City Branch had little traffic past Henderson after 1936. The ICC approved this segment for abandonment on August 28, 1985. The UP made a few more trips to Boulder City to deliver new transformers (the last on December 19, 1985), then donated the branch past milepost 10.80 to the state of Nevada in December 1986 and renamed the remainder it kept the BMI Branch. The UP

recently reclaimed a small portion of the branch past milepost 10.80 to reach a customer.

### LAS VEGAS SPURS: BLUE DIAMOND, NELLIS, AND FIBREBOARD

Gypsum quarries in southern Nevada have supplied plaster and wallboard to southern California since the 1920s. In 1924 Blue Diamond Materials Co. opened a gypsum mine at Blue Diamond, 15 miles southwest of Las Vegas. To ship the raw gypsum to Blue Diamond's Los Angeles plant, the LA&SL built the 10.69-mile Blue Diamond Spur from Arden west to Blue Diamond, placing it in operation on May 27, 1925. In 1941 the company built a wallboard plant at Blue Diamond. Flintkote Corp. acquired Blue Diamond in 1959 and closed the operation in the early 1980s when the deposit became exhausted. The UP abandoned the spur in 1985 and removed the rails in March and April 1987. All of the spur was on a rising grade of up to 2.35 percent, with curves of up to 10°.

With war threatening in 1940–41, the U.S. Army Air Corps built the Las Vegas Gunnery School at North Las Vegas. The LA&SL brought troops and fuel to the new air base on the McCarran Spur, about three miles in length, built from Valley to the base in 1941. The base was renamed Nellis Air Force Base in 1949 and the spur became Nellis Air Base Spur at that time. The spur on the base proper was removed in 1985; a stub still serves a scrap yard just off the main line.

Fibreboard Paper Products Co. (now Pabco Gypsum Co.) built a new gypsum wallboard plant at a quarry 15 miles northeast of Las Vegas in 1964. To serve it, the LA&SL built the 11.46-mile Fibreboard Spur in 1964–65. The spur leaves the main line at Apex, climbs to a summit, then drops 700 feet on grades of up to 1.90 percent. Maximum curvature is 9°.

### THE HILL FIELD BRANCH

In 1891 the Great Salt Lake & Hot Springs Railway began running excursions to Beck's Hot Springs, four miles north of Salt Lake City. Reorganized as the Salt Lake & Ogden Railway in 1896, the line was extended to Ogden by 1908 and electrified in 1910. In 1917 its name changed to Bamberger Electric Railroad, for its president (also Utah's governor), Simon Bamberger. Passenger service ceased in 1952 and freight operations on January 1, 1959. On that day the UP acquired (for $450,000) 8.46 miles of the Bamberger, from Bridge Junction in Ogden to Arsenal, in order to provide service to Hill Air Force Base. This became UP's Hill Field Branch. It is now called the Hill Field Industrial Lead.

### THE LITTLE MOUNTAIN BRANCH

In 1967 the UP acquired 2,383 acres on Bear River Bay near Little Mountain, Utah, on which it planned to build evaporation ponds to extract minerals from the Great Salt Lake. On February 3, 1969, the ICC authorized UP's 13.27-mile Little Mountain Branch. In December 1970, after the ICC dismissed an appeal from the SP and Rio Grande for trackage rights over the branch, the OSL began construction, and in September 1971 began operating the Little Mountain Branch, the last branch added to the South-Central District. The trackage at the $28-million extraction plant, operated by Great Salt Lake Minerals & Chemicals Corp., is shared with SP's own Little Mountain Branch.

## OTHER SUBTRACTIONS FROM THE SOUTH-CENTRAL DISTRICT

After the Leamington Cut-off opened, the former Salt Lake & Western from Cutler to Boulter became the Fairfield Branch. The LA&SL gained approval to abandon from Topliff to Boulter, 13.3 miles, on August 29, 1918, though some of these rails remained in place until 1927. The remainder of the branch served the Topliff quarries of American Smelting & Refining Co. and U.S. Smelting, Refining & Mining Co., which shipped limestone to their smelters for fluxing until 1937. On June 3, 1938, the LA&SL received approval to abandon 6.14 miles from Five Mile Pass to Topliff, plus 7.03 miles of quarry spurs at Topliff. The LA&SL was about to abandon the rest of the Fairfield Branch in 1942, but held off when a quarry at Five Mile Pass began shipping refractory clay for construction of the Geneva Steel Works. This clay was used in the mortar for the millions of firebricks in Geneva's blast and open-hearth furnaces and its coke ovens. This business at an end, the LA&SL finally abandoned the Fairfield Branch in 1952.

By the late 1930s, ore deposits in the Tintic District were running out. The Northern Spy Extension, 2.79 miles, went first, in 1937. It appears that the former New East Tintic Railway was pulled up in 1939. The LA&SL purchased Rio Grande's share of the Mammoth Branch in 1944, then abandoned it in 1958. Of the three Shays that handled ore on the Mammoth Branch, the LA&SL sold the smallest in 1918, and retired the other two in 1948, along with their engine house at Tintic. These were the only Shays the UP ever owned. The Eureka and Silver City Branches subsisted on occasional carloads of ore until 1978, when they too were abandoned.

After 1899 many complicated changes were made to the main-line and branch-line trackage in and near downtown Los Angeles. On November 7, 1924, the LA&SL began using SP's Central Station, and the initial point of the Pasadena Branch then moved from First Street to Bridge Junction. In 1931 the LA&SL and SP double-tracked 1.32 miles of the Pasadena Branch between Rock Junction and the SP diamond at Alhambra Avenue for the use of SP freights. In 1939,

when the LA&SL began using LAUPT, it double-tracked and relocated 3.1 miles from Alhambra Avenue to Downey Road. At the same time the junction with the Glendale Branch (Rock Junction) moved to a new location and became Glendale Junction, and the initial point of the Pasadena Branch returned to First Street.

In 1899 the Los Angeles Terminal built a 1.1-mile spur off the Pasadena Branch from Arroyo Park to Millard Canyon. The LA&SL abandoned the Pasadena Branch as follows: in 1900 from Altadena to Arroyo Park (2.1 miles); in 1929 from Millard Canyon to Pasadena (2.4 miles); in 1969 from Pasadena to Avenue 33 (8.2 miles); and in August 1985 from Avenue 33 to Pasadena Junction (2.2 miles). The remaining 0.9 miles of the Pasadena Branch, between Pasadena Junction and First Street, were then added onto the Glendale Branch.

In 1924 the LA&SL granted trackage and agent rights on the Glendale Branch between mileposts 4.5 and 9.0 to the Glendale & Montrose Railway, an interurban running between Glendale and La Crescenta. The G&M electrified this portion of the Glendale Branch and began handling the LA&SL's business west of milepost 4.5, allowing the LA&SL to abolish its mixed train to Glendale. In 1927 the LA&SL abandoned the Glendale Branch between Verdugo Park and Glendale (0.82 miles) because this portion had no business and was paralleled by the G&M. After the G&M went bankrupt in 1930, the LA&SL acquired G&M boxcab 22 (it became UP E-100) to operate the Glendale Branch west of milepost 4.5. The LA&SL's steam-powered local would bring its train up to Delay Drive, where the boxcab was kept, and swap engines.

On June 6, 1938, the LA&SL obtained trackage rights over SP's parallel main line between Glendale Branch mileposts 1.96 and 4.84 and abandoned the branch between those points. In 1941 the LA&SL

dieselized the branch and sold the E-100 to UP subsidiary Yakima Valley Transportation Co. In 1956 the LA&SL obtained more SP trackage rights between new Glendale Branch mileposts 0.35 (near Glendale Junction) and 3.06 (Arroyo Junction) and abandoned the branch between those points, retaining only a 1.25-mile portion between Arroyo Junction and Forest Lawn. The UP abandoned this portion in 1990 because of light traffic and transferred what remained of the Glendale Branch, 1.96 miles from First Street to just west of Glendale Junction (most of this was former Pasadena Branch), to the main line. The main line now began at milepost -1.96, a location 0.86 miles west of Mission Tower. In 1994 UP sold its main line between Soto Street Junction (milepost 2.1) and milepost -1.96 to the Southern California Regional Rail Authority (Metrolink), retaining trackage rights into LAUPT.

The OSL has abandoned various branches in the Salt Lake City-Ogden area since 1906, when it abandoned about 0.5 miles of the Syracuse Branch (the former Ogden & Syracuse) west of milepost 4.7. Another 2.6 miles came up on August 31, 1955. The remaining 2.1 miles to Barnes are now the Syracuse Industrial Lead. In 1942 the OSL severed the Evona Branch (the original Utah Central main line, bypassed by the Sandy Ridge Cut-off in 1906) between mileposts 2.62 and 3.78, where it met the cut-off, because of street improvements and because the Ogden sugar factory had closed on September 13, 1941. In 1945 the OSL abandoned another 1.03 miles of the Evona Branch, cutting it back to Sugar Works Junction, milepost 1.59. This remainder is now the Evona Industrial Lead. In 1944 the OSL abandoned the entire 1.09-mile Five Points Branch (built by the OSL&UN in 1892) because of street improvements and lack of business.

# ADDING MAIN LINE CAPACITY

*As we know, the commerce of America moves east-west, not north-south.*
—Roger Puta, 1982

For its first decade the Salt Lake Route as built was adequate for its traffic. By 1916, however, business had grown to three passenger trains and three freights each way daily, all dispatched by timetable and train orders. On railroads in populated country, an agent/operator in a depot about every 10 miles issued train orders to keep traffic fluid, and in between trains sold tickets and handled freight business. But in the desert, an operator had no business to handle. Signaling was the economical alternative to hiring a plethora of operators, even assuming operators could be hired to live in a little shack in the middle of a vast desolation of sand.

The LA&SL first signaled 58 miles from Los Angeles to Riverside, which in 1916 had numerous locals to fruit-packing houses and a 54-car passing siding every 4 miles. On this stretch, Union Switch & Signal Co. installed an Automatic Block System (ABS), using Style S upper-quadrant, three-position semaphores wired on the Absolute Permissive Block (APB) principle, completing Los Angeles to Pomona in 1916, and Pomona to Riverside in 1917. Existing interlockings at SP crossings in Pomona and Ontario and at a PE crossing at Magnolia Avenue in Riverside were wired into the system. (The Ontario interlocking became manual in 1941 when SP abandoned most of its Chino Branch.)

In August 1916, just after this project began, the LA&SL contracted with Federal Signal Co. to supply ABS between Rox and Modena, 112 miles, this territory chosen because of limited sight distances and many helper movements. Federal Signal supplied its Type 4A upper-quadrant semaphores, which were similar to US&S's Style S semaphores. By January 1917 the LA&SL's newly organized signal department had completed Rox to Caliente, 62 miles. The LA&SL then decided to shift the ABS territory 4 miles to the west. When completed in 1918 the ABS ran from Guelph, 4 miles west of Rox, to Tomas, 4 miles west of Modena.

In July 1917 Federal began supplying Type 4A upper-quadrant semaphores for an ABS installation between Lynndyl and 8th South Street in Salt Lake City, where the Passenger Line met the Provo Subdivision. This 118-mile subdivision then had 29 scheduled trains daily between Garfield and Salt Lake City, a number inflated by commuter runs to and from the Garfield smelter. The Freight

Line from Buena Vista into Salt Lake City was not signaled. The LA&SL's signal department also installed these signals, completing the work in 1917. The cost of these two installations was about $1,500 per mile.

For all three of its early installations the LA&SL chose to use Absolute Permissive Block (APB), a system invented by General Railway Signal in 1911 for use on single track, instead of the earlier overlap system favored by the Harriman roads. APB allows one train to follow another between two sidings, very handy on long grades. Signals arranged on the overlap principle permit only one train between two sidings at a time. (A block in Absolute Permissive Block territory is *Absolute* for opposing trains, and *Permissive* for following trains, ensuring that an opposing train waits at a siding, but allowing a following train to proceed at restricted speed. Overlap can usually be distinguished from APB in old photographs by the position of signals between sidings: overlap signals are typically staggered, whereas APB signals are typically directly opposite each other. Intermediate signals in CTC installations are typically arranged on the APB principle.)

This was probably the only time Federal supplied signals to the UP system, which gave most of its business to US&S. These were the only major installations of upper-quadrant, three-position semaphores on the UP System, which until 1926 almost exclusively used lower-quadrant, two-position US&S Style B semaphores. Most interestingly, these were the only major signal installations on the APB principle on the UP system prior to the late 1930s. The UP was a stubborn advocate of the cheaper and simpler overlap system, despite the fact that APB could handle more trains on single track than the obsolete overlap system. At least in signaling the LA&SL was both highly independent of UP practices and more up-to-date, though this would change when the UP purchased Clark's 50-percent stake of the LA&SL in 1921.

The LA&SL planned to install ABS during 1918 from Daggett to Guelph, and Tomas to Lynndyl, but when the USRA took over the nation's railroads on January 1, 1918, it ordered almost all signal work to stop nationwide, leaving the LA&SL with dark territory on 395 miles of its 784-mile main line. Work did not resume for eight years, though three interlockings were installed in the 1920s: at Ironton in 1924, Hobart Street in Los Angeles in 1926, and the Badger Avenue Drawbridge at Terminal Island in 1926. Not until December 1926 did the LA&SL, now under UP's control, order ABS from US&S to begin closing the LA&SL's gaps. By then semaphores had become obsolete, so US&S Style P-3 color-lights (a three-lamp signal) were ordered instead. However, the UP used its standard overlap system for these installations instead of Absolute Permissive Block. The LA&SL activated the 59 miles of ABS from Las Vegas to Farrier (formerly Guelph) and the 71 miles from Tomas to Milford on May 28, 1927. This was UP's first major installation of color-lights.

While this work was underway, the LA&SL ordered more US&S Style P-3 color-lights for ABS from Milford to Lynndyl, 89 miles, and from Daggett to Las Vegas, 175 miles. Poor Tonopah & Tidewater was stuck paying for a four-lever (LA&SL East, LA&SL West, T&T North, and T&T South) interlocking at Crucero, housed in a little tower. Its operator cleared trains until 1940, when the T&T ceased operations. The Milford to Lynndyl ABS was activated on November 5, 1927; when the last ABS section between Daggett and Las Vegas was cut in on November 10, 1927, the LA&SL was finally signaled from end to end. These installations cost about $3,000 per mile—ABS signaling had doubled in price in ten years because of inflation.

To expedite heavy traffic in the late 1920s, the LA&SL installed remote-control switches (controlled by the local operator) in 1928–29 at Crucero, Kelso, Cima, Las Vegas, Moapa, Islen, Crestline, and Tintic, and in 1930 built a 4-mile remote control installation between Pierce and Bracken to handle Boulder Dam traffic. The Depression put a stop to more signal improvements until 1938, when color-lights were installed on double track between 9th Street and Alhambra Avenue, 1.9 miles, to reach Los Angeles Union Passenger Terminal. A remote-control interlocking was installed at 9th Street Junction in Los Angeles in 1940, using General Railway Signal Type SA searchlights.

In 1941, as traffic began to really pick up, the LA&SL respaced the signals from Milford to Lynndyl for longer braking distances and finally upgraded them from overlap to APB so the main line could handle more trains. In 1942 the same improvements were made between Las Vegas and Rox, and Tomas and Milford, for the same reason— more traffic. The Kelso remote-control installation was extended east to the west switch at Hayden in 1942, making it into a four-mile interlocking so that helpers could return to Kelso more expeditiously, and work began on a Centralized Traffic Control (CTC) system from Yermo to Daggett in summer 1942.

It was soon obvious that these little measures were not enough. Prior to the war, the LA&SL ran three passenger trains each way daily, the streamliner *City of Los Angeles* each way every third day, and three eastbound and four westbound freights daily, for which ABS was adequate. By June 1942 the number of trains had increased to 10 daily each way (by June 1943 the number had increased to 15 to 20 daily each way), beyond the capacity of a hilly, single-track ABS railroad. Westbound loads and eastbound empties had increased 150 percent over prewar levels: during a typical week, freight traffic eastbound averaged 7.2 trains daily with 193 loads, 301 empties, and 17,796 gross tons; and freight traffic westbound averaged 9.6 trains daily with 395 loads, 70 empties, and 23,011 gross tons. The *Challenger* now ran in two sections each way daily; most days the *Pacific Limited* did likewise. There were also some 12 troop trains weekly running in bunches of 4 to 6, which tied things up beyond belief.

The entire LA&SL was beyond saturation. On the heavily graded 171-mile Second Subdivision between Yermo and Las Vegas, almost every freight-train crew ran over the limit (13 hours 41 minutes on duty) after which overtime started. On busy days they could not make it over the road without violating the 16-hour law, and left their initial terminal with two crews on board. In desperation yardmasters let empties accumulate in yards and dispatchers abandoned whole trains in sidings, which further tied up the railroad. Because helpers could not return to Kelso in a timely manner, and freights spent most of their time in sidings, a locomotive shortage was about to bring the LA&SL to a standstill.

While Meadow Valley Wash and Clover Creek Canyon were even more of a bottleneck, that territory had shorter crew districts– Las Vegas to Caliente, 125.3 miles, and Caliente to Milford, 117.3 miles–and those crews could generally make it over the road in 16 hours. The OSL and OWR&N were likewise choked, but those lines likewise had shorter crew districts, along with some double track or alternate routes. The 171-mile crew district from Yermo to Las Vegas, previously unremarkable, became UP's worst bottleneck. In July 1942 the UP realized it had to immediately begin installing CTC on this stretch.

In the summer of 1942, while US&S began shipping material to Las Vegas, 20-man UP signal gangs swarmed over the Second Subdivision. Thirty-two sidings received full CTC equipment; most

were lengthened to 120-car capacity. One end of each siding was thrown over to a 19-foot center to allow installation of the station-leaving signal between the main track and the siding. The existing P-3 color-lights were reused for the automatic (intermediate) signals, respaced for adequate braking distances, and converted to APB. New H-2 searchlights were installed at power-switch locations, reusing the old masts and cases. All signals were made approach-lit. Semaphore-type motor-car indicators were installed for the safety and convenience of track maintainers. Yermo to Las Vegas was wired to a machine at Las Vegas controlled by the Second Subdivision Dispatcher, using US&S's two-wire multiple-time code system. Yermo to Daggett was wired to a machine at Yermo, handled by an operator under the direction of the First Subdivision Dispatcher in Los Angeles. The CTC was discontinuous at Kelso and Yermo to minimize wiring complications at these yards.

The signal gangs completed the CTC from Daggett to Yermo in fall 1942, giving this section the honor of UP's first CTC installation.

They next placed in service the 19-mile helper district from Kelso to Cima, on December 6. During January to March, 1943, 10-to-20-mile sections between Cima and Las Vegas were cut in as each was completed. Then the signal gangs worked west from Kelso, cutting in the final section from Harvard to Yermo on June 16, 1943. Until September 1, 1944, when the D&RGW completed 284 continuous miles from Dotsero, Colorado, to Helper, Utah, this was the longest CTC installation in the U.S.

The benefits of CTC were at once recognized: previously 14 locomotives were required for helper service at Kelso; this was cut to seven. Freights began covering the Second Subdivision in 10 hours or less. The Second Subdivision's 17 train-order offices (13 of them 24-hour) were cut back to four one-man agencies plus the 24-hour agency at Kelso.

The signal gangs then moved to the next hot spot, installing 69.1 miles of CTC in 1944 over the Blue Mountains from Pendleton to La Grande, Oregon, on the OWR&N. That fall they returned to

AT LEFT: At dusk on March 11, 1992, with no eastbounds in sight, the eastward absolute signal at west Kelso, California, has defaulted to its most restrictive aspect. *Jamie Schmid*

ABOVE: At Hayden, California, on December 26, 1964, Extra 404 East, the CN (Colton Fruit), has gone into the controlled siding. In observance of UP rule 715(A), its head brakeman has crossed to the other side of the main to inspect Extra 184 West, which has nearly 100 gondola loads of Utah coking coal bound for Kaiser Steel at Fontana. In 1942 the LA&SL interlocked the main line between Hayden and Kelso (Kelso is visible in the distance) to expedite the return of helpers to Kelso.
*Gordon Glattenberg (collection of Martha Mills)*

ABOVE: In terms of adding capacity, CTC is the most important improvement in the LA&SL's physical plant to date. As part of the Los Angeles–Riverside Junction CTC project of 1948–49, the UP extended a second main track from Downey Road to East Los Angeles, where a "Snowball" Ski Special highballs east for Sun Valley, Idaho, during January 1966. The lead to East Yard is at left. *Alan Miller*

AT LEFT: On the evening of August 26, 1990, the SLOAZ (Salt Lake City to Oakland Trailers) heads west on the No. 1 Track into CTC territory at Grant Tower, just west of UP's Salt Lake City Union Station. The Rio Grande controls Grant Tower interlocking; its limits include these searchlight signals. Technically, single-lamp (searchlight) and three-lamp signals are both color-lights, but the term color-light is now usually construed to mean just the three-lamp style. *David Rector*

AT RIGHT: Locomotives come and go, but signals last almost forever. The US&S style P-3 color-light at milepost 237.6 between Kelso and Hayden has done its job for 66 years. On December 23, 1993, the moon displays a partial lunar aspect while this signal glows only with the light of the dying day. The lamps in this eastward automatic signal will remain dark until a train enters their track circuit. *Mark Hemphill*

install CTC from Las Vegas to Caliente, 125 miles, wired to a second CTC machine in the Las Vegas dispatching office. Six sidings were extended to 120-car capacity as part of this project; all sidings were equipped with full CTC installations. Las Vegas to Carp was activated by January 1, 1945; Caliente to Carp was activated a few months later. Total cost of the Daggett to Caliente CTC was $2.8 million, or $9,300 per mile, three times what it cost to put in ABS in the 1920s–railroading was getting to be expensive.

By pouring its considerable resources into a big problem, the UP had solved it in a big hurry. However, this was an example of the Jeffers-era UP standing still while events sped by. As the UP finished up its very first CTC project, little Rio Grande was well on its way to completing CTC over its entire main line. The UP, in fact, was about the last large railroad in the U.S. to start installing CTC. This conservatism cost the UP dearly in inflated wartime prices for signaling material, as well as excessive operating costs on its single-track ABS territory.

During 1946, while the CTC gangs returned to the OWR&N and OSL for more big projects, the CTC was made continuous through Yermo, Kelso, and Las Vegas to lessen terminal delays, and the semaphores between Caliente and Tomas were replaced with US&S color-lights in preparation for what was then the largest CTC project ever: 324.5 miles from Caliente to Buena Vista. The order for the section west of Milford went to US&S in June 1947, followed by Milford-Buena Vista in July. Each section was wired to its own CTC machine in Salt Lake City, housed in a new Utah Division Dispatchers' Office, an air-conditioned, "fireproof" building built in 1947–48.

As part of the work, line changes were made to reduce curvature at Strong, Bloom, and Black Rock. The sidings at Bloom and Strong were moved three miles west and three miles east, respectively, to get them off 0.60 percent grades. Its operating experience between Yermo and Caliente showed the UP that CTC required fewer sidings than ABS, so it removed 16 single sidings and 1 second siding between Milford and Buena Vista and made 5 sidings into single-switch spurs. The remaining sidings were lengthened to at least 122 cars, and some to 137–143 cars. New #14 turnouts and H-2 searchlight high and dwarf signals were installed at all power switches. The existing P-3 color-lights were reused for the automatic signals, respaced for increased braking distances. Some intermediates were equipped to display a fourth aspect of flashing yellow, "Advance-Approach." Slide fences at numerous locations in Clover Creek Canyon and motor-car indicators were included in this project, which the signal gangs completed in late 1948.

Wrapping up CTC on the LA&SL main line, the UP placed an order with US&S in September 1948 for signaling material from Los Angeles to Riverside Junction, using H-2 searchlights at control points and P-5 color-lights for the automatic signals. These were wired to a CTC machine at the Los Angeles dispatching office. Included in the project were four miles of new second main track from Downey Road to milepost 7.16 at East Los Angeles, and passing track extensions between East Los Angeles and Riverside Junction. The single-track CTC was completed in 1949, and the two-main-track CTC from First Street to milepost 7.16 in 1950. A three-mile stretch from Downey Road to East Los Angeles was left out of the CTC to avoid complications in the terminal area (this gap was filled in during the late 1980s). The LA&SL's last ABS semaphores were eliminated in this project. Other than terminal-area gaps at Los Angeles and Salt Lake City, the entire LA&SL main line was either CTC or ABS double track by 1950, six years ahead of similar signaling improvements on the OSL and OWR&N.

The benefits of CTC on the LA&SL were manifold. Trains could now enter and leave sidings at 20 mph without stopping to throw the switch. Under ABS trains were "lost" for long periods between open stations, whereas CTC gave the dispatcher a chance to change his mind at each siding, allowing meets to be closely timed. Trains could now proceed on signal indication and no longer had to wait on sidings when, despite there being track and time to advance them against superior or opposing trains, the dispatcher had neither the means nor the time to give every train involved a new train order.

Faster over-the-road speeds coupled with dieselization in 1948 enabled the UP to combine several crew districts on the South-Central District. Effective for trainmen on April 11, 1948, and enginemen on January 11, 1949, the crew changes at Caliente and Lynndyl were abolished, making a 243-mile district between Las Vegas and Milford and a 207-mile district between Milford and Salt Lake City. On these same dates Provo Subdivision crews likewise began running through Lynndyl on a new 176-mile Provo-Milford district, and passenger crews began running through Yermo, for a very long 334-mile Los Angeles-Las Vegas district. Milford's dispatching office was consolidated to Salt Lake City in 1948. The terminals at Lynndyl and Caliente were largely abandoned and removed by 1950. UP's switch between Pacific Time and Mountain Time, which had previously taken effect at Caliente, was shifted west to Las Vegas, where it remains today.

New agreements also allowed road trains to perform up to four hours' switching on line at certain locations such as Tintic, which allowed the UP to abolish the Shay operation at Tintic in 1948 and scrap the Shays. The Provo yard crew now began handling the

Geneva Steel Works. In 1951 a six-mile CTC installation between Provo and Geneva and extension of yard limits from Provo to Pipemill allowed the yard goat to run to Geneva without train orders. This was a minimalist CTC job; it had not a single power switch, only one lever (east or west), and seven signals.

Since 1949 the most apparent signaling change on the LA&SL main line has been installation of speed signaling at many sidings, upgrading of those sidings from 20 mph to 30 mph, installation of Advance Approach aspect on many intermediates, and further consolidation of dispatching offices. In 1968 a new CTC machine at Salt Lake City replaced the two CTC machines at Las Vegas, and on June 25, 1975, the Los Angeles office was consolidated with Salt Lake City. Three dispatchers then handled the LA&SL, splitting their territories at Las Vegas and Milford. The Salt Lake City office closed in May 1989, when it was cut over to the new Harriman Dispatching Center in Omaha.

The crew districts established with the installation of CTC on the South-Central District have remained stable to present, though the UP has tried to eliminate Yermo for freight crews as well as passenger crews. Certain fast trains, such as the 1st and 2nd LAX eastbound, and the VAN and SUPRV westbound, began running through Yermo on March 3, 1979, and some double-stacks also ran through. But delays on the Santa Fe and high away-housing costs at Los Angeles put a stop to this run-through in 1992. The old OSL crew districts on the South-Central District from Salt Lake City to Provo, Salt Lake City to Ogden, and Ogden through McCammon to Pocatello, Idaho, remain in effect at present.

The same cannot be said for the South-Central District's divisional boundaries. Prior to 1931 the LA&SL split at Caliente into two divisions, the Los Angeles and the Salt Lake. To save on staff during the depression, the two were combined as the Los Angeles Division. Reflecting the need for closer management as traffic picked up with depression's end and war's onset, on August 1, 1941, the Los Angeles Division was again split at Caliente, the LA&SL east of that point going to the enlarged Utah Division, which stretched to McCammon, Idaho, and the LA&SL west of that point going to the new California Division. On January 1, 1948, with the disappearance of Caliente drawing near, the California Division was extended eastward to Salt Lake City. This lasted until September 11, 1949, when the California Division was cut back to Las Vegas (Caliente was now gone), and the Utah Division was extended west to Las Vegas. The Utah Division now ran from McCammon to Ogden, and Ogden to Las Vegas, and the California Division from Las Vegas to Los Angeles.

This structure persisted until 1982, when the ICC approved the UP-MP-WP merger, and the WP became UP's Western District. On April 29, 1986, the Utah Division was eliminated, its territory split at Smelter and Sandy between the California and Idaho Divisions. Since 1986 the UP has shuffled its divisions several times. As of December 1994 the former LA&SL is part of the Los Angeles Service Unit, except for the Salt Lake City–Ogden terminal area, which is part of the Western Terminals Service Unit. The former OSL from Ogden to McCammon is part of the Cheyenne Service Unit. It is likely that new and different service units will further confuse old divisional boundaries in the future.

On December 31, 1987, the OSL was merged into the UP, and the following day the LA&SL was merged into the UP. The one-day delay was necessary because the LA&SL was half-owned by the OSL (dating to 1903) and half-owned by the UP (dating to 1921). As corporate entities, the LA&SL and OSL no longer exist.

ABOVE: *Tim Zukas*   INSET: *Mark Hemphill*

# PART II

# BASIN & RANGE

## *The Route of the South-Central District*

At 8:35 A.M. on April 21, 1985, Meadow Valley Wash slumbers in the pallid light of a hazy spring morning. The smell of damp sage permeates the calm air. Meadow Creek gurgles placidly around stones and underneath cottonwoods that have grown tall in the 75 years since this valley floor was last wiped clean by a flood. At valley's edge the main line of the South-Central District climbs towards Caliente and Crestline. The track winds around rock stained orange by hot, iron-laden water, passes the east switch at Boyd, passes the toe of an alluvial fan spilling its debris from the mouth of a ravine, then vanishes into the canyon's interlocking fingers. Down at creek level the county road retraces the original grade of 1903. The LA&SL's High Line of 1911–12 is about as far as it can get from the creek without climbing the canyon walls. You can guess which, road or railroad, is the more likely to be reasonably intact after the next flood.

Every locomotive and car seems to look alike these days, but nature has ensured that this route will never look like any other. Only this route has a Meadow Valley Wash, where the railroad runs trains according to the whim of rainstorms. Only this route needed a Kelso oasis, where deep wells provided succor for steam engines, and nurtured palm trees that shaded UP's herald on the windy morning of December 23, 1993.

There are two ways to look at railroads: (1) railroads mold the land, or (2) the land molds railroads. People who work for and write about railroads often slip into the trap of thinking that railroads beat nature into submission. They see big locomotives "conquering" the grade, seldom stopping to think that it is really the other way around. If nature had not put a mountain range in the railroad's path, the railroad would certainly not need those big locomotives. Nor do they stop to think why the railroad went over that mountain range in the first place, which usually has something to do with what nature placed on the other side, such as a natural harbor. The mountain range might contain a treasure-trove of coal or copper. The rainfall that washes out the main line in those mountains also makes crops grow down in the plains. All sense of why a railroad chooses one valley for its route and not another is lost in the thrill of big locomotives and flashy domeliners.

But nature is what makes the railroad. Nature sets the grades and curves; a locating engineer's only choice is to either accept what nature doles out or spend enormous sums of money to try and smooth out the little bumps (forget the big bumps). Nature either blesses a railroad with traffic or starves it into poverty. While railroads in large part made agriculture, mining, and industry in the West possible, they did not create farms, mines, or cities, though they often tried. Nature creates wealth. People harvest it, graze it, mine it, log it, smelt it, refine it, and forge it, and the railroad hauls it away.

In the case of Meadow Valley Wash, nature determined that the Salt Lake Route would run through this canyon; it was the only practical route. Nature determined where the Salt Lake Route would build its track in this canyon, though the lesson had to be taught twice. Nature determined that coal runs west on this railroad and oranges run east, and not the other way around. Nature determined that this would be the first route on the UP to dieselize.

The builders of the SPLA&SL were driven by their goal of connecting Los Angeles and Salt Lake City with the shortest line possible, coupled with their desire to minimize grades and curvature and expensive construction. Because in 1900 there was almost zero population and meager resources between Los Angeles and Salt Lake City, there was no need to zigzag to a town or detour to a mine. Thus one must look to the geology and geography of this region to understand why this route looks the way it does.

Almost all of the South-Central District lies within the Basin & Range Province, a region where North America is being stretched on an east-west axis. In the last 30 million years the Great Basin has almost doubled in width, breaking the crust apart along faults perpendicular to the direction of motion. The blocks between the faults have risen or lowered alternately: one block goes up to become a long, skinny range, the next block drops down to become a long, thin basin, and so forth, basin-range-basin-range-basin-range, for 400 miles across the Great Basin, as if God had dragged a rake and left furrows. Rain and snow have worn down the ranges, filling in the basins with sediments thousands of feet thick.

Given this topography, there was only one real choice without making the construction very expensive: stick to the basins, which are smooth, and skirt the jagged ranges. Because the route from Los Angeles to Salt Lake City runs across the bias of the north-south basins and ranges, wherever possible the engineers sought to cross the ranges to minimize circuity. In a few places prehistoric lakes and glacier-fed rivers had forced outlets through the mountains, opening pathways through Afton Canyon and Meadow Valley Wash on the SPLA&SL (also Bear River Canyon and Red Rock Pass on the OSL). There was no engineering problem per se; construction in the basins was cheap and easy, and by paying no attention to the possibility of floods, construction through the canyons was pretty cheap too. Thanks a lot, nature! But the basins are dished, not flat, and there is also the matter of climbing from sea level at San Pedro to 4,200 feet at Salt Lake, and unavoidable summits at Cajon Pass, Cima Hill, Crestline, and Boulter Summit, thus some 550 miles of the 785-mile SPLA&SL main line runs uphill or down on grades of significance. Thanks for nothing, nature!

Nature established the route, then it established the division points. Given the lack of settlements along the route, the SPLA&SL created its division points according to the availability of water, proximity to grades, and the distance a crew could run in one day, about 100 miles. The crew districts ran from Los Angeles to San Bernardino, 67 miles; San Bernardino to Otis (Yermo after 1908), 96 miles; Otis to Las Vegas, 171 miles; Las Vegas to Caliente, 125 miles; Caliente to Milford, 117 miles; Milford to Lynndyl, 89 miles; and Lynndyl to Salt Lake City, 118 miles. Helpers were stationed at San Bernardino, Kelso, and Caliente. Nature then dealt the SPLA&SL some traffic: veins of copper, silver, and lead in the Great Basin; seams of coal in the Wasatch; fields of wheat, vegetables, and sugar beets in Utah's sheltered mountain valleys; California sunshine for oranges, movies, and tourists; and under San Pedro Bay a hidden treasure: oil. Then the Salt Lake Route rolled the dice and began to play the game of railroading.

## THE PROMISED LAND

*You won't have to buy an overcoat to wear in sunny California. And whenever you get hungry, all you'll have to do is pick oranges off the trees along every street.*

—Anonymous cowboy to itinerant roustabout Frank Waters, 1924

In the 1920s Los Angeles was the "ultimate goal of that Manifest Destiny that had impelled America's westward expansion," in the words of Frank Waters. It was Hollywood and Howard Hughes, Lockheed and Douglas Aircraft, Union Oil and Chevron, sunshine and easy money. It was, supposedly, the prototype for modern high-tech America, free of Big Steel and King Coal, free of Jim Crow and The Man, free of small-town suspicions and old-world antagonisms.

By the 1950s New York journalists had decided that the city of Los Angeles was a metaphor for our entire modern culture, even though it is a city so geographically diffuse it hardly has either center or edge. Similarly, the UP has no real focal point in Los Angeles, no immense yard or engine facility or backshop, no great company passenger terminal capped with an imposing headquarters tower. Instead, UP's facilities in Los Angeles are spread 188 miles from Yermo to East San Pedro. If there is a focal point to the UP in Los Angeles, though this is a shaky distinction, it is the wye at Downey Road. This is where the SPLA&SL began building east toward Utah in 1901. The north leg of the wye once led to the passenger station on First Street and the Alameda Street freight house, later to SP's Central Station, and now leads to Los Angeles Union Passenger Terminal. The south leg leads down the San Pedro Branch to the side-by-side Ports of Los Angeles and Long Beach. Santa Fe's San

Bernardino Subdivision (formerly the Third District) crosses the San Pedro Branch just south of Downey Road. This crossing is protected by Hobart Tower.

ABOVE: In the 1920s, railroads built everything as if they meant it to last forever. In 1926 the LA&SL built Hobart Tower with thick concrete walls and a clay tile roof, making it fireproof, exulted the trade press. The tower, now owned by the UP and Santa Fe, and operated by the UP, houses a 56-lever General Railway Signal electric interlocking machine, which controls the crossing of UP's San Pedro Branch and Santa Fe's Third District main line. On January 24, 1988, UP's Harbor Hauler has just left East Yard, which begins immediately east of Downey Road. The Hobart operator has lined it through the plant, and the hauler's two B23-7's chuff through the east leg of the wye at Hobart Tower on their way to the Port of Long Beach with "K" Line containers. Santa Fe's

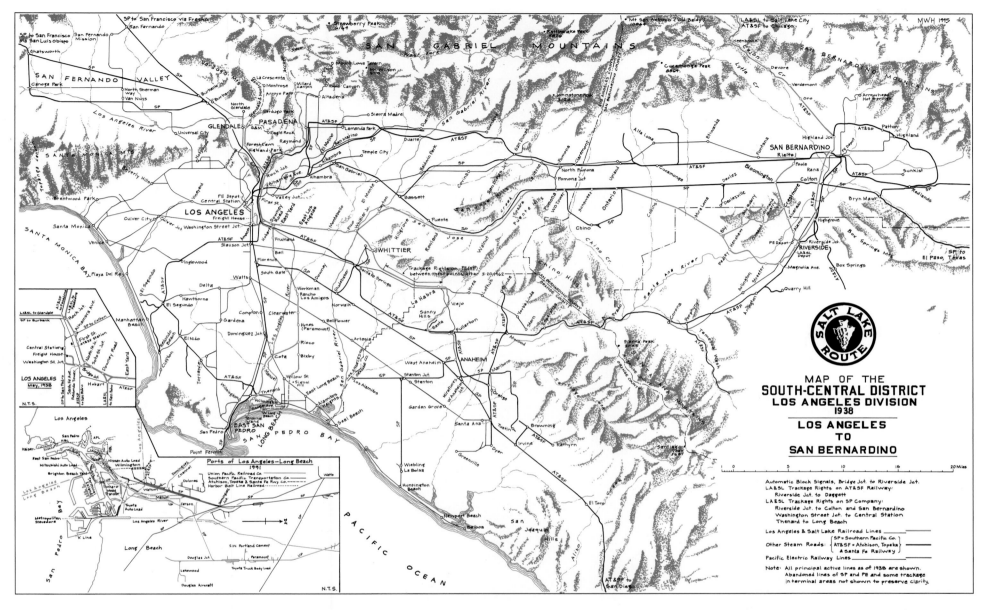

MWH 1995

MAP OF THE
**SOUTH-CENTRAL DISTRICT**
LOS ANGELES DIVISION
1938

**LOS ANGELES
TO
SAN BERNARDINO**

0      5      10      15      20 Miles

Automatic Block Signals, Bridge Jct. to Riverside Jct.
LA&SL Trackage Rights on AT&SF Railway:
    Riverside Jct. to Daggett
LA&SL Trackage Rights on SP Company:
    Riverside Jct. to Colton and San Bernardino
    Washington Street Jct. to Central Station
    Thenard to Long Beach

Los Angeles & Salt Lake Railroad Lines _____
Other Steam Roads: { SP = Southern Pacific Co.
                     AT&SF = Atchison, Topeka
                     & Santa Fe Railway }
Pacific Electric Railway Lines _____

Note: All principal active lines as of 1938 are shown.
    Abandoned lines of SP and PE and some trackage
    in terminal areas not shown to preserve clarity.

freight main line between Los Angeles and San Bernardino, built by subsidiary California Central Railway in 1888, is in the foreground. Hobart Yard, Santa Fe's principal yard in the Los Angeles Basin, is just to the right. Over 75,000 eight-hour tricks have begun at Hobart Tower since it was built in 1926. *Alan Miller*

AT RIGHT: Early interlocking plants were Rube Goldberg contraptions, where the operator threw a tall lever inside the tower which moved a series of rods and levers to mechanically actuate a signal or switch. The levers interlocked with each other to keep the operator from establishing conflicting or opposing routes. Colloquially, they were called "armstrong plants," because the power to move the heavy and often balky linkage was furnished by the operator's strong arms. Electric interlockings like Hobart Tower's General Railway Signal Model 2 machine, built in 1926 and enlarged in 1930, were an enormous improvement over armstrong plants, because they allowed signals to be controlled at much greater distances, because it was faster and easier to set up a route, and because they required less maintenance. The GRS factory in Rochester, New York, and competitor Union Switch & Signal at Swissvale, Pennsylvania, built thousands of interlocking machines, eliminating the jobs of thousands of switch tenders. Today, computer-controlled interlockings have replaced the jobs of thousands of tower operators. *Dave Crammer*

## EAST YARD

*As California went, so did the nation. California today is the United States tomorrow.*
　　　　　　　　　　　　　　　　　　—Gerald Nash, historian, 1972

Between 1880 and 1930 Los Angeles County was the fastest-growing metropolis in the U.S. In 1880 there were only 33,000 people in the whole county. In 1930 there were 2,208,000, and on January 1, 1994, there were 9,230,000! The LA&SL and UP have had to endlessly enlarge and expand their facilities to keep up. The LA&SL built a big freight house on Alameda Street south of downtown in 1923, and expanded it several times and built several warehouses during the 1920s to handle the city's insatiable appetite for autos,

appliances, and freight-all-kinds. The original SPLA&SL yard and engine facilities at Fourth Street in Los Angeles were soon cramped and hemmed in on all sides by the city, so in 1924-25 the LA&SL built (at a cost of $1,750,000) a new yard and engine terminal called East Yard, out in the country at East Los Angeles. On a 230-acre site, the LA&SL laid out a 1,000-car receiving yard, a 700-car eastbound classification yard, a 880-car westbound classification yard, and a 446-car repair yard. Shop and engine facilities included a 20-stall brick roundhouse, a 195-foot-by-254-foot locomotive backshop; a coach, steel car, and blacksmith shop; a car repair shop, and a storehouse where to speed things up a storeman raced through the aisles on roller skates. The pleasant climate allowed the LA&SL to use heavy timber framing and sheet-metal siding on most of the shop

buildings instead of the usual masonry and concrete. Not all yard tracks were laid at first; more were added as business increased in the 1920s. Space was also provided to more than double the size of the roundhouse and the shop buildings at East Yard, but most of this planned-for shop expansion never took place.

More tracks were added at East Yard in 1942–44 in response to war traffic. The three yards originally contemplated in 1926 were now complete: A Yard handled westbounds, B Yard handled locals, and C Yard handled eastbounds. A ten-track coach yard was built at the west end. Eight open-air stalls were added to the roundhouse in 1941, and a 135-foot turntable was installed in 1945 to accommodate the Challengers which began running west to Los Angeles in 1937.

When the UP dieselized the South-Central District in 1947-48, it built a small, three-track fueling and inspection facility with pits and raised platforms at East Yard. These open-air inspection tracks were roofed over in 1952, and the steam engine backshop was converted to service diesels in 1951–52. The turntable and all but three stalls of the roundhouse were removed in 1952, the remaining stalls came out in the early 1960s, and the backshop was demolished in March 1973. A new quarter-mile-long freight house at East Yard was completed in 1960, and the yard was enlarged again.

In 1953 the UP began its first-ever piggyback service at Los Angeles, but the business did not require much in the way of facilities until the early 1960s, when the need for a better ramp became pressing. In 1964 the UP built a new ramp at East Yard with a capacity of 220 trailers on flatcars, "and ingeniously designed ramp equipment, adaptable to all types of piggyback flat cars," which was a fancy way of describing ramp tractors. The UP's very first Drott 40-ton-capacity straddle crane was purchased for East Yard in early 1968, "permitting loading or unloading of a trailer in the remarkable time of two minutes." A second 40-ton Drott crane arrived in 1969.

In 1970-71, to expedite classification of carload and piggyback traffic at East Yard, the UP spent $2.8 million to convert B Yard into a 16-track hump yard and to build a three-track piggyback facility. The piggyback yard received a fourth loading/unloading track in 1977. That year UP's TOFC and COFC business increased by 26 percent. East Yard was soon swamped with trailers and containers. Unlike 1924, East Yard was now surrounded by the city, leaving no room for expansion. The available acreage at East Yard could not accommodate everything, so the freight cars had to go, out to a new $9 million, 24-track, 1,500-car flat-switched yard built at Yermo in 1980–81. This allowed the UP to tear out C Yard, the yard tower, and the car shop to make space for more trailer and container parking. Yermo became the principal collection and blocking point for all loose cars into and out of Los Angeles.

But even this was not enough. In 1987–88 a $14.5-million expansion doubled the size of the intermodal yard, making East Yard the largest intermodal facility on UP's system. This project added three 7,000-foot loading/unloading tracks for a total of seven (they are called Drott 1–7 for the manufacturer of the straddle cranes), purchased three Mi-Jack R1000 straddle cranes at $700,000 each, and enlarged parking to accommodate 2,213 trailers and containers. East Yard's seven Drott tracks are now worked by six Mi-Jack R1000 and two Le Tourneau ST-100 straddle cranes. Container parking now takes up most of the land once occupied by the carshop, locomotive backshop, roundhouse, and coach yard. Reflecting the shift both to Yermo and to intermodal and

unit trains, the UP deactivated East Yard's hump in 1990. The East Yard diesel house is now UP's only locomotive facility west of Salt Lake City on the LA&SL.

AT LEFT: On their first revenue trip west, U50's 31–33 wait to return east on November 23, 1963 (GE had just displayed the 31 at the Chicago Railroad Fair). The aging timber-framed locomotive backshop looms above them. *Alan Miller*

ABOVE: Looking west from the Crest Tower on July 20, 1992, SW10 1210 is busy storing cars in the bowl tracks. At left the intermodal yard is awash in stacked containers. The two-track main line is at far right. Crest Tower houses the controls for the bowl switches and now inactive hump retarders. As of 1993 only 3 switch engines were active on the day trick at East Yard, down from 12 in the late 1980s. *Dave Crammer*

THREE PHOTOGRAPHS BELOW: Modern locomotives require much less maintenance than their predecessors, and freight cars likewise need less attention, in part because boxcars, refrigerator cars, and stock cars, and their doors, cooling units, etc., all of which eventually break, have been replaced by simple intermodal platforms. Along with computers that have replaced clerks, the result is that yards are not nearly as labor-intensive as they were two decades ago. Nevertheless, it still takes people to run East Yard: hostler-herder Jaime Gonzales hoses down an SD40-2 in December 1993; welder Gilbert Chavira repairs a draft gear pocket the same month; and yardmaster Dave Simpson uses a radio, a telephone, and the limited view from Crest Tower to keep up with his yard on July 20, 1993. A yardmaster's lunch in the days of steam might have been roast beef sandwiches wrapped in wax paper, and proper attire was a white shirt and dark tie. In 1993, lunch is a salad with Paul Newman's "all natural" ranch dressing, and casual dress is the rule. *Dave Crammer*

# THE OIL PORTS: THE LUCK OF THE UP

*The corporation may some day become a good medium-sized crude oil company operating a profitable railroad on the side.* —Economist Kiliaen V. R. Townsend assesses the UP, January 10, 1949

The first successful oil well in the U.S. struck oil on August 27, 1859, at Titusville, Pennsylvania. By the mid-1860s people concluded that southern California's tar pits gave evidence that California was also a good place to drill for oil. Within a decade enough oil was found in southern California to make it an important oil state, and by 1910 California's wells were producing 22 percent of the world's total supply of oil. The great Signal Hill Field, discovered by Shell in 1921 when this small hill behind the city of Long Beach was being subdivided for homes, made millionaires out of those who were lucky enough

to own one of the lots, and even the heirs of people buried in Long Beach's Sunnyside Cemetery received royalty checks. Long Beach and Los Angeles became major oil-exporting ports, most of the oil hauled by tankers through the Panama Canal to the East Coast, or used to fuel the ships themselves.

Late in 1936 an independent driller found oil in commercial quantities beneath the LA&SL's land at San Pedro Bay, 2,700 acres on Rattlesnake Island (by then renamed Terminal Island) and the adjoining salt flats originally owned by the Los Angeles Terminal Railway. It was soon apparent that this pool, named the Wilmington Field, was very large. To protect its oil from being drained off by wells on adjoining land, the Union Pacific became an oil company just about overnight. By April 10, 1937, the UP had 81 wells in progress at Wilmington, and was producing 3,200 barrels of oil daily. The following year the Wilmington Field netted the UP $4.7 million. The field made a huge contribution to UP's treasury in the waning years of the depression, and boosted the railroad's net income in 1937 by nearly one-tenth. The SPLA&SL had cost the UP about $60 million to build and equip. By 1951 the Wilmington Field was returning that amount in profit every 24 months. It was the greatest prize the UP had ever won. It was also pure luck.

AT LEFT: During February 1979, UP's Harbor Local crosses the Henry Ford Avenue Drawbridge (originally the Badger Avenue Drawbridge) onto Terminal Island. The vertical lift towers of the Heim Bridge at right dwarf the railroad's 1926-built bascule bridge. Both bridges cross the Cerritos Channel, which connects the inner harbors of the Ports of Los Angeles and Long Beach. This Sunday-through-Friday local went on duty at East Yard in Los Angeles in the afternoon, and turned on the wye on Terminal Island for its return trip to East Yard. During the 1980s the UP used four daily locals on the San Pedro Branch, with colorful names such as the Tuna Fish Local, Mead Local, and Paramount Local, to handle its loose carload business. *Joe Blackwell*

BELOW: GP40 882 switches Dow Chemical on Terminal Island early in 1992, a few months before this former New York Central unit was damaged by fire and retired. At right is UP Resources well 566A, one of over a thousand producing oil wells the UP has drilled at San Pedro. UP's and other companies' wells in the Wilmington Field pumped out so much oil by the early 1950s that the entire area, 16 square miles, subsided from 2 to 24 feet. Further subsidence was only halted through the injection of enormous quantities of sea water into the oil-producing strata, about 100,000 barrels per day by 1959, which, as a benefit, increased the production of oil. Los Angeles now uses more oil than its wells can produce, and by the 1970s Los Angeles-Long Beach was principally an oil-importing port. In 1979, for example, 32 million tons of oil (one-half of the total cargo handled at the ports that year) were pumped out of supertankers at the ports, most of it coming from Alaska's Prudhoe Bay Field, America's biggest-ever oil find. *Dave Crammer*

BELOW: Navigating through a stinking tableau of catalytic crackers, scrap heaps, derelict vehicles, and leaky 55-gallon drums, UP Extra 3190 West comes around the wye connecting track from UP's San Pedro Branch to SP's Long Beach Branch in August 1983. This unit grain train is destined for the Port of Long Beach. The wye connecting track takes off from the UP at Thenard, which is just west of the west switch at Manuel. A second connection at Thenard (in the distant background) allows UP's unit trains to run in the other direction on SP's Long Beach and San Pedro Branches to the Port of Los Angeles. Continuing on UP's San Pedro Branch across the SP diamond leads to Mead Transfer, the Henry Ford Avenue Drawbridge, and Terminal Island.

The original San Pedro Branch ran down Ocean Avenue, the main street in Long Beach. For many years the LA&SL wanted to build a cut-off that would bypass downtown Long Beach. It prepared its first plans in 1920, but because of arguments about the cut-off's precise location and payment for grade separations, the project was delayed. The LA&SL relocated its track on Terminal Island in 1924-28 to accommodate widening of the main channel, and in 1926 it built the southernmost 2 miles of the cut-off, from Terminal Island across Cerritos Channel to the Wilmington District, via the Badger Avenue Drawbridge, which gave the LA&SL access to a new Ford assembly plant at Wilmington. But the rest of the cut-off remained unbuilt. The LA&SL made 24 different locations, each removing the cut-off a little further from the city, until an agreement was finally reached in

December 1931. Work began on May 7, 1932, after right-of-way litigation was concluded, and the cut-off opened for business a year later. The 1932-built section ran 7.58 miles from Wilmington to Rioco, where it met the existing San Pedro Branch; it included six grade-separation structures at major streets and an 11-span bridge over the Los Angeles River flood-control channel. The branch through downtown Long Beach was abandoned in 1932, leaving stubs at each end that served local industries: 2.48 miles from Bixby to Terminal Island, which included the 185-foot Scherzer rolling-lift drawbridge across the Long Beach harbor channel (abandoned in 1934); and 2.78 miles south of Rioco, now the Lakewood Industrial Lead.

The LA&SL built a small yard at Mead Transfer as part of the cut-off, which the UP now uses to interchange its loose carload business to and from the Port of Los Angeles to the Harbor Belt Line. The LA&SL, SP, Santa Fe, Pacific Electric, and the City of Los Angeles's Municipal Terminal Railroad created this switching road in 1928. The Harbor Belt Line provides equal access to all the wharves at Los Angeles for a flat fee per loaded car. *Rob Leachman*

# THE LOS ANGELES BASIN

*The highly developed citrus-fruit belt between Riverside and San Pedro, Calif., furnishes the carrier with a heavy and profitable traffic.*
—ICC Valuation Report, 1922

East of Los Angeles the Salt Lake Route traverses the Los Angeles Basin from west to east, threading the gap between the San Jose Hills and the Puente Hills, skirting the south side of the Pedley Hills, and climbing from 158 feet above sea level at East Los Angeles to 881 feet where it meets the Santa Fe at Riverside. In 1880 this was very empty countryside, much of it open range. By 1910 citrus groves, truck farms, and walnut trees had displaced the range cattle whose smelly hides were rolled down the bluffs at San Pedro Bay and laboriously loaded onto sailing ships. Small farm towns like Hillgrove, Walnut, and Mira Loma were soon strung along the Salt Lake Route like beads on a string. Night locals worked from dawn to dusk to gather loaded Pacific Fruit Express reefers from the dozens of packing houses between East Los Angeles and Riverside.

Beginning in World War II these towns began to grow, and grow some more. One orange grove after another fell to the insatiable craving for land, land, and more land. The only limit to a town's growth was when it collided with another growing town. Checkerboard streets, cookie-cutter houses, and look-alike malls filled up the Los Angeles Basin like water. They covered the bottom, they lapped at the sides, and now they have begun to spill over the rim through mountain passes and into the desert beyond.

ABOVE LEFT: On January 6, 1975, Santa Fe's Colton Tower operator has held UP Extra 719 East, giving preference to an SP transfer. The UP brakeman returning to his train has just paid a visit to his brother, the tower operator.

In 1883 the California Southern, building north from San Diego towards Cajon Pass, had to cross the SP main line at Colton. When the California Southern men attempted to install their diamond on August 7, the SP blocked them with several locomotives. A crowd assembled, the mood grew ugly, and bloodshed seemed imminent. Luckily, cool heads on both railroads quickly reached an agreement to install the diamond.

Typically, the railroad that wants the diamond has to pay to protect train movements through the diamond from collisions, such as with an interlocking controlled from an adjacent tower. The Santa Fe, California Southern's successor, built a tower at Colton in 1894. It was destroyed by a Santa Fe derailment on January 9, 1917. To rapidly restore the interlocking to service, the Santa Fe disassembled a tower at another location and reassembled it at Colton. The second tower, equally owned by the Santa Fe, LA&SL, and SP, closed at 8:00 A.M. on November 7, 1978, and was demolished in early 1980. Santa Fe now controls Colton interlocking from its dispatching center in Schaumburg, Illinois.

With Santa Fe's sale of its former Second Subdivision between San Bernardino and Los Angeles for commuter trains, every UP, SP, and Santa Fe train between Los Angeles and eastern points must cross this diamond at Colton, making it perhaps the busiest diamond in the West. SP crews sometimes call Colton "Knee-Pad Junction," because they claim they have to beg the Santa Fe for a signal to get across.
*Doug Harrop*

BELOW LEFT: The SPLA&SL's first route between Riverside and San Bernardino was complicated and tedious. SPLA&SL passenger trains entered SP's Riverside Branch at Riverside Junction, took this branch to Colton, crossed over the SP main line, took SP's San Bernardino Branch from Colton to San Bernardino, made a reverse move into SP's San Bernardino depot, then entered Santa Fe's First District at San Bernardino to travel over Cajon Pass, and regained company rails at Daggett. SPLA&SL freight trains entered the Santa Fe at Colton. On February 1, 1916, the Santa Fe agreed to let all SPLA&SL trains enter Santa Fe's Third District main line at Riverside Junction, saving the SPLA&SL considerable time and tedium. The LA&SL retained its rights on SP's Riverside and San Bernardino Branches until 1956, for local business.

The Santa Fe was slow to double-track its Third District between San Bernardino and Riverside Junction, because most of its passenger trains used its Second District between San Bernardino and Los Angeles. Colton to San Bernardino was double-tracked by 1912. In 1930 the Santa Fe double-tracked 3.1 miles between Highgrove and Riverside; signal work

included a new interlocking tower at Riverside Junction and US&S searchlight-type ABS to Highgrove. In 1944 it double-tracked from Colton to the Santa Ana River Bridge east of Highgrove, at which time ABS with interlockings at the ends of double track replaced the existing manual block system. The bridge was double-tracked in 1975, closing the last gap in the double track between Riverside Junction and Daggett. The tower at Riverside Junction closed on September 21, 1979, and was razed in early 1982.

At Riverside, the Salt Lake Route built the most elegant and intricate of its Mission-style depots in 1904. On January 17, 1982, UP Extra 3674 West, an 84-car export coal train, rumbles past the depot on Salt Lake Avenue. These two blocks of street running were eliminated in 1983 when the junction with the Santa Fe was moved 1.4 miles west to West Riverside. The depot, damaged by fire in 1982, was donated to the city, refurbished, and is now a restaurant. *Vance Pomerening*

ABOVE: On a fine, clear December morning in 1987, an extra section of the CSLAZ (Canal Street–Chicago to Los Angeles Trailers) zooms through an enclave of rolling pastureland at milepost 26, just east of Walnut. This location is now called Diamond Bar, an old name resurrected for the new east end of two main tracks at milepost 25.5. In January 1992, the UP reached a $17-million deal with the Southern California Regional Rail Authority (Metrolink) for operating rights over 56 miles from Los Angeles Union Passenger Terminal to West Riverside. This required the UP to add 36 miles of second main track, and make CTC and grade-crossing improvements to accommodate five commuter trains each way daily. Three Metrolink trains began running between LAUPT and San Bernardino on June 14, 1993. As of June 1994, UP had added 28.5 miles of the second track. Stations stops on the UP are made at Montebello, City of Industry, Pomona, Ontario, and Pedley. *Ron Butts*

## CAJON PASS

*I then proceeded...until I got near the head of the Inconstant River... instead of traveling southeast around the bend of the stream, I struck directly across the plain nearly S.S.W. to the gap in the mountain.*

— Jedediah Strong Smith crosses the Mojave Desert and rediscovers Cajon Pass, 1826

East of San Bernardino the LA&SL shakes loose of its entangling branches and industrial leads, and climbs into the mountains on the Santa Fe track it entered at Riverside Junction. Here the Santa Fe follows Cajon Creek into a fortuitous gap between the San Gabriel and San Bernardino Mountains, where the San Andreas Fault is relentlessly tearing California in two. Above Cajon station the mountains pull back from the creek. The

valley broadens into a gullied bowl, rimmed by mountains on east and west, and a summit ridge on the north. The Santa Fe winds back and forth, seeking the best grade, until it rolls over the summit ridge at Cajon Pass, 25.6 miles east of San Bernardino and 2,697 feet higher (after 1972). This is the gateway to the Mojave Desert.

The east side of Cajon Pass is comparatively gentle. The Santa Fe runs diagonally down the sloping, sandy alluvium that fans out from the mountains, then turns north as the grade lessens, and runs across the Mojave Desert to Barstow.

The Mojave Indians and the coastal Indians used this pass as a trade route, for shells and turquoise. Father Francisco Garcés was probably the first European through it, in 1776, searching for a trail that connected the northern New Mexico and southern California missions. Garcés found what he was

looking for, but the Spaniards never used it. His trail lay cold until fur trappers led by Jedediah Smith rode southwest from the Great Salt Lake to southern California in 1826. For the next 22 years occasional caravans of Mexican traders and American fur trappers trekked over Cajon Pass to the San Gabriel Mission. Mormons scouting for places to settle picked up the trail in southern Utah and came down it to San Bernardino in 1847. Liking what they saw, they came back in force in 1850–51. Yet it was forty-niners, not Mormons, who improved the pass for wagons, in December 1849. For the next two decades, until the Central Pacific and Union Pacific met at Promontory, Utah, wagons often came this way from Salt Lake City during the winter. The first railroad to do work in the pass was the Los Angeles & Independence, which fought off the SP to do some grading in Blue Cut in 1875, and started on a 3,700-foot tunnel through the summit ridge before giving up in 1877.

The next railroad to think about the pass was the California Southern, the 1880 creation of San Diego citizens hoping to see their city and its excellent natural harbor surpass Los Angeles. To do that, they needed a rail connection. The Atlantic & Pacific, the company controlled by the Santa Fe and the Frisco, then building west toward California, needed a friendly port on the Pacific Coast, i.e., a port not controlled by the SP. Recognizing their mutual needs, on July 10, 1880, the A&P and California Southern agreed to meet on the west bank of the Colorado River at Needles, California (the Santa Fe bought 50 percent of the California Southern on November 7, 1884, and merged it into its system on January 17, 1906).

The California Southern built north from San Diego, and reached San Bernardino on September 13, 1883. The Atlantic & Pacific crossed 545 miles of arid desolation to reach Needles on August 8, 1883, leaving a 250-mile gap still to be filled. But waiting at Needles was the SP, which had quickly built a line from Mojave, California, to Needles to block the Santa Fe's way into California. The SP, however, got caught cash-short by the financial crisis of 1883. When the Santa Fe told the SP to hand over its Needles–Mojave line or risk being paralleled, the SP reluctantly realized the game was up, and leased the Needles-Mojave line to the A&P on August 20, 1884, "therefore losing its monopoly of California," noted the *New York Times*.

This reduced the gap between the A&P and the California Southern to just 81 miles, via Cajon Pass. William Raymond Morley, the Santa Fe's brilliant locating engineer, inspected Cajon in 1880 and declared, "This is nothing; we can go through here easily enough." And they did. In April 1884 crews began work at San Bernardino and Waterman Junction (Barstow after January 1, 1886). By July, 15 miles of track extended towards the pass from each end. After a Chinese grading crew finished digging a large cut near the summit (Terrass Cut, between Dell and Gish), the rails were connected. On November 14, 1885, the first train crossed Cajon Pass, and Santa Fe's route to San Diego was complete.

AT LEFT: At dawn's first light on March 28, 1987, a heavy westbound freight eases over the apex of Cajon Pass. The two-unit helper that shoved from Victorville to Summit will also provide dynamic braking on the 3.0-percent descent to Cajon on the 1885-built South Track. The helper engineer has pulled his throttle back to idle, moved the dynamic brake handle into "set up" position for the required ten seconds, and begun to slowly increase braking effort to keep this train from obeying gravity too quickly. The engines of his two units have revved up to provide excitation current to the traction motors for dynamic braking, their sound a mellow counterpart to the cold spang of wheels striking rail ends and the creaking rhythm of heavily laden grain hoppers. As the train begins to fall toward San Bernardino, the helper engineer will ease his dynamic brake handle to the right, observe the ammeter needle sink counterclockwise towards its 700-ampere limit, and when he is confident that dynamic braking and air brakes have balanced the train against the force of gravity, perhaps he will admire the splendid sight of glistening snow on the San Gabriel Mountains 5,000 feet above his train. *Eric Blasko*

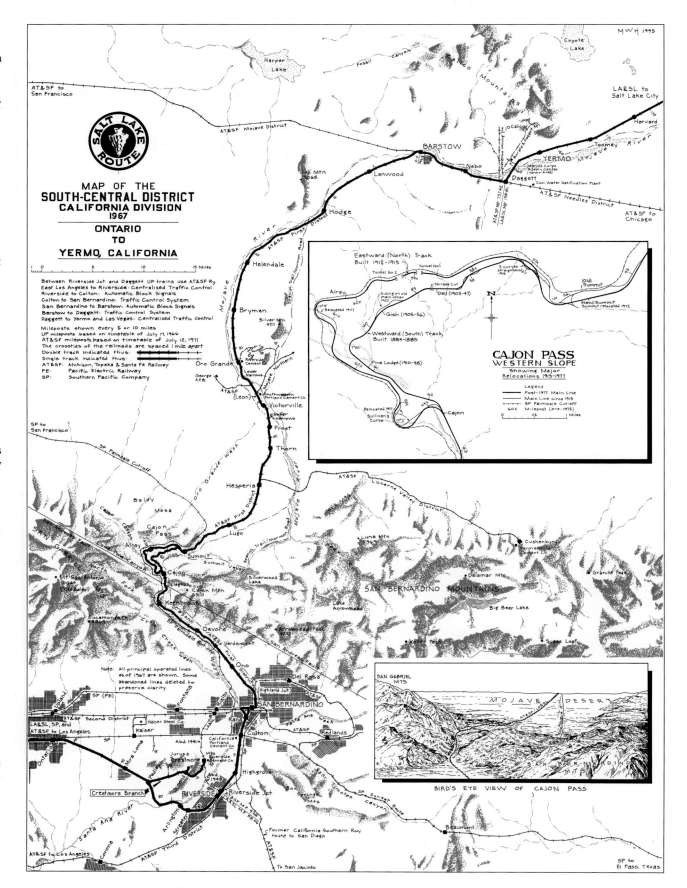

MAP OF THE
SOUTH-CENTRAL DISTRICT
CALIFORNIA DIVISION
1967
ONTARIO
TO
YERMO, CALIFORNIA

CAJON PASS
WESTERN SLOPE
Showing Major
Relocations 1913-1977

BIRD'S EYE VIEW OF CAJON PASS

*El pueblo de Nuestra Señora la Reina de Los Angeles*—the village of Our Lady the Queen of the Angels—mushroomed into a huge city by 1910. Retired farmers and storekeepers, mostly from the Midwest, sick of frigid winters and blistering summers, flocked to Los Angeles after selling out during the economic booms of 1904–06 and 1910–13, to sit back in the warm sun and the ocean breezes, and watch oranges grow. The city's growth put tremendous pressure on all the railroad routes into Los Angeles, as did the heavy eastbound movement of fruit and produce.

The alignment of the California Southern over Cajon Pass was nothing to be proud of; it hooked around every obstacle bigger than a boulder. California Southern locating engineer Fred Perris, a former forty-niner, had avoided a summit tunnel by using a 3.0-percent ruling grade from Summit down to Cajon, where the grade decreased to a more reasonable 2.2 percent for the remaining 18.5 miles to San Bernardino. His alignment was suitable for a frontier railroad with four or five little trains daily, but by 1914 the Santa Fe and the Salt Lake Route put an average of 34 trains daily onto this twisty single-track mountain railroad, plus light helper engines. And there were a lot of helpers—about 13 on the pass at any given time.

All eastbound passenger trains longer than five cars required a helper; the ten-car transcontinental passenger trains required three engines, as did eastbound freights of 1,750 tons or more. Westbound tonnage freights required a single helper on the 1.60 percent from Victorville to Summit. Passenger trains were limited to 30 mph down the 3.0 percent, freights to 15 mph, with 10-minute stops at Cajon and Devore to cool wheels. Uphill speeds were seldom faster than 15 mph.

The traffic was not just congested, it was congealed. The SPLA&SL felt its trains spent too much time parked in sidings watching Santa Fe trains go by, so in September 1911 it announced plans to build its own line from San Bernardino to Daggett, which would have a ruling grade of 1.0 percent from Riverside to Keenbrook, 2.20 percent from Keenbrook to Summit, and 1.0 percent from Summit to Otis (Yermo). By December 1913 the Salt Lake Route had completed its survey, which now began at Ontario, but made no move to begin construction.

Meanwhile, the Santa Fe started to loosen the gridlock by double-tracking 3.4 miles from San Bernardino east in 1910. In 1912 it extended the second track up the canyon to Cajon, eliminating or reducing curves as it went, and equipped the double track with Automatic Block Signals (ABS), using Union Switch & Signal Type S upper-quadrant semaphores (Santa Fe's standard until 1923). In November 1912 the Santa Fe began grading a separated, reduced-grade eastward track from Cajon to Summit. Taking advantage of the wider valley above Cajon, the engineers were able to lengthen the distance from Cajon to Summit by 10,230 feet, which reduced the grade from 3.0 to 2.2 percent. About 1.1 million cubic yards of rock and soil were moved, much of it by extra section gangs, to grade the new line. Tunnels 1 and 2, 380.1 feet and 467.5 feet long, respectively, were dug just east of Alray, the new line's only siding (named for Al Ray, a Santa Fe roadmaster). They were lined with concrete after completion. The new eastward track was placed in service on November 1, 1913. Because it lay to the north of the old track, trains operated left-handed from San Bernardino to Summit. US&S Type S ABS was extended from Cajon to Summit in 1914.

Signals and double-track on Cajon's stiff west slope made operations fluid again, and the lessened grade allowed the Santa Fe and SPLA&SL to trim one helper off most trains. Mollified, the SPLA&SL signed a new trackage-rights agreement with the Santa Fe on August 13, 1915 (it took effect on February 1, 1916), and shelved its independent survey. The agreement also sped up SPLA&SL trains by extending the trackage rights from Colton to Riverside Junction, and allowed the SPLA&SL to conduct on-line business between Daggett and Colton without penalty.

On the east side, the Santa Fe double-tracked from Daggett to Cottonwood (Hicks after 1913, and Hodge after 1926) in 1910, equipped this with US&S Type S ABS, and installed General Railway Signal interlockings at Daggett and Cottonwood in 1911. In 1917 manual block signals were installed at nine block stations from Hicks to Summit linked to the dispatcher by telephone. While manual block required an operator around the clock at each station, it was a good system for a busy single-track railroad in the pre-CTC era. It sufficed until 1924, when a second track and US&S Type R color-light ABS were added between Summit and Hicks. This job was completed in November 1924. Left-hand operation was then extended from Summit to Frost, where a flyover allowed eastbound trains to duck under the westward track and revert to normal right-handed operation without the choke point that a crossover would introduce. At San Bernardino, however, trains still had to cross over, in front of the yard office at A Yard.

When traffic rebounded in the late 1930s, the Santa Fe installed spring switches in 1938 on the leaving switches at Devore, Keenbrook, Cajon, Alray, Lugo, and Hesperia, and color-light signals, both three-color and searchlight types, began to replace the semaphores. During World War II, the number of train movements zoomed to over a hundred on an average day. There was thought given to triple-tracking portions of the pass until the ICC allowed westbound trains to be lengthened from 50 to 90 cars, and eastbounds to 100 cars. Sidings were lengthened accordingly.

FAR LEFT: Big, modern units, two SD60M's and an SD60, take their train through 467.5-foot Tunnel 2 on the North Track between Alray and Summit on May 15, 1991, seemingly without effort. Hidden in a cut just to the right is SP's Palmdale Cut-off, which parallels the North Track between Summit and Devore. SP built the 79.8-mile cut-off in 1966–67 between Palmdale and West Colton so that SP trains to and from northern California could bypass bottlenecks in Los Angeles. SP engineers surveying on Cajon in the early 1960s were surprised to meet a crew of UP engineers surveying a long tunnel under the pass to Ontario. The two roads discussed a partnership; after the UP lost interest, SP went ahead with the Palmdale Cut-off. *Scott R. Snell*

NEAR LEFT: High-speed power—two DDA40X's and an 8000-series "Fast Forty" SD40-2—lift hotshot LAX up the 2.2 percent on the North Track between Pine Lodge and Alray shortly after sunrise on a December 1977 morning. Pine Lodge disappeared from the timetable in 1948, and Alray was reduced to a short set-out track in 1972. *Bob Finan*

BELOW: The LAF coils through Sullivan's Curve (just above Cajon on the North Track), on a pristine winter day in February 1978, bound for an evening arrival at the pig ramp in East Yard. At left is Southern Pacific's Palmdale Cut-off. When possible, westbounds run down the North Track because its maximum speed is 30 mph versus 20 mph on the South Track. Named for early-day rail photographer Herb Sullivan, Sullivan's Curve was one of three 10° curves on the 1913-built eastward track. The first was just east of Cajon where the line curved west and crossed Cajon Creek, the second was Sullivan's Curve, and the third was just below Alray. The Santa Fe widened all three to 6° to 6.5° in 1977 (probably they would have all been 6° curves if the upper ones had not been penned in by SP's adjacent 6° curves). *T. J. Donahue*

59

After the construction of the new eastward track in 1913, Cajon Pass proved remarkably resistant to further realignments for the next 59 years, except for a few revisions made necessary by excess precipitation. The Santa Fe, it has been noted, has always been a railroad to spend a great deal of money to go fast, but since there was little chance of ever going fast over Cajon Pass, it has concentrated its relocation dollars elsewhere, such as on the Arizona Divide. And so today the Santa Fe still tolerates a 3.0-percent grade in the middle of its main line.

Terrass Cut, the big cut dug by Chinese laborers in 1885 at milepost 59 just west of Dell, was a recurrent problem, shedding rocks and mud onto the track every winter. Heavy rains during the winter of 1921–22 caused the south side of the cut to fail completely. The tremendous weight of the saturated material slumping into the cut forced the ground beneath the track to bulge upwards until trains could no longer be operated. Steam shovels were brought in to recover the cut. Some of the earth they dug out was used to build a new straightened-out main-line grade at Gish, the heavily curved original main line at Gish becoming a 70-car siding.

Floods between March 2 and 4, 1938, caused by the heaviest rainfall in southern California in 61 years, closed the Santa Fe from Barstow to Los Angeles. Rain began to fall on February 27,

and by March 4 the total precipitation at Los Angeles was 11.15 inches, which saturated the soil and caused every river in the Los Angeles Basin to overflow its banks, flooding large areas of the city with 3 to 4 feet of water. There were 27 washouts aggregating 3.62 miles of track on the First District between Barstow and San Bernardino, and at five locations mud and rock slides covered the track to a depth of 20 feet or more. The LA&SL detoured its passenger trains via Sacramento, California, until the Santa Fe reopened on March 10. After the flood the Santa Fe decided that about 2 miles of its grade along the east bank of Cajon Creek, from west Cajon to Cozy Dell, were too vulnerable to flooding and mud slides from Cleghorn Canyon, so in 1939 the Santa Fe moved it to the west bank. Four years later Cajon Creek damaged the relocated track below Cajon, demonstrating that washouts in this canyon are not easily suppressed.

By the mid-1960s, as trains became heavier and cars became longer, a problem arose on Cajon that could be solved only by relocation. Approaching Summit from the west there were two curves where the eastward and westward tracks came together and the climb ended, a 10° left-hand curve followed by a 6.5° right-hand curve. This was a frequent site for pulled draw-

bars, and on a few occasions long cars on the head end of eastbound trains were pulled over on the 10° curve. A series of S-curves at Summit gave long, heavy trains trouble. Further, the signaling system normally limited each track to one direction of traffic, making the pass very inflexible.

To solve all of these problems at once, in May 1972 the Santa Fe began work on a $4.3-million, 3.3-mile line relocation at Summit, and began installing Traffic Control System (Santa Fe's nomenclature for CTC) between Barstow and San Bernardino to allow trains to move in both directions on both tracks by signal indication. The relocation project moved Summit to the south, lowered the top of the pass by 51 feet (from 3,826 feet to 3,775 feet above sea level), and straightened the curves at Summit to a maximum sharpness of 4°. All of the passing sidings between Barstow and San Bernardino were pulled up in favor of pairs of No. 24 crossovers at Hodge, Frost, Lugo, Summit, Cajon, and Verdemont (by 1976 Santa Fe had added crossovers at Lenwood; by 1978 milepost 29.4; by 1982 Keenbrook; and by 1983 East Victorville). The first train ran through Summit on the new South Track on September 20, 1972, and on the new North Track a few days later. The Santa Fe then abandoned the old main line at Summit.

ABOVE: The curve that caused most of the trouble was the big 10° curve on the North Track just west of Summit where trains turned through 141° of a circle. The GP30 on the point of Extra 703 East during January 1971 fits fine on this curve, but the trailing double-diesels exhibit an alarming amount of overhang. *Keith Ardinger*

AT RIGHT: The first UP train over the new South Track at Summit following Santa Fe's dedication ceremony on October 2, 1972, was Extra 6931 West. The original line is visible at far left, just below SP's Palmdale Cut-off. Cuts like these would have been impossibly expensive for the California Southern in 1885, unrealistic for anyone other than a Pennsy in 1914, but in 1972, using ripper-toothed bull-dozers, wheel loaders, paddle-wheel scrapers, and off-road dump trucks, "dirt cheap" took on a whole new meaning. *Keith Ardinger collection*

AT LEFT: A look west on the relocated main line at Summit during February 1978 shows the large cut from which the photo at right was taken. The original line passed in front of the ridge from right to left, then ducked through the ridge just to the right and above the new line. The train is a KUW, for Kaiser Unit West, an 84-car, 11,000-ton unit train of coking coal from Kaiser's Sunnyside Mine at Sunnyside, Utah, to Kaiser Steel at Fontana, California, via D&RGW to Provo, UP to Barstow, and Santa Fe to Fontana. The use of Santa Fe helpers on UP trains and vice versa is common. This trio of GP35's is cut in to avoid folding up the light caboose; they will stay with the train to San Bernardino for additional dynamic braking. With helpers,

retainers on westbound trains heavier than 4,500 tons are not required on the 3.0 percent so long as the brake-pipe reduction does not exceed 18 pounds. If it does, the train must be stopped immediately and retainers turned up. In any case the maximum speed for heavy trains is at present 15 mph from Summit to Cajon on the South Track, and 20 mph on either track from Cajon to San Bernardino. *T. J. Donahue*

# THE MOJAVE DESERT

*Two ounce vial of ammonia to apply freely to bite wound after
opening and squeezing out poison. Saturate the wound thoroughly
for two hours or more to neutralize poison. If wound on arm or leg,
ligature belt or cord twisted tightly between wound and heart to prevent
poison reaching blood vessels and vital parts. After treatment of two
or three hours, wound should be cauterized by burning small amount
of gunpowder on it and searing with hot nail or iron to prevent  blood
poisoning.*
　　　　　　　　　　　　　　　　　　　*—Barstow Printer,* 1911

At 54,000 square miles, the Mojave Desert is larger than any
one of the 27 smallest states. The lowest point in the desert is
Death Valley, where the all-time high air temperature for the
U.S. was recorded:134°. Ground temperatures may reach 190°.
Precipitation in the Mojave is seldom more than 4 inches per
year, most of it during the winter months, often as snow.
Where the rainfall exceeds 7.25 inches annually, sagebrush
thrives; elsewhere, creosote bush predominates, a plant which
spreads in concentric rings by cloning itself. Some of these
clones have persisted for 9,000 years. Where the soil is too salty
for creosote bush, desert holly and cattle spinach grow, excret-
ing excess salt through their pores. The desert is often slightly
wetter at higher elevations, and there the Joshua-tree appears.
Mormons named them for the resemblance of their upturned
limbs to Joshua's upraised arms as he led the Israelites to the
Promised Land.

Settlers established ranches along the Mojave River during the 1860s. The Mojave Indians were soon starved out
or exterminated. Cattle were turned out into the desert
in large numbers to graze. In 1910, for example, the Rock
Springs Cattle Co. at Kelso grazed 8,000 head. The armies
of cattle grazed the desert to death and trampled the streambeds. Stripped of edible vegetation, the desert eroded, and
could no longer support cattle. It has not recovered, and may
never.

Many minor discoveries of gold and silver were made in
the Mojave in the nineteenth century. Two little mining railroads ran from Daggett to silver mines at Calico, and a third
to a nearby borax deposit, between 1887 and 1907. In the
long run limestone deposits east of Victorville, crushed and
fired in kilns to make cement and lime at Oro Grande, Leon,
and Cushenbury, have been more important than precious
metals.

In World War II the government filled the Mojave full
of military bases, including a Marine Corps supply center at
Yermo, George Air Force Base (now closed) at Adelanto, and
Fort Irwin north of Yermo. Fort Irwin is now the National

Training Center. Army units as large as divisions from around the country periodically pack up everything they own, from tanks to tents, load it on trains, and take it to Fort Irwin to challenge Fort Irwin's resident "Russian" motor rifle regiment.

AT LEFT: On either side of Victorville, the railroad follows the Mojave River through its Upper and Lower Narrows, miniature gorges about 1,000 feet long and 150 feet high. On the afternoon of April 12, 1990, Extra 3388 West growls out of the shadows of the Upper Narrows about a mile west of Victorville. Frost splitting has caused almost perfect spheroidal weathering of the old granite. Wind has carried off the dirt and dust, but there is not enough water to roll the rocks away. *Eric Blasko*

ABOVE: Cajon's east side is like a shallow bowl. The railroad rapidly loses 1,107 feet in 19 miles between Summit and Victorville, then flattens out, descending from Victorville to Barstow at half the rate it did previously. The speed restrictions end below Oro Grande, so

eastbounds roll fast through the Mojave Desert until they slow to enter Barstow. At sunset on a June day in 1977, UP Extra 81 East flies through the desert at Hodge, behind an inimitable UP consist of two DD35A's, two DD35's, and one each of an SD40-2, GP30B, and SD24B. Hodge was named for the Hodge brothers, who homesteaded here in 1913. *Don Jocelyn*

AT RIGHT: At Daggett the UP regains its own track, swings across the Mojave River to Yermo, then strikes off into the wilderness. The home signal at the east switch at Manix is stark black against the sunset on January 2, 1987. In a few hours it will blink to life as a westbound enters the approaching block, beckoning it towards mountains backlit by the electrical blaze of the nation's second largest city. *Mark Simonson*

## AFTON CANYON

*Afton Canyon is a beautiful and rugged gorge, traversed by the railroad.* —From *Along the Union Pacific System*, 1928

The Mojave River arises from snowmelt in the San Bernardino Mountains, and flows northeast in a curving path. When there is not enough water for the river to flow above the surface, it percolates through the sandy bed, often reappearing miles downstream. John Frémont remarked on the river's curious properties in 1844: "As we followed along its course, the river, instead of growing constantly larger, gradually dwindled away...We continued along the dry bed, in which, after an interval of about 16 miles, the water reappeared in some low places...A short distance below, this river entirely disappeared."

Father Francisco Garcés, the first European to see the Mojave River, called it *Arroyo de los Màtires*, "Gulch of Martyrs"—ironic, since that fate befell him in 1781 at the hands of the Yuma Indians. Jedediah Smith's name for the Mojave River was more rustic but no less vivid; he called it the Inconstant River. He too was later killed by Indians, in 1831. John Frémont listened to the name of the local Indian tribe, and wrote down Mohahve. Corrected for spelling, it stuck. Lieutenant R. S. Williamson was the first to look at the canyon as a possible railroad route, during the Pacific Railroad Surveys of 1853. Cartographers had assumed the Mojave flowed into the Colorado, until Williamson set them straight.

For its final 4 miles, until its end at the Mojave River Sink, the river flows through Afton Canyon between the Cady and Cave Mountains. Before there was an Afton Canyon the mountains were contiguous, and the Mojave River filled a prehistoric lake that covered much of the western Mojave Desert. Geologists call this Manix Lake, for the railroad station. Eventually the river cut a gorge and emptied the lake.

Afton Canyon was at first called Cave Canyon, for three small caves where Indians used to camp. It was later renamed Afton for the railroad station at its west end. The largest cave disappeared when the SPLA&SL drove 542-foot Tunnel 1 through an oxbow ridge. Locals claimed a portion of the cave was hidden behind the tunnel's timber lining. In 1957 the UP found that ground pressure had caused the lining to deteriorate. Since the ridge Tunnel 1 ran through is composed of poorly cemented gravels and conglomerates, and is not especially tall, the UP decided to daylight rather than enlarge and concrete the tunnel, removing about

330,000 cubic yards of overburden between May 1 and August 1957, the work done between 4 P.M. and 10 A.M. because of daytime temperatures up to 118°. It was the last timber-lined tunnel in service on the LA&SL.

FAR LEFT: At 2:46 P.M. on January 10, 1983, the 2-VAN motors uphill at milepost 193.7, near the location of the long-gone station of Cliffside. The 1-VAN went by 45 minutes earlier. A 1.0-percent westward grade begins here and continues with few breaks for 11 miles to Field. The 2-VAN's 9,000 horsepower is more than enough to take its 45 piggyback flats and caboose uphill through the 40-and 45-mph curve territory in Afton Canyon at a reasonable speed, but back on the 70-mph straight track west of Dunn, the 1.0 percent will deny it the ability to accelerate to the speed limit. In 1983 the VANs were the premier westbounds on the LA&SL. The UP had to be on its toes to carry trailers from Chicago to Los Angeles in competition with the shorter, faster Santa Fe. *Jamie Schmid*

TOP LEFT: Between trains on November 13, 1988, a desert tarantula hunts for dinner in Afton Canyon. Large and furry—females may grow to a legspan of four inches—they are dangerous only to insects, lizards, and small animals. Their venom is usually no more poisonous to people than a bee's, and they rarely attack people. Somehow this tarantula has lost part of a leg. It may be running on seven legs for a long time, as female tarantulas may live for 20 years. *Eric Blasko*

ABOVE: At 2:05 P.M. on March 22, 1988, Extra 9158 West's 15 piggyback flats and 7 auto racks sing through the 5° curve at milepost 194 between Basin and Afton. During spring a small amount of water often flows through Afton Canyon, and vegetation grows in the riverbed. Most of what is seen here is creosote bush, greasewood, and shadscale. The last two shrubs are very tolerant of salty soils. Their shoots and leaves provide forage for grazing animals, especially sheep, though greasewood can be toxic when overeaten. The canyon walls are practically sterile of plant life, lacking precipitation and suitable soil. When Father Garcés and his four Indian companions passed through the canyon from east to west 212 years prior, on March 9, 1776, they noted the grass was good but the water tasted salty. In the 1860s, when white men settled along the river, it was often visible for its entire 94-mile length to where the river loses itself in the Mojave River Sink. Now, because most of its water is appropriated for irrigation, the Mojave seldom looks like an actual river. *Jamie Schmid*

Contrary to what might be expected for a railroad in a desert, water has been the source of most of the LA&SL's woes. Cloudbursts inconsequential in a wet climate are very exciting in the desert, where the plant life is sparse and ill prepared to soak up large amounts of water, the gravelly surface is virtually waterproof, and the streambeds cannot channel large amounts of water. The calamity of January 1, 1910, in Meadow Valley Wash was the worst flood the Salt Lake Route has experienced to date, but there have been others.

On February 15, 1927, a cloudburst spawned a flash flood that weakened the bridge over San Jose Creek at Clayton, California, (milepost 13.75). It collapsed underneath the eastbound *Los Angeles Limited*, killing its engineer. In 1938 a large tropical storm moved northeast into California. Heavy rains began falling on February 27 and by March 2 every river

in southern California had overflowed its banks. The Santa Fe's side-by-side spans over the Mojave east of Victorville survived, but the river overturned one pier of the LA&SL's bridge between Daggett and Yermo, two spans dropping into the roiling current. Confined between the walls of Afton Canyon, the Mojave River was especially destructive. The two bridges on either side of Afton station and the bridge at Baxter were destroyed. These were multiple 60-foot deck-plate girder spans with midstream piers. Too short and too close to the streambed, they crimped the river like an hourglass, until the river angrily cast them aside. Tunnel 1 became an aqueduct with water eight feet deep. The pile trestle to the limestone quarry across the river at Baxter vanished, and the grade was washed out in numerous places between Afton and Baxter, as well as between Daggett and Crucero. The Tonopah &

Tidewater was inundated as the Mojave River Sink filled up.

In Meadow Valley Wash and Clover Creek Canyon, the precipitation was not as severe, and the High Line performed well. A concrete pier at the eighth crossing of the wash at milepost 419.3 near Carp was undermined, putting a severe dip into the bridge. Washouts at Barclay, Islen, Minto, Carp, and Vigo trapped a freight near Carp. Both the Pioche and the Mead Lake Branches were washed out. In the Los Angeles Basin, two bridges on the San Pedro Branch, bridges across Arroyo Seco on the Glendale and Pasadena Branches, and portions of the Anaheim Branch were damaged, and 42 spans of the Santa Ana River trestle on the Rialto Branch disappeared. Flooding washed out the main line along the east bank of the Los Angeles River, at Mira Loma, and east of Pomona.

Bridge and building crews drove pile trestles to fill the gaps, reopening the main line east of Las Vegas on March 11. The damage in Afton Canyon was much worse and the line was not reopened between Las Vegas and Daggett until March 22. Santa Fe's main line over Cajon Pass reopened on March 10.

The UP learned another lesson about desert floods. It replaced the small, short, deck-girder spans at Afton and Baxter with much longer combinations of 200-foot Pratt trusses and through girders. The two bridges at Afton were

replaced in 1938, and the 120-foot two-span deck-girder bridge at Baxter (Basin after about 1960) was replaced with a 460-foot through bridge in 1939. The bridge at Yermo was rebuilt in kind. A new 85-span pile trestle over the Santa Ana River restored service on the Rialto Branch.

AT LEFT: At 7:03 A.M. on March 27, 1987, two SD40-2's drift downhill eastbound between Afton and Basin with 25 cars, all pig-gyback. No matter how trivial a desert stream might seem, sooner or later it will fill up with muddy water. *Eric Blasko*

ABOVE: The engineer of a westbound just east of Afton in October 1974 has dropped the visor to protect his vision from the evening sun. Muted under the harsh light of high noon, in the setting sun the variegated rock in Afton Canyon takes on brilliant hues of crimson, saffron, and cochineal. *Don Jocelyn*

## BASIN, WHERE THE RIVER COMES TO DIE

*The answer is simple: it stopped raining.*
—Erma Peirson, naturalist, 1970

Released from the confines of Afton Canyon at Basin, the Mojave River gives up. People have harvested its water for their fields and lawns, the sun has collected a sweat tax every inch of the way, and now there is nothing left. If there was a trickle of water in the canyon, it stops. If there was a smudge of hopeful grass along its meandering trickle, it withers. If there were the footprints of a small nocturnal creature come down to its damp sandy banks to drink under the light of stars and moon, now there are bones. At Basin begins the edge of the Mojave River Sink, a great desolation where the wind greedily scours the parched surface for grains of sand, and carries them off to its hoard in the Devil's Playground.

Long ago (geologists' two favorite words), this basin contained a pluvial lake, from the Latin *pluvia*, "rain." When the glaciers moved south, and the desert's climate turned cold and wet, rain sluiced down the gullies of the fault-blocked mountains of the Basin & Range Province, and collected in the enclosed basins between the ranges. If there had been enough rainfall, the pluvial lakes would have become larger and larger until they overflowed their impoundments, and using cutting action they would have established a full-fledged drainage system in the Basin & Range Province, some streams flowing south into the Colorado River, others north into the Columbia and Snake Rivers. But there was not enough rainfall for this to happen, even during the ice ages. And after each ice age, when the climate returned to its normal state of drought, the pluvial lakes shrank until they were no more, leaving their shorelines stranded like seaweed at high tide, and depositing a scum of glistening white salt crystals on the basin floors.

In wet years, enough rain falls to refill some of the ancient pluvial lakes with playas, or temporary lakes. Sometimes the playas will last for a few years, but more often their water, only a few feet deep and spread out over many square miles, succumbs quickly to evaporation. Playas are less common now than they were a century ago; if there is any sort of perennial stream that helps replenish a playa, people have assiduously garnered this water for themselves with dams and ditches.

The Mojave River Sink is the first of a series of playas, connected like stair steps, that collect water from 3,500 square miles of desert. If enough water comes down the Mojave River to fill its sink, it overflows and runs across the desert past Crucero to Soda Lake. Once Soda Lake fills a few feet deep, it overflows north into Silver Lake (this valley used to lie below sea level, and the Mojave River over time has brought enough silt and sand downstream to raise the valley floor a thousand feet). If water kept flowing into Silver Lake, it would eventually spill over into the Amargosa River, and water would run north through the Silurian Valley to fill up Death Valley. But it has not rained that much in a long time.

In the recorded past Soda Lake and Silver Lake have filled with water several times. The Tonopah & Tidewater, which blithely laid its track right on these lake beds in 1906, got drowned out in 1910 when the river ran at its highest level since 1862, and had to raise its track across Silver Lake by six

inches. In January 1916 the lake filled again, even deeper, and this time the T&T had to move its track over to Silver Lake's eastern shore. There was enough water in Silver Lake after the Mojave River flood of 1938 to hold regattas for several weeks, and to put the T&T out of service for several months. Floods during the spring of 1969 reached Silver Lake and water remained there for several months. But when the rains stop, the river stops running, and the lakes soon dry up. The Mojave River dies at Basin because it stopped raining about 16,000 years ago.

Left: At 6:31 A.M. on March 6, 1988, a hazy sunrise glints from the side of a short eastbound double-stack and piggyback train at Basin. Released from the 40- and 45-mph territory in Afton Canyon, the train rushes past the west switch at Basin, 34 miles of 70-mph track ahead of it. From Basin to the bottom of the sink just east of the former station of Cork, the railroad descends 254 feet, giving eastbounds a bit of a head start on the long climb that begins at milepost 208 and ends 3,237 feet higher at the top of Cima Hill.

Above: The morning of December 2, 1988, is 35° cold. The wind moans a dreary tune across the coarse alluvium, tugging experimentally at the stubborn creosote bushes, snatching up tumbleweeds and flinging them across the desert. Westbound at Basin at 7:45 A.M., four howling SD40-2s fight the 0.6-percent grade out of the Mojave River Sink, 10,000 tons of soda ash hung on their drawbar. Blurry in the dusty air are the tawny sands of the Devil's Playground, nestled against the grizzled scarps of Cowhole Mountain, Old Dad Mountain, and the Kelso Mountains, league after league of worn-out mountain tops marching across the desert like frozen waves in an ocean of slowly moving sand.
*Two photographs, Eric Blasko*

One day in a long journey...time seems to have died on the afternoon of December 22, 1979, at Basin, California. There is no whisper of a breeze, no rustle of leaves to interrupt the desert's funereal silence.

Look east down the track: there, a pinprick of light, glowing like an ember in the dancing heat. Out there on the 9-mile tangent that points like an arrow to the mouth of Afton Canyon, a train is coming this way. Now the radio crackles to life. The L.A.–Cima dispatcher in Salt Lake City is calling this train. It is the PLA, a drag freight from Pocatello, Idaho, to Los Angeles. The dispatcher reminds the PLA that it has a pickup to make from the CTC siding at Basin. There is a ballast-pit spur at Basin facing east. An eastbound that went by earlier pulled 22 loads of ballast from the spur,

and set them into the controlled siding so that the PLA can pick them up without making a runaround. The dusty old company hoppers, side sheets bulged outwards and top chords hammered down from years of abuse, are now resting on the siding.

The dispatcher has specific instructions for the PLA: "Stop back of the east switch to hold the pickup east of the east switch." To translate, he wants the PLA to leave its train on the main short of the east switch, take the power down the main past the west switch, back the power onto the ballast cars, push them back onto the train, then head the whole train into the siding to let the VAN run through on the main. The VAN, a hot piggyback train, is coming up fast behind the PLA.

At 2:05 P.M. the PLA arrives at Basin, but instead of stopping

back of the east switch as instructed, it pulls down the main to the west switch, where the power leaves the train and backs into the siding to pick up the ballast hoppers. The radio remains silent, even though the dispatcher surely saw that his instructions went for naught when the PLA cleared the block east of the east switch and the track light blinked out on his CTC board. The PLA's crew apparently has had a long day; they are so close to dinner in the Yermo clubhouse they can almost taste it, and they figure they have just forced the dispatcher's hand. Now, they think, he will have to let them run ahead of the VAN to Dunn, the next siding 9.6 miles to the west, and maybe they will be able to run ahead of the VAN all the way to Yermo, and sit down to dinner a few minutes early.

No way. The dispatcher holds the PLA on the main at Basin and runs the VAN through the siding. At 2:30 P.M. the PLA's head-end brakeman crosses the track to inspect the VAN while it reins in its 16,200 horses and moseys through the 20-mph siding. At 2:38 the VAN passes the PLA. At 2:45 the VAN clears the first intermediate west of Basin and the PLA gets a yellow "Approach" signal allowing it to leave Basin—much later than it would have left if they done what the dispatcher had told them to do. Almost certainly tomorrow, if not tonight, the PLA's crew will receive a strong message from the trainmaster.
*Two photographs, Jamie Schmid*

## THE DEVIL'S PLAYGROUND

*Spread out below us lay the desert, stark and glaring, its rigid hill-chains lying in disordered groupings, in attitudes of the dead.*                   —Surveyor Clarence King in eastern California, 1866

From the summit of Cajon Pass the LA&SL runs downhill for 114 miles, down to a place hot and hellish—the Devil's Playground. It has descended over 2,800 feet from Cajon Pass to reach this miserable wasteland of sand dunes and vicious heat. The railroad is flat for about a mile between the former siding at Cork and Balch, then it starts to climb to the top of Cima Hill, 3,237 feet higher. The LA&SL may not look the part, but it is a very mountainous railroad, because its route cuts across the grain of the north-south running ranges of the Basin & Range Province. The 140-platform, 28-car double-stack trains the UP began hauling east from Los

Angeles in October 1986 were too long and too heavy (weighing as much as 10,000 tons) to put all the power on the head end, so the UP had to give them a two-unit helper from East Yard in Los Angeles to Milford, Utah. At 572.6 miles, it was the longest manned helper operation in the U.S. and Canada. The helpers, like the double-stacks they pushed, changed crews in Yermo and Las Vegas.

ABOVE: In nature's graveyard, 230 miles east of Los Angeles, three SD60M's and two DASH 8-40C's combine to put 19,400 horsepower on the point of the LAAP3Z-11 at 7:45 A.M., and a C30-7 and an SD40-2 add 6,000 more horsepower on the rear. The train's weight is 7,886 tons; length is 8,260 feet. If you could carry enough water, you could hike 3,000 feet up to the summit of the forbidding Bristol Mountains in the background, and look down on Santa Fe's main line on the other side. The UP abolished the double-stack helpers in early 1993.

ABOVE: Thirty-two minutes later, the HKYR-09 rolls downhill on dynamics past the same location. The intermediates in the background mark the former east switch of Flynn, a 5,602-foot CTC siding pulled out in the late 1970s. The HKYR is a Hinkle, Oregon, to Yermo maid-of-all-work, laden today with 30 coal loads from the Rio Grande at Provo, covered hoppers of cement and Wyoming soda ash, and lumber from the Pacific Northwest, for a total of 75 loads, 2 empties, and 9,403 tons, very heavy for a non-unit train. Three big new units, two SD60M's and a DASH 8-40C, have lugged it up the backside of Cima Hill, a feat which would have greatly taxed three SD40-2's. The LAAP3Z-11 is now halfway up Cima Hill (look above the hoppers), the exhaust of its units smudging the morning sky. At night, you can see headlights coming from 25 miles away out here, and wonder where the trains will meet.
*Two photographs, Jamie Schmid*

# THE KELSO CLUB

*Train or engine crews desiring to eat at Kelso must notify dispatcher as much before arrival as practicable, but not later than at Kelso initial switch.* —UP Special Rule 871 (R), 1975

During the Miocene Epoch, the climate in the Basin & Range Province was very wet. Rain eroded the young, raw mountains to a fraction of their original size. Their rock crumbled into sand and washed down ravines to the bottom of the mountains, where the water deposited it in alluvial fans. As each alluvial fan grew in size, it joined with its neighboring alluvial fans. Ultimately each range became surrounded by a broad, smooth, gentle slope of eroded material. These are called *bajadas*, Spanish for "slope" (pronounce the "j" like an "h").

East of the Devil's Playground the mountains close ranks, and their respective bajadas merge. The SPLA&SL's surveyors ran their line as far as possible in the flats, then looked for a gap through the mountains. The only suitable place was Kessler Summit, where a bajada sloping west from the Mid Hills and New York Mountains meets a bajada sloping east from an old cinder cone, forming a high connecting ridge. On the east side of the ridge, the surveyors were able to plot a line that descended on a 1.0-percent grade into the Ivanpah Valley. But on the west side the valley is narrower and the valley floor rises more rapidly, and from Kelso to Kessler Summit the surveyors plotted a 2.2-percent grade to minimize construction costs and reduce the circuity inherent in a looping 1.0-percent approach to Kessler Summit.

Because bajadas are nothing more than tilted desert, it was no more difficult to lay track over Kessler Summit than it was to lay track on flat ground. The problem came when it was time to start running trains, because the west slope has 17.3 miles of 2.2-percent (compensated) grade. The severity of this grade is exacerbated by the lack of curvature; curves, because they resist the wheel flanges, help to retard downhill trains. "As many a hogger reminded me," recalled Walter Thrall, as a student fireman in 1941, "it took real skill to bring a long, heavy train down that mountain."

Soon after the SPLA&SL was completed, the station at the top was renamed Cima *(SEE-mah)*, Spanish for "summit." At the bottom of the 2.2 percent, 2,077 feet below Cima, the Salt Lake Route built a helper terminal called Kelso. Every eastbound got one or more helpers at Kelso, and if they were really heavy a helper met them at Balch. The helpers frequently ran over Cima Hill to Desert for westbounds that could not make the 1.0 percent unassisted.

Because Kelso was about as far from civilization as one could go without coming out the other side, the SPLA&SL had to build Kelso from scratch: a roundhouse for a half-dozen helper engines; dwellings for engine crews, blacksmiths, boiler makers, machinists, section men, and their families; fuel tanks, sand towers, tool sheds, etc.; a store, schoolhouse, and post office; and, most important, wells, a softening plant, and storage tanks to dispense the water essential for making steam, boiling coffee, taking baths, and watering the depot lawn.

Kelso's centerpiece was the Kelso Club, built in 1923 to

replace an earlier depot. It was a paradigm of Mission-style depot architecture, carefully proportioned and conservatively embellished. While its white stucco walls, red clay tile roof, and dark-green trim were typical for the LA&SL's depots, here, in the midst of an endless desert, it was a brilliant splash of color in a canvas of khaki and olivine.

Inside was a lunchroom, open around the clock, and a waiting room that doubled as Kelso's social center. Upstairs there were bedrooms lining a corridor, each just big enough to hold two narrow iron beds. An arcade along the depot's track side provided a shady place to sit on benches and watch the comings and goings of trains, helpers, and people. Around the depot grew a lush oasis: a lawn, palm trees, cottonwoods, hedges, and flower beds. But where the watering stopped, the desert began, as sharply as if the sod had been cut with a knife.

Kelso bustled during World War II; more trains meant more helper engines. Iron miners began mixing with LA&SL railroaders in 1942, when Kaiser Steel opened the Vulcan Mine nine miles south of Kelso to supply iron ore to its new blast furnace in Fontana, California. The bustle was just temporary; war's end and dieselization in 1947–48 took away most of the helpers, and the miners decamped when the Vulcan Mine shut down in 1949–50. On February 3, 1959, Kelso's last helper job was abolished. After the agency closed in 1962, the town shriveled to a handful of section men and their families.

The Kelso Club's doors stayed open for 23 more years, because of a contract provision that gave train crews the right to stop at Kelso for lunch. Finally the UP abolished this archaic practice, and closed the depot at midnight, June 30, 1985. The UP was just about to demolish the depot when the efforts of area residents and rail enthusiasts saved it. Now the Bureau of Land Management is refurbishing the Kelso Club to be a museum and visitor center for the Mojave Desert.

The Kelso Club will survive in body. But without rooms for seven bucks a night, iced tea served up in frosty UP glasses, and trains stopping for sack lunches, Kelso's soul is gone.

AT LEFT: On December 23, 1993, a westbound soda-ash train idles at Kelso while the conductor walks both sides to knock down the retainers he turned up at Cima an hour before. The fresh white paint, the new roof, and the barren ground around the Kelso Club echo what the club looked like when it was brand new. Except for the drought-tolerant palm trees, the vegetation that flourished here promptly expired when the UP turned off the water in 1985. The cottonwoods, once home for a multitude of birds and insects, became brittle husks without water, and were bulldozed away by the BLM.

AT RIGHT: On March 14, 1984, a westbound unit coal train stops at Kelso for the crew to pick up lunch and to allow the brakemen time to knock down the retainers they turned up at Cima. The Kelso oasis was not notable for its size; you could cross it in a matter of seconds by walking from the depot's platform to the depot's arcade. No, the Kelso oasis was notable for its sheer existence. This was, you see, the only lawn in about 2,000 square miles! The contrast between desert and oasis was never more remarkable than it was at Kelso. This tiny patch of transplanted life made you realize just how far from home you had come.

BELOW: To practically all of its infrequent visitors, such as the Marines from Twentynine Palms, who come this way on their weekend trips to Las Vegas, Kelso is but a bumpy grade crossing and a stop sign. There is no sign readily visible from the county road to tell desert travelers that this annoying interruption in their high-speed trip has a name. Should one care to get out of their air-conditioned car and walk around to the front of the Kelso Club, there, above the entrance, one can read the elegant, elongated Roman letters that announced to train passengers that Kelso was a place of importance. Most people just slow for the grade crossing, then step on the gas and never look back. *Three photographs, Mark Hemphill*

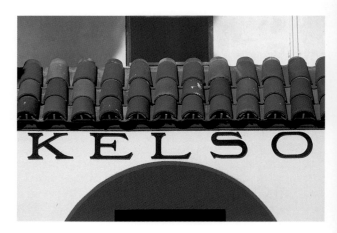

March 14, 1984: a hot, dry wind has blown hard through Kelso all day. It sears your skin, cracks your lips, and fills your mouth with grit and your eyes with tears. Tumbleweeds bound over the tracks, carom off the bunk cars, and sail into the desert. A coal train comes down Cima Hill into Kelso, its headlight just a golden glimmer in the dusty air. It is one of two 11,000-ton unit trains that have been working west from Las Vegas since early morning, their progress slowed by the crosswind, meets with several superior eastbounds, and the grueling 1.0 percent climbs from Las Vegas to Erie and from Desert to Cima. Their crews have worked up an appetite since morning. After leaving Cima each crew radioed in its order to the Kelso lunchroom. An hour later their sack lunches await them in a line on the lunchroom counter, each bag tagged with the name of a crewman. While the brakemen turn down the retainers, the engineers and conductors collect the lunches. After they leave,

the day-shift counterwoman totes up her receipts while a retired rancher slowly sips a cup of coffee.

At four o'clock the school bus arrives from Baker, drops off five children who live in the modular homes on the east side of the tracks, then turns around and hightails it back to Baker. While the first coal train pulls out, and the engineer of the second returns to his cab, brown bag in hand, the children huddle together for protection from the gale. The moment the caboose of the first train clears the depot, they look both ways, then happily run for home.

At day's end the wind dies out. The cottonwood trees around the Kelso depot come alive with the noisy chatter of hundreds of birds. After dark the platform lamps come on, little pools of yellow light on the brick platform. Bats swoop and dip through the trees, homing in on the insects that dizzily circle the lampposts. The swing-shift counterman props the lunchroom

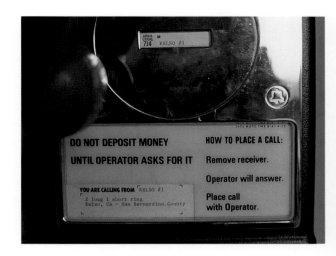

door open in hopes of a cooling breeze. His transistor radio broadcasts Hank Williams through the screen door into the calm desert night, and Jeannie Pruitt sings about her satin sheets for the ten-thousandth time. A few men from a maintenance gang enjoy a smoke on the steps of their bunk cars, then retire to bed. The pay phone on the depot wall offers a scratchy connection with the rest of the world. After a few rings an operator in Los Angeles answers, then pauses as you tell her your location, dumbfounded that big Pacific Bell has a pay phone identified only as Kelso #1.

At 10 P.M. the coffee is still hot and the hamburgers are served up on UP Streamliner china. An eastbound stops with its caboose even with the depot to pick up its lunch, then throttles up for the climb to Cima. At midnight a westbound drops down Cima Hill. Its dynamic brakes wail in the distance for what seems like an hour. When the home signal at East Kelso waves it onward with a high green over two reds, its engineer kicks off the air and shuts off the dynamics. There is a momentary lull in the noise, then he pushes his throttle into power. The diesels gathers their feet under them and shoot towards Kelso. A few minutes later the train slams past the depot like the thunderclap of Armageddon, jarring the roof tiles and rattling the window sashes in their frames. Then the train is gone, its clamor fading into the distance. A few minutes later the counterman clicks off his radio and turns off the platform lights.

One radio and a half-dozen lamps have defended this outpost of man against the encroaching darkness all evening. Now that they are extinguished, the darkness rushes in and reclaims Kelso for its own. Starlight almost bright enough to read by brings the dark creosote bush into stark relief against the pale sand. Out here in the desert, far from any city, the Milky Way is a light show that bests all the flashing, twirling neon in Las Vegas. *Telephone and caboose, Mel Patrick; other photographs, Mark Hemphill*

# CIMA HILL

*... the underlying intent of all is the common desire to prevent the most feared event in railroading–the irrevocable loss of control of trains descending mountain grades.*

—National Transportation Safety Board, 1981

If you compare Cima Hill to other western grades such as Donner, Tehachapi, and Cajon's North Track, Cima Hill climbs higher in the same distance. Yet Cima Hill looks benign. It has no tight curves, no tunnels, no deep cuts, and no high fills. At first glance it just does not look like a mountain grade.

The LA&SL was very aware of the danger that lurks here. All westbounds stopped at Cima and made an air test and walking inspection. No train left Cima with more than 70 tons per operative brake. Empty cars kept at Cima were added to trains exceeding this limit. Trains stopped at both Chase and Dawes to cool wheels, and at each place a walking inspection was made. Trainmasters spent much time observing brake tests and inspections on Cima Hill, and firemen spent years learning the road before promotion to engineer.

In time these precautions seemed unnecessary to the UP in light of dynamic brakes and pressure-maintaining brakes. The UP no longer required walking inspections at Cima, Chase, and Dawes. The limit of 70 tons per operative brake disappeared, even for trains with inoperative dynamic brakes, and no longer were empties kept at Cima for extra braking effort. Road foremen and trainmasters spent less time checking on their crews. Respect for Cima Hill was replaced by a feeling that runaways were something from link-and-pin days, and dynamic brakes became UP's principal method of controlling speed.

At 10 A.M. on November 17, 1980, UP Extra 3119 West left Las Vegas with SD40 3119, twenty bulkhead flats loaded with new ties, and a caboose. A mechanized tie gang near Yermo had run out of ties, and was sitting expensively idle. Extra 3119's engineer, David LeRoy Totten, 31, had completed UP's engineer training program on January 17, 1979, scoring over 96 percent on the final exam. He was judged "a very apt student," and was known as a stickler for the rules. But he was not experienced, especially with mountain-grade operation.

At 1:29 P.M. Extra 3119 West stopped in the north passing track at Cima to set retainers, required by the rules since the 3119's dynamic brake was not working. Extra 8044 West, the 2-VAN-16, with DDA40X 6946 on the point, passed Extra 3119 West at Cima and began descending the hill. The 3119 followed the VAN out of Cima. Just after it cleared the west switch, at 1:59 P.M., Totten began setting air. He made several more brake applications, trying to maintain the 15-mph speed limit, but each time his train slowed only for a moment, then started to accelerate again. At 2:09 P.M. he called the dispatcher, concern in his voice: "I keep setting air and it won't slow down." The dispatcher could then have put the VAN into Dawes siding to get it out of the way, but did not.

Totten was never again able to reduce the speed of his train. By 2:13 P.M. he had set 30 pounds of engine brakes. The conductor opened his caboose valve to activate emergency braking, but did not tell Totten he had done so. The emergency application did not propagate to the 3119, so the pressure-

maintaining feature began feeding air into the brakepipe, releasing the train brakes. Extra 3119 West began to accelerate rapidly. Had the 3119 been equipped with a brakepipe flow indicator, Totten might have realized what had happened, and placed his brake valve in emergency to cancel the pressure-maintaining feature. But at the time UP did not use this device. Because most of the tie cars did not have working brakes, the retainers had little effect. The 3119's independent brake was now the only functioning brake on the entire train.

At 2:15 P.M. the gap between Extra 3119 West and the VAN had narrowed to about 5 miles. Totten called the dispatcher, told him he had made a full-service application, was traveling at 25 mph, and was accelerating. The dispatcher asked Totten if this meant he would not be stopping at Dawes to cool the wheels! Realizing that Extra 3119 West was rapidly gaining, the VAN's engineer released his brakes and put his throttle into power.

At 2:21 P.M., Extra 3119 West was between switches at Dawes moving 62.5 mph, and the VAN was just past Hayden at full throttle moving 65 mph. At east Kelso, the VAN's overspeed tripped at 75 mph, and by the time it could be overridden its speed had dropped to 68 mph. Although its head brakeman thereafter interrupted the overspeed feature, this slowdown likely saved the VAN from a disastrous derailment on the 2°03' curve at milepost 231, as the eight-wheel trucks of DDA40X 6946 would probably not otherwise have negotiated this curve. Extra 3119 West shot through Kelso about a minute behind the VAN, gaining speed at 6 to 8 mph per minute. It went through the curve at milepost 231 at nearly twice its legal speed of 60 mph, but somehow remained on the track.

At 2:29 P.M., Extra 3119 West, moving about 118 mph, caught the VAN, moving about 85 mph, at milepost 230.6,

five miles west of Kelso. Four separate episodes of collision and derailment ensued. Extra 3119 West first struck the VAN's caboose, crushing its platforms and causing it to uncouple, derail, turn over, and slide down the embankment on its side. The VAN's conductor and rear brakeman were thrown to the floor, the conductor receiving multiple severe injuries which were fatal in minutes. The brakeman was critically injured. Extra 3119 West then struck three auto racks, one at a time. The first two derailed, overturned, and slid down the embankment. The third climbed over the 3119 and stripped off its carbody. Totten and Extra 3119 West's 22-year-old head brakeman received massive and instantly fatal injuries. Most of the ties hurtled off into the desert. SD40 3119, the VAN's caboose, and 23 freight cars were destroyed.

The National Transportation Safety Board concluded that (1) Extra 3119 West weighed about 2,245 tons, but because of

UP's practice of underestimating the weight of ties, its crew was told they had 1,495 tons; (2) UP's rules for mountain grade operation were based on tons per operative brake, yet UP did not limit the tonnage a train or locomotive could take down Cima Hill; (3) the UP inadequately maintained the brakes on tie cars in company service and failed to properly test and inspect Extra 3119 West at Las Vegas; (4) Extra 3119 West needed at least 14.4 effective brakes to balance the 2.2 percent grade with a full service application and no working dynamic brake, but at least 13 cars did not have fully effective brakes, and probably 6 had no working brakes at all; (5) it took the UP two days to repair the brakes on 20 similar tie cars for a test train, which needed 20.5 effective brakes and a 17 pound brakepipe reduction to balance the grade at 15 mph; (6) an expert engineer called out of retirement was able to safely take the test train down Cima Hill without dynamic brakes; (7) the engineer of Extra 3119 West was not an expert; (8) the dispatchers' office failed to take any action when advised

of the emergency, and had no protocol for runaways; and (9) UP's rules for mountain grade operation were inadequate compared to those of the SP, BN, Rio Grande, and B&O. The NTSB absolved David LeRoy Totten of blame.

Ten months after the runaway, the NTSB found that the UP had continued to operate trains over Cima Hill without proper inspection and testing: "...The movement of heavy trains down long, steep grades is a difficult and dangerous business under the best conditions. The Safety Board believes that the UP's rules and instructions, as well as the mannner in which its operations are conducted, do not adequately take these principles into consideration. This may explain why the runaway and the difficult-to-control train have become a problem relatively unique to the UP in the past few years."

ABOVE LEFT: Light westbounds with plenty of dynamics may run 35 mph without retainers from Cima to Kelso. This is the 1-VAN with five SD40's/SD40-2's, at Hayden on January 9, 1983. This hill is so straight that on most of it eastbounds are permitted 70 mph (79 for passenger). *Jamie Schmid*

BELOW LEFT: Unit coal, grain, and soda-ash trains all stop at Cima to turn up retainers. On December 23, 1993, conductor Richard Vizcarra trudges through a bitter gale at Cima to set retainers on his soda-ash train, up one side of 80 cars and back down the other, taking about an hour. *Mark Hemphill*

ABOVE: At 9:26 A.M. on January 10, 1983, Extra 3637 West skips the wheel-cooling stop at Dawes because it has sufficient functional dynamic braking for its tonnage. Its dynamic brakes and train air brakes must exert at least 207.5 tons of force to hold its 79 loads of soda ash and a caboose at a constant speed. The dynamics will account for not more than 120 tons of this force; the train air must provide the rest. *Jamie Schmid*

On November 23, 1986, Cima Hill has been very quiet. Down at Kelso it is warm, but 2,000 feet higher, on top of the hill, it is rather chilly. Late in the day an eastbound emerges from the Devil's Playground. At first it is only a dark spot floating in the glassine air. Eventually it takes on the shape of a train—a long, heavy, under-powered train, the LANP, a drag freight from Los Angeles to North Platte, Nebraska. Its ascent of Cima Hill is laborious, so slow that despite the light wind a dirty smear of exhaust lingers above its three units.

About an hour after passing Kelso the LANP passes the east switch at Chase. The home signal at east Chase flicks on, its two red searchlights glittering like rubies against their pale back-drop, the bajada below the distant Providence Mountains. Now the deep, urgent beat of EMD and GE diesels at maximum throttle can be discerned.

In the day's last light the LANP plods upwards through the Joshua trees that dot the top of Cima Hill above Chase. Should one of these units grow tired of its hard labor and slack off, this train will surely stall.

These diesels are true to their task. They climb painfully through the pair of 2° curves below Cima, then crawl over the apex. The train gradually gains speed, from 8 mph to 9 mph. Then 10. Then 12. By the time the last empty hopper rumbles past the Cima store, and the blinking light of the rear-end device disappears on the other side of the apex, the train is moving along smartly at 35 mph.
*Two photographs, Mark Hemphill*

# ERIE SUMMIT

*The line and grade should fit the country. An 0.4 per cent grade should not be attempted in 1 per cent country, but it should be demonstrated beyond question that the country is 1 per cent country; sufficient traffic may convert a 1 per cent country into an 0.4 per cent country.*

*—The Elements of Railroad Engineering, 1937*

The profile of the LA&SL in the Mojave Desert can be modeled with a row of shallow soup bowls, the type found in fancy restaurants. Drape a string down the row. You will notice the string is flat where it crosses from rim to rim, and down in the bottoms of the bowls as well. But most of the string runs uphill or down. Now line up more bowls to make 20 or so parallel rows, and place hand saws teeth-up between each row. Run your string diagonally from corner to corner, going through the gaps between the tip of one hand saw and the handle of the next.

In essence you have recreated the situation that confronted the SPLA&SL's locating engineers in 1902. This occurred because most of the Basin & Range Province has no drainage system—each basin is self-contained, like the soup bowls—and because the mountains, though small, are steep sided, sharp, and impenetrable, like the hand saws.

The SPLA&SL's locating engineers had a choice. One possibility was to build cheaply by running the line through the middle of the basins (the bottoms of the soup bowls) and to accept the steep grades and high operating costs this would entail. Another was to build expensively by establishing a level line along the fringes of the mountains from summit to summit (around the rims of the soup bowls), which would minimize grades and lower operating costs.

Of great interest, because this was a Harriman road, the engineers decided to build cheaply. Harriman had established an 0.82-percent ruling grade during his reconstruction of the UP proper, yet this standard did not extend to the SPLA&SL farther west than the Leamington Cut-off. Everywhere else the SPLA&SL had a ruling grade of 1.0 percent, and it had three districts with heavier grades than any encountered east of Ogden. While the difference between 0.82 and 1.0 percent might seem trivial, any locomotive on a 1.0-percent grade will haul 18 percent less tonnage than it can up an 0.82-percent grade. Also, fuel consumption is higher and speeds slower. These differences add up to big money if there is a lot of tonnage being hauled.

Most other railroads which built from scratch in the twentieth century expended huge sums to engineer favorable low-grade main lines, notably the Virginian, 0.2 percent eastward in favor of its coal traffic, the SP&S, 0.4 percent eastward, and the WP, 1.0 percent in both directions.

Heavy traffic was expected to justify these expensive lines, an expectation realized on the *Virginian* within seven years yet never seen on the WP or SP&S. It would appear that Harriman weighed the Salt Lake Route's cost of construction against its projected cost of operation and expected traffic, counted on most of the tonnage running downhill from 4,200 feet at Salt Lake City to sea level at San Pedro, and decided the SPLA&SL did not warrant a big-ticket alignment.

AT LEFT: Kelso and Las Vegas are roughly the same altitude, but to travel between them trains must climb a total of 2,600 feet to summits at Cima and Erie. From Cima the railroad plunges into the Ivanpah Valley, an enclosed basin, on a total of 26 miles of 1.0 percent. It runs across the normally dry bed of Roach Lake for three miles, climbs 7.5 miles of 1.0 percent to Erie, then sweeps down into Las Vegas on a total of 17 miles of 1.0 percent. This is a tough railroad either way. At 11:05 P.M. on March 13, 1992, the LAAP4Z-12 extends its snout around the corner of the mountain at milepost 316 east of Sloan, gingerly taking 6,779 tons of double-stacks down 12 miles of 1.0 percent from Erie to Arden. Out of sight is helper LAP42K-12, using dynamics to tug on the tail of the python. In the steam era a 1.0-percent grade was a helper grade for a heavy train; Las Vegas often gave

westbounds a helper to Cima, 80 miles away, and gave eastbounds a helper to Apex. Tunnel 2, in the background, was abandoned in a 1943 line relocation that straightened out a sharp curve—the original curve and its replacement can be compared in this view from a nearby mountain. *Jamie Schmid*

BELOW: A half hour before the double-stacks come down the hill, the CSRLA-12 crawls up the 1.0 percent at milepost 317 east of Sloan, a 10,891-ton export coal train with three big units instead of four SD40-2's. The drawback to such unit reduction is that there is no room for error; if you have to cut out one or two traction motors, you're finished, period. This train loaded at the Sufco (Southern Utah Fuel Co.) loadout at Sharp, Utah, and will unload at the Port of Los Angeles.

Despite being a very steeply graded railroad, the original SPLA&SL main line was surprisingly free of the heavy rock work that typifies mountain railroading. Outside of Clover Creek Canyon, most of its rock work was confined to 12 miles between Arden and Erie. Since the contractor could not justify a large crew to quickly build this one small stretch, he used a temporary track to put the main line into service. The permanent line opened on May 26, 1905. *Jamie Schmid*

## LAS VEGAS

*When the working stiffs came in, a lot of undesirable characters followed and set up establishments that would take their pay from them.*

  –Frank Crampton, mining engineer, describes Las Vegas circa 1910

Arising from four springs in the Spring Mountains, Las Vegas Wash flowed 5 feet wide and 2 feet deep, nurturing grassy meadows until it emptied into the Colorado River. A scout from the party of New Mexico trader Antonio Armijo stumbled across it just after Christmas 1829. Armijo named the meadows *las vegas*. They were a welcome respite for hot and dusty caravans on the Old Spanish Trail and the military road from Salt Lake City to San Diego.

Mormon colonists arrived in the meadows in June 1855. They built a large adobe fort to protect their houses and animals, grew corn, melons, and oats, and attempted without success to instruct the Paiute Indians in religion and agriculture. Isolation and hardship caused dissension leading

to the colony's demise in 1857. The meadows were resettled in 1865 by ex-prospector Octavius Decatur Gass, who provided lodging, food, and fodder for travelers and prospectors until 1882, when he lost his Rancho Las Vegas to Archibald Stewart because of inability to pay a debt. After Stewart died in a card game shoot-out, his wife continued to run the ranch.

Observing that this location would make an ideal division point, the OSL bought an option from Mrs. Stewart in June 1901, and in 1902 Clark purchased the ranch and its water rights for $55,000. C. O. Whittemore, Clark's attorney, platted "Clark's Las Vegas Townsite," and sold the lots in a boisterous auction on May 15, 1905. The town became the seat of the new Clark County (named for Senator Clark, of course) on July 1, 1909. The SPLA&SL built a 14-stall brick roundhouse and a standard SPLA&SL six-track yard. Armour & Co. built a 100-ton ice plant in 1907 (Pacific Fruit Express bought it a little later). The Las Vegas Land & Water Co., an LA&SL subsidiary, set up a water system for both the railroad and the town. A passenger coach sufficed as a depot until a Mission-style depot was built in 1909. The same year work began on a $400,000 locomotive shop, its concrete-and-steel

main building 150 feet by 380 feet. Completed in 1911, it was the SPLA&SL's principal shop, and added about 400 men to the railroad's Las Vegas payroll. Its powerhouse supplied electricity to the whole town as well as the shop. Additional yard tracks were added for war traffic in 1942 and 1943. More tracks were laid in 1950. The yard blocked most eastbounds until the new yard opened at Yermo in 1981.

Aside from the obligatory two-block red-light district, Las Vegas circa 1920 was a sleepy company town of 2,300 people who bought their water, land, ice, and electricity and often rented their house from the railroad, and either they worked for the railroad or their livelihood depended upon railroad paychecks. The start of work on Boulder Dam in 1928 ended UP's big influence in the town's politics. The city began buying its electricity from the dam in the late 1930s, and bought the railroad's water system in 1953. Yet even by 1940 the population was a mere 8,400. Military bases, industry, and casino gambling during the 1940s increased the area's population to nearly 50,000 by 1950. Now Las Vegas has close to a million people; it may soon overtake Salt Lake City–Ogden.

AT LEFT: On November 12, 1988, Extra 3412 East awaits a crew at the main line fueling facility behind the Union Plaza Hotel, which stands on the site of UP's Las Vegas depot. By 1968 this location was too valuable for a depot, so UP's Upland Industries began building the 23-story, 504-room hotel on the depot grounds, demolishing the depot once passenger service ended in 1971. The UP leased the hotel following its 1971 completion to Sam Boyd (as in Sam's Town Casino) and Frank Scott, who separately operate the hotel's casino, so technically the UP is not in the gambling business.

The UP and City of Las Vegas have never agreed on much of anything, but in 1988 they agreed that UP's 235-acre Las Vegas Yard would make a good site for a casino-convention complex that might revitalize the stagnant downtown casino district. In February 1988 the UP decided to move the yard north to Wann; by May 1989 UP had opened an auto ramp at Wann. However, residents of North Las Vegas did not want UP's yard in their neighborhood, so in December the UP decided to move the yard to Arden, and the main line fueling facility to Boulder Jct. But area residents were no more enchanted about having the yard in their backyard. When the UP's deal to sell the Las Vegas yard to a developer fell through in April 1990, the city tried to pressure the UP into leaving by finding numerous fire code violations at UP's lumber-unloading facility. The UP retaliated by threatening to stop shipping lumber to Las Vegas, which would have severely crimped construction. Grudgingly, the UP and the city accommodated each other. The UP built three side tracks at Arden and a small set-out yard at milepost 342, and opened a new fueling facility at Yermo on April 7, 1992. The UP began tearing out its Las Vegas Yard in 1993. *Eric Blasko*

ABOVE: UP's Las Vegas diesel house, quiet on January 31, 1980, was originally the Las Vegas shop powerhouse. During the nationwide shop craft employees' strike of July 1, 1922, the UP retaliated against Las Vegas strikers who prevented scabs from entering the shop by turning off the power, forcing the town back to kerosene lamps. The UP broke the strike with replacements, whom it forced to join a company union. Because Las Vegas had supported the strikers, the UP punished Las Vegas by sending its work to Caliente and by building a new shop at East Los Angeles, idling 300 men in a town of 2,300. Although the Las Vegas shop eventually reopened, it never regained importance. It was not converted to work on diesels, and by 1960 it was gone. It is probably just as well that the UP tore down the powerhouse in July 1986. *Vance Pomerening*

BELOW: During September 1969, UP's Las Vegas station slumbers in the heat. Today, Las Vegas would probably look like SP's division point at Carlin, Nevada, except for three strokes of luck: Boulder Dam, Los Angeles, and quick divorces. A Las Vegas divorce became all the rage after Mrs. Clark Gable, the former Ria Langham, arrived in early 1939 to fulfill Nevada's six-week residency requirement. In the months following celebrities, society mavens, and businessmen's wives flocked to Las Vegas to get divorces, the press greeting the famous at UP's station. Possibly the UP decided its not-so-old Mission-style station was too old-fashioned a backdrop for photographs of the stars; it began work on a new air-conditioned Art Moderne station in June 1939. *Emery Gulash*

## DESERT CROSSING

*January 23: "We ate a horse." January 24: "Ditto." January 25: "Ditto." January 26: "Ditto, we ate a male mule."*
                                                —Antonio Armijo's diary entries in the Mojave Desert, 1830

The Mexican packers called the dry stretches between water holes *jornadas*, "journeys." An exceptionally dry stretch, such as the 50 bone-dry miles from Las Vegas to the Muddy River at Moapa, was *a jornada del muerto*, a "journey of the dead." In 1844 pathfinder John Frémont found it "dotted with the white skeletons of horses that had failed to effect a crossing," according to historians LeRoy and Ann Hafen. (The Paiutes called the Muddy River the "Moap," thus Moapa.) The railroad, because it crossed vast distances quickly, and carried large quantities of water with it in tenders and tank cars, eliminated the water problem of old. The SPLA&SL conquered the jornada from Las Vegas to Moapa with deep wells at Dry Lake, which today still serve to water UP's hog trains. However, when the SPLA&SL began using the desert water

in its locomotive boilers, a problem not experienced by the caravans arose: large quantities of dissolved solids in the desert wells. To a horse or a person the alkaline water merely tasted bad, but it gave boilers fits. After running on a diet of desert water over one crew district, an SPLA&SL locomotive was typically foaming over and in acute need of a boiler wash. Bad water also greatly diminished firebox, flue and boiler life, and caused numerous engine failures and train delays.

In the early 1920s the UP attracted attention for its success with long locomotive runs, having more of these in 1924 than any other U.S. railroad. The UP accomplished these inter-district runs by building many water-treatment plants. The LA&SL, which was one of UP's worst water districts, received water softening plants at East Yard in Los Angeles, Kelso, Las Vegas, Rox, and Dry Lake in 1923, Arden in 1924, Desert and Moapa in 1925, Lynndyl in 1926, Salt Lake City in 1927, Caliente, Modena, and Nephi in 1928, Erda and Carp in 1929, and Lund in 1931. By October 1924 the UP was running passenger engines through from Los Angeles to Caliente, 460 miles, an exceptional accomplishment for a notoriously bad-water railroad.

AT LEFT: At 9:36 A.M. mountain standard time (MST) on April 24, 1985, Extra 3724 East growls up the arid lower reaches of Meadow Valley Wash just west of milepost 407 (the UP switches from pacific time to mountain time at Las Vegas instead of at the Nevada–Utah line). This portion of the wash is called Huntsman Canyon. Hoya siding can be seen on the background tangent. The original line ran where the county road now runs, at far left in this view, and crossed Meadow Creek at an elevation lower than the three 100-foot through plate girders installed here in 1911. This train is solid empty covered hoppers, except for one high-wide load. *Tim Zukas*

ABOVE: On April 24, 1976, DD35A 74 leads a combined PASHW-24/SLLAM-23 (Potash loads-West/Salt Lake City-Los Angeles Manifest) past the former siding at Garnet. The consist of this train is all bulk, 29 loads of Utah coal and 64 loads of Idaho potash, at least 9,000 tons, and heavy enough to make two of the three trailing SD45's run hot on the 1.0-percent to Apex. The background tangent is the site of Garnet siding, a 70-car CTC siding pulled out in 1971.

Before CTC, the LA&SL was a typical steam-era single-track railroad, with sidings at 5-mile intervals, closer together in places such as the 2.2-percent west slope of Cima Hill. The UP had no idea what to expect when it installed its first-ever CTC between Daggett and Las Vegas in 1942–43; long, single-track CTC was a new concept, dating to a 1937 installation of 112 miles on the CB&Q from Akron to Derby, Colorado. It is not surprising that in 1942 the UP believed it needed a CTC siding every 5.5 miles between Yermo and Las Vegas, and gave 32 sidings (two each at Kelso and Cima) full CTC installations. Most of these were previously 4,700-foot sidings; as part of the project they were extended to a nominal length of 5,600 feet. Afton, Glasgow and Roach remained short and received everything but power switches; these were added in 1944, making them fully functional (if short) CTC sidings. New Dunn, King, Cork, Sutor, Bard, and Pierce were downgraded to house tracks with leave-siding signals only. In 1945, when the UP installed CTC from Las Vegas to Caliente, every siding likewise received full CTC.

As it turned out, a siding every 5 miles gave the Las Vegas CTC dispatchers more flexibility than they needed. When the UP equipped the 324 miles from Caliente to Salt Lake City with CTC in 1947–48, it knew more, and 21 sidings were either removed or converted to house tracks. Likewise, the UP pulled out 11 full CTC sidings and 8 of the 9 short sidings between Yermo and Caliente starting in 1944. By the late 1970s the LA&SL typically had a siding every 10 to 11 miles, which worked fine so long as traffic was not very heavy and most trains were short and fast. In 1980, however, when export coal trains began running west on the LA&SL, the UP realized it had pulled out a few sidings too many and had to start putting some back in. Garnet was reinstalled, though not exactly in its previous location. *Jamie Schmid*

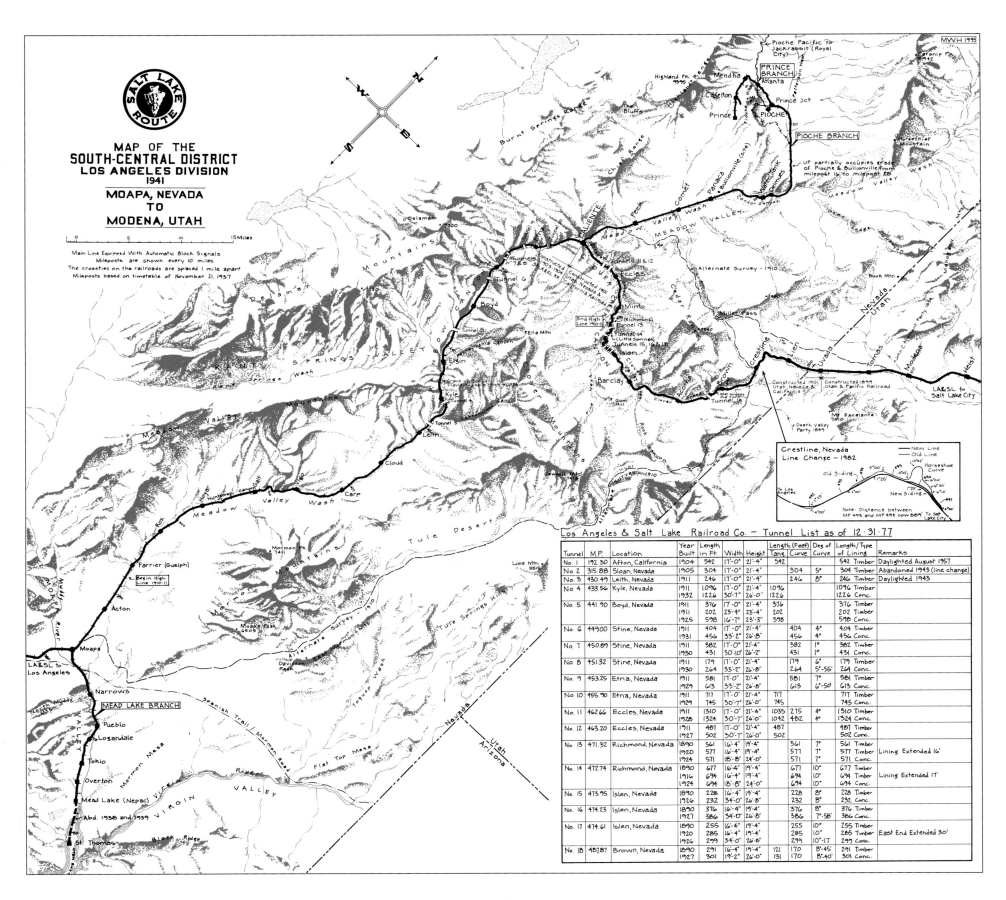

## MAP OF THE SOUTH-CENTRAL DISTRICT LOS ANGELES DIVISION 1941 MOAPA, NEVADA TO MODENA, UTAH

MWH 1995

Main Line Equipped With Automatic Block Signals
Mileposts are shown every 10 miles
The crossties on the railroads are spaced 1 mile apart
Mileposts based on timetable of November 21, 1937

Crestline, Nevada
Line Change — 1982
— New Line
— Old Line

Note: Distance between MP 493 and MP 494 now 869'

Los Angeles & Salt Lake Railroad Co. — Tunnel List as of 12-31-77

| Tunnel | M.P. | Location | Year Built | Length In Ft. | Width | Height | Length (Feet) Tang | Des of Curve | Length Curve | Length/Type of Lining | Remarks |
|---|---|---|---|---|---|---|---|---|---|---|---|
| No. 1 | 192.30 | Afton, California | 1904 | 542 | 17'-0" | 21'-4" | 542 | | | 542 Timber | Daylighted August 1957 |
| No. 2 | 315.88 | Sloan, Nevada | 1905 | 304 | 17'-0" | 21'-4" | | 304 | 5° | 304 Timber | Abandoned 1943 (line change) |
| No. 3 | 430.49 | Leith, Nevada | 1911 | 246 | 17'-0" | 21'-4" | | 246 | 8° | 246 Timber | Daylighted 1943 |
| No. 4 | 433.56 | Kyle, Nevada | 1911 | 1096 | 17'-0" | 21'-4" | 1096 | | | 1096 Timber | |
| | | | 1932 | 1226 | 30'-7" | 26'-0" | 1226 | | | 1226 Conc. | |
| No. 5 | 441.90 | Boyd, Nevada | 1911 | 376 | 17'-0" | 21'-4" | 376 | | | 376 Timber | |
| | | | 1911 | 202 | 23'-4" | 23'-4" | 202 | | | 202 Timber | |
| | | | 1925 | 598 | 16'-1" | 23'-3" | 598 | | | 598 Conc. | |
| No. 6 | 449.00 | Stine, Nevada | 1911 | 404 | 17'-0" | 21'-4" | | 404 | 4° | 404 Timber | |
| | | | 1931 | 456 | 33'-2" | 26'-8" | | 456 | 4° | 456 Conc. | |
| No. 7 | 450.89 | Stine, Nevada | 1911 | 382 | 17'-0" | 21'-4" | | 382 | 1° | 382 Timber | |
| | | | 1930 | 431 | 30'-10" | 26'-2" | | 431 | 1° | 431 Conc. | |
| No. 8 | 451.32 | Stine, Nevada | 1911 | 179 | 17'-0" | 21'-4" | | 179 | 6° | 179 Timber | |
| | | | 1930 | 264 | 33'-2" | 26'-8" | | 264 | 5°-55' | 264 Conc. | |
| No. 9 | 453.25 | Etna, Nevada | 1911 | 581 | 17'-0" | 21'-4" | | 581 | 7° | 581 Timber | |
| | | | 1929 | 613 | 33'-2" | 26'-8" | | 613 | 6°-50 | 613 Conc. | |
| No. 10 | 455.90 | Etna, Nevada | 1911 | 717 | 17'-0" | 21'-4" | 717 | | | 717 Timber | |
| | | | 1929 | 745 | 30'-7" | 26'-0" | 745 | | | 745 Conc. | |
| No. 11 | 462.66 | Eccles, Nevada | 1911 | 1310 | 17'-0" | 21'-4" | 1035 | 2.75 | 4° | 1310 Timber | |
| | | | 1928 | 1324 | 30'-7" | 26'-0" | 1042 | 482 | 4° | 1324 Conc. | |
| No. 12 | 463.20 | Eccles, Nevada | 1911 | 487 | 17'-0" | 21'-4" | 487 | | | 487 Timber | |
| | | | 1927 | 502 | 30'-7" | 26'-0" | 502 | | | 502 Conc. | |
| No. 13 | 471.32 | Richmond, Nevada | 1890 | 561 | 16'-4" | 19'-4" | | 561 | 7° | 561 Timber | |
| | | | 1920 | 577 | 16'-4" | 19'-4" | | 577 | 7° | 577 Timber | Lining Extended 16' |
| | | | 1924 | 571 | 18'-8" | 24'-0" | | 571 | 7° | 571 Conc. | |
| No. 14 | 472.74 | Richmond, Nevada | 1890 | 677 | 16'-4" | 19'-4" | | 677 | 10° | 677 Timber | |
| | | | 1916 | 694 | 16'-4" | 19'-4" | | 694 | 10° | 694 Timber | Lining Extended 17' |
| | | | 1924 | 694 | 18'-8" | 24'-0" | | 694 | 10° | 694 Conc. | |
| No. 15 | 473.95 | Islen, Nevada | 1890 | 228 | 16'-4" | 19'-4" | | 228 | 8° | 228 Timber | |
| | | | 1926 | 232 | 34'-0" | 26'-8" | | 232 | 8° | 232 Conc. | |
| No. 16 | 474.23 | Islen, Nevada | 1890 | 376 | 16'-4" | 19'-4" | | 376 | 10° | 376 Timber | |
| | | | 1927 | 386 | 34'-0" | 26'-8" | | 386 | 7°-58' | 386 Conc. | |
| No. 17 | 474.61 | Islen, Nevada | 1890 | 255 | 16'-4" | 19'-4" | | 255 | 10° | 255 Timber | |
| | | | 1920 | 285 | 16'-4" | 19'-4" | | 285 | 10° | 285 Timber | East End Extended 30' |
| | | | 1926 | 299 | 34'-0" | 26'-8" | | 299 | 10°-11' | 299 Conc. | |
| No. 18 | 487.87 | Brown, Nevada | 1890 | 291 | 16'-4" | 19'-4" | 121 | 170 | 8°-45' | 291 Timber | |
| | | | 1927 | 301 | 19'-2" | 26'-0" | 131 | 170 | 8°-40' | 301 Conc. | |

88

## Meadow Valley Wash

*[In the Southwest], warnings are posted where highways dip in and out of normally dry, bridgeless washes:*
*DO NOT ENTER WHEN FLOODED. The grammatical ambiguity amuses English teachers: Who is*
*flooded? But the point should be clear even to jokesters.* —David Lavender, western historian, 1980

Meadow Valley Wash is not particularly old, geologically speaking. It was formed about a million years ago when a large fresh-water lake in an old caldera (where the town of Panaca is now) cut an exit through the caldera's southern rim at Caliente and drained into the Colorado River. The wash's volcanic past is most apparent in Rainbow Canyon at Boyd, where hot, iron-laden water has stained the rock vermilion. Other solutes left their own distinctive colors: green from copper; black from manganese. The bright white cliffs at various locations are ash deposits.

Meadow Valley's geologic history was of little interest to the OSL&UN's surveyors in 1887. What they saw was a perfect path to California from the railhead at Milford. From the broad summit ridge at Crestline, they could make a steady descent to the Muddy River Valley at Moapa. From Moapa they could run through open country all the way to the Santa Fe at Barstow. The day they made this discovery there was no longer any question as to where their route would go.

ABOVE: A minute after 1 P.M. on September 13, 1992, the 6248 West, mixed double-stacks and TOFC, cruises down Meadow Valley Wash at milepost 405, two miles east of Hoya. At present the wash is uninhabited between Moapa and the section house at Carp. The lower wash is composed almost entirely of outwashed sand and gravel; the soil, such as it is, is too sandy and the creek too intermittent to support agriculture. In the foreground are two Mojave yuccas, or Spanish dagger, about the largest plant this climate will permit. At far left is the county road, which is usually washed out, buried in sand drifts, or too muddy for travel between Moapa and Carp. UP's access road is preferred by desert travelers, for obvious reasons. *Garland McKee*

Dieselization and CTC, completed on the LA&SL in 1949, allowed the UP to remove about one-third of the LA&SL's sidings between Yermo and Salt Lake City, the nadir reached when Flynn came out in the late 1970s. The unexpected advent of export coal trains in spring 1980 caught the LA&SL short. On a typical day in 1975, the UP ran about 12 through trains through Caliente, usually six fast piggyback trains, four to five slower manifests, and one to two unit coal trains. By spring 1981, unit coal, grain and soda-ash traffic had increased the count through Caliente to as many as 25 trains a day. Most of the capacity problems were encountered between Uvada and Yermo, where grades are long and the sidings were too far apart, too short, or both. An adequate plant had suddenly become inadequate, as had happened during World War II.

In a flurry of earth moving and track laying in 1981–82, the UP spent $22 million to reinstall or lengthen 13 CTC sidings between Uvada and Yermo, build a new classification yard at Yermo, and make terminal improvements at Provo, Milford, East Los Angeles, and at the Ports of Los Angeles and Long Beach. A second main track was installed between Las Vegas and Boulder Junction, incorporating Bracken siding. The $6.5-million Crestline line change eliminated its horseshoe and lengthened Crestline from 6,212 to 6,490 feet. In Clover Creek Canyon, a new 5,812-foot siding was installed at Richmond, and Eccles went from 6,014 to 15,105 feet. Caliente was lengthened to 14,080 feet and mid-siding crossovers were installed. In Meadow Valley Wash, Carp was extended from 5,045 to 5,872 feet and Galt reinstalled as a 6,100-foot siding. Garnet was reinstalled as a 6,282-foot siding. Sloan was lengthened from 5,212 to 6,288 feet, Joshua from 5,226 to 6,062 feet, and both sidings at Cima were lengthened, from 5,088 and 5,272 feet to 6,271 and 6,355 feet. A 9,191-foot siding was added at Kelso, and Sands went from a 588-foot spur to a 6,100-foot siding. A 1.1-mile, $1.8-million line change between mileposts 480 and 482, east of the former siding at Barclay, reduced curvature from 9°15' to 5°, reduced total curvature by 70°42', and shortened the railroad by 0.07 miles.

the east switch, while the Ford train clears the main and comes down the siding to the west switch, where it stops. The dispatcher can now place the east switch back to normal, and the five big units on the double-stack and the helper's two SD40-2's throttle up to leave Galt seven minutes after they arrived.
*Two photographs, Jamie Schmid*

AT RIGHT: On September 14, 1989, a crew field-welds a rail at the junction of new concrete ties and older wood ties west of Caliente. The UP installed its first 6,340 feet of concrete ties in 1982 at Crestline, as part of the Crestline line change. Although concrete ties have been around since the early 1900s (an early user was the Riverside, Rialto & Pacific), technical problems were difficult. U.S. installations were limited at first to railroads such as the Black Mesa & Lake Powell in 1974. The UP was so cautious about its first concrete ties that they went between switches at Crestline, so if they gave trouble trains could be routed through the siding.

Because concrete ties need special rail fastenings and different ballast, and have different track dynamics than wood ties, they cannot simply be slid under the rails in place of worn-out wood ties. Wood ties are still more economical for most installations; the UP limits its use of concrete ties to heavy-curve and heavy-tonnage areas such as Meadow Valley Wash and Clover Creek Canyon, where they hold alignment and gauge much better than wood ties. Beginning in 1987 the UP began installing concrete ties on curves 7° or sharper between Hoya and Crestline. As of July 1991, the UP had installed more than 17 miles' worth in these canyons. *Mel Finzer*

The High Line lifted the LA&SL out of easy reach of Meadow Creek, but by no means did it tame the creek. Any time there are heavy rains in the mountains above Meadow Valley Wash, the UP knows that trouble is coming. On August 20, 1984, for example, a flash flood washed out the main line at Farrier. A westbound coal train came upon the washout unaware; the first three units splashed through, but the fourth unit and 24 coal loads derailed in a heap, closing the railroad for 48 hours.

Even small storms can cause problems, if not for the railroad, then for desert travelers. The county road, which is paved from Caliente as far as Elgin, is often closed by flash floods, and below Carp the county road should be approached with great caution after inclement weather. As photographer Mel Patrick found out in February 1979, the water in the wash's upper reaches one day travels to its lower reaches by the next day.

"The day before, a little flood came down the wash at Caliente and wiped out the paved county road just south of town. Now I was foolishly going into the wash from the south end, not realizing that there was a lot of water coming down the wash. So I went in from Moapa, took some pictures around Vigo, and started to head back out. At Rox, where the road crosses the wash, rising water cut me off. Where the wash had been perfectly dry in the morning, now it was covered with a foot of water, and rising fast as I watched. In the space of the next hour the water rose to about three feet deep. I really didn't know how high the water was going to go, so I parked my car on the highest ground I could find and waited.

"After a while, along came a UP welding truck. They insisted that their truck could quite easily ford the creek, and so they drove in. Big mistake. When the water reached the level of the fan it picked up water and splashed it all over the engine, soaking the ignition system. The truck died right there in the middle of the water. I suggested that they simply put the truck in gear and use the starter motor to pull the truck out. They didn't think it would work, but it did. I was rather amazed how the starter had no trouble pulling the truck forward and out of the creek, but I guess you had better have a big truck battery with a lot of amp-hours to do this trick. I walked across the creek, getting very wet, so I could photograph this process.

"After they got the truck up on dry ground, they took out the spark plugs, dried everything, and got the truck restarted. They also had to drain the water out of the truck's upper gas tank. They gave me a lift to Moapa, where I had to hitch a ride into Las Vegas, no easy feat on an interstate highway, I might add. I borrowed the pickup of a friend of a friend in Las Vegas and came back the next day, but the water was still too high to cross. Three days later we came back again, and I was able to drive my car out."
*Three photographs, Mel Patrick*

ABOVE: At Leith the mountains close in on Meadow Valley Wash, and from there to Caliente the creek is at all times penned in by mountains 2,000 to 3,000 feet higher. Nevertheless, this is not a sheer-walled canyon in the sense of a Royal Gorge or even a Feather River Canyon, but more of a ragged cleft through mountains torn by innumerable side canyons, creeks, gulches, and ravines. By late afternoon, much of the canyon floor is deep in shadow, but as the end of day approaches, the sun's rays sometimes find a path around some obstructing peak and down a narrow tributary into the main canyon, lighting up a small portion of the railroad. At 6:08 P.M. on March 23, 1988, the evening sun spotlights the east switch at Elgin. A 33-car eastbound, mostly TOFC and auto racks, has held the main to meet a westbound APL double-stack train. Now it throttles up, leaving on a green. Twelve minutes later the light was gone, bringing blue-gray darkness to the bottom of the canyon. *Eric Blasko*

## The High Line and Its Tunnels

*As a matter of fact, all the railroads of the United States have been built to present standards piece-meal over a long period of years, and, with only one or two exceptions, the new property as completed ready for service was a vastly different property from what it is today.*
*—The Elements of Railroad Engineering, 1937*

Depending upon the source consulted, between 1900 and 1921 Senator Clark was either an idiot savant or the LA&SL's benevolent parent, and the UP was either a brutal tyrant or the epitome of progressive railroading. Historians of the Southwest often see Clark as a knight who strove to bring real progress to an undeveloped region, and see the UP as an arrogant outsider. Historians of the UP often see Clark as a freebooter, obstructionist, or megalo-maniac, and see the UP put upon by Clark's infuriating inability to grasp the nuances of Class I railroad operation.

Most often these interpretations arise during analysis of the two times when the relationship between Clark and the UP was undergoing change, either during their marriage in 1902 when they commingled their railroads into Harriman's "Community of Interest," or during their divorce in 1921 when the UP bought out Clark's half. The claim has been made that the UP had to bring the LA&SL up to par after 1921, presumably because Clark had pigheadedly resisted the UP's entreaties for modernization. (According to this theory, the UP made things right and Clark made things wrong; since each owned 50 percent, this is difficult to fathom.) However, most of the LA&SL improvement projects of the 1920s, such as signaling and bridge replacement—which Clark is alleged to have resisted—actually began in 1917, then were post-poned by USRA control beginning in 1918, as were most railroad improvement projects nationwide. A review of UP's capital expenditures during the 1920s indicates that improve-ments to the LA&SL were in proportion to improvements on the whole UP system, and not indicative of improvements to a run-down railroad. By itself, California's tremendous growth during the 1920s would seem to have demanded most of these improvements regardless of what Clark had or had not done.

Records expressing UP's dissatisfaction with the LA&SL's condition may just indicate that the LA&SL had been too independent for UP's tastes. When UP president Carl R. Gray toured the LA&SL in 1921, "the condition of its branches left on his mind a very sorry impression; they had to be improved and new ones built," according to Maury Klein. Yet of the four branches (as distinct from spurs) built after this date, the Anaheim was a continuation of work in progress, the Boulder City was actually an industrial spur built in response to the sudden appearance of a big customer (Boulder Dam) in otherwise worthless territory, and the Cedar

City was at least as much an industrial spur in response to another big new customer (Columbia Steel) as it was the opening up of new territory. Only the Fillmore can be construed as a branch that opened up new territory (and its contribution to UP's traffic appears insignificant).

Whatever the rationale, the UP did spend a great amount of money on the LA&SL between 1921 and 1930. One of the most expensive projects it undertook, costing over $4 million, was the preparation of the heavy-grade, heavy-curve territory in Meadow Valley Wash and Clover Creek Canyon for double-tracking, by enlarging to double-track dimensions 11 of the 16 tunnels in these canyons, and replacing their timber linings with concrete. This project, which began in 1924, was very likely a reaction to rapidly increasing traffic on the LA&SL in the post-recession year of 1923, when its revenue ton-miles grew by 26 percent.

Four tunnels in the canyons—5, 13, 14 and 18—were not enlarged to double-track dimensions during this project, though they were enlarged from their previously constricted dimensions and concreted. Tunnel 5 below Boyd remained single-track, probably because the badly frac-tured basalt above it dictated against double track. Tunnels 13 and 14 at Little Springs and

Tunnel 18 at Brown also remained single-track, probably because the canyon was considered too cramped for a second track at these locations.

When first built, all of the LA&SL's tunnels had been lined with timber for their entire length, indicative of poor rock conditions. By 1924 the timber in the six original OSL&UN tunnels was 34 years old, and as might be expected they were the first to be concreted (along with Tunnel 5 at Boyd, which apparently had some ground pressure problems). By 1932, the project was complete, excepting only Tunnel 3 at Leith, which remained timber-lined until daylighted in 1943. The tunnel crews performed this work while trains continued to roll, an extraordinary accomplishment in hot, rugged, and remote country which went unnoticed by the trade press.

FAR LEFT: Early on the morning of October 17, 1988, the 9102 West rumbles through Tunnel 4 west of Kyle, the oversize bore reverberating with the noise of the piggyback train. The home signal at the west switch of Kyle can be seen through the tunnel. It appears that none of these tunnels has had a second track. If a second track ever is required, the tunnel floors will probably have to be lowered because in the 1920s no one anticipated double-stacks. *Eric Blasko*

NEAR LEFT: The 9106 West pops out of 598-foot Tunnel 5 west of Boyd on November 10, 1989, pushing a plug of cold air out of the mountain. The UP shield cast into Tunnel 5's west portal in 1925 was last repainted (by a railfan) in 1980 and is now beginning to fade again in the desert sun. If the slide fences around the portal and the profusion of joints in the rock above this tunnel are any indication, this mountain is not particularly solid. *Doug Harrop*

ABOVE: According to the 1928 guidebook *Along the Union Pacific System*, Rainbow Canyon begins at Etna and ends at Leith, and is very scenic: "The rock formations of the walls are quite individual in character and present many fantastic shapes, such as castles, Indian heads, etc." Rainbow Canyon is also narrow and confined, which led the SPLA&SL to build its original main line near creek level. That in turn led to considerable destruction when Meadow Creek came to life on the morning of January 1, 1910. At 8:38 A.M. on March 19, 1985, the VAN curls out of Tunnel 8 on the High Line between Etna and Stine. A future flood will have to spread from wall to wall and also rise some distance before it can threaten the High Line. *Eric Blasko*

# Caliente

*After giving birth to Caliente and nourishing it through infancy, the railroad granted that town a vigorous adolescence.*
                                                      —James W. Hulse, historian, 1971

The meadow where Clover Valley and Meadow Valley joined together was homesteaded in the early 1870s by Charles Culverwell, whose ranch supplied meat and draft animals to Pioche. First called Culverwell, then Clover Valley Junction, then Calientes (from the Spanish *caliente*, "hot," for the hot springs north of town), the "s" was dropped in 1903. A noisy construction camp flourished here in 1900, populated with "ten-day men" who worked ten or so days to earn a few dollars, then left. Culverwell, "the mayor of Calientes," sold his land to both the SPLA&SL and the OSL, holding up overeager OSL graders with a shotgun in 1901 when they forgot to pay him.

Because this was a wide spot with water, the SPLA&SL built a division point here in 1904–05. A 20-stall roundhouse (until 1911 it was a principal shop), 6-track yard, depot, and a row of company houses transformed Culverwell's ranch from a muddy construction camp into a smoky railroad town of 600 people. To handle war traffic, the UP extended the turntable from 92 to 126 feet in 1941, added more yard tracks (bringing Caliente up to 12 tracks) and more rooms at the club house in 1943, and built two more water tanks in 1944. Then the war was finished, and so was Caliente's career as a railroad town. Dieselization in 1947–48 decimated the roundhouse forces, and CTC in 1948 eliminated the crew change for trainmen on April 11, 1948, and for enginemen on January 11, 1949. The yard closed in 1948. One helper hung on until about 1953, and an agent until 1983. Today about 1,100 people call Caliente home, but few of them work for the UP.

ABOVE LEFT: At 11:24 A.M. on November 12, 1988, an LAAP snakes up Meadow Valley Wash into Caliente, past meadows where Angus cattle graze on a pretty autumn day. These cliffs are made of tuff, a dry (not molten) crystalline rock ranging in size from dust to boulders that is ejected by volcanoes. Tuff accumulates in layers, similar to sedimentary rocks. *Eric Blasko*

ABOVE RIGHT: At 10:06 A.M. on November 10, 1988, the CSLAZ (Canal Street–Chicago to Los Angeles) rolls quietly past Caliente's depot. Its four units returned east through Caliente on the LAAP shown in the previous photograph. The work train waiting on the siding will follow the CSLAZ down the wash to dump ballast. All that now remains of Caliente's yard is a setout track occupied this gray morning by gondolas loaded with concrete ties. It must have been interesting to switch trains at Caliente, as the yard was on a 0.70-percent grade. Outfit cars are parked on the northeast leg of the wye, which once led up Meadow Valley at left to Pioche. The main line runs east up Clover Creek at right. The roundhouse was in the middle of the wye. *Eric Blasko*

BELOW RIGHT: To replace a frame depot which burned on September 9, 1921, Caliente received a new Mission-style depot in 1922, a 58-foot-by-207-foot combination station/hotel. Architects John and Donald Parkinson of Los Angeles set the pattern at Caliente for most of the LA&SL's modern depots, with the Mission style. A clubhouse built in 1928 provided additional rooms. The UP gave the depot to the town in 1971; it is now the town hall, police station, and library. *Mel Finzer*

# THE HIGH LINE, PART II

*I have stood in the middle of a broad sandy wash with not a trickle of moisture to be seen anywhere, sunlight pouring down on me and on the flies and ants and lizards, the sky above perfectly clear, listening to a queer vibration in the air and in the ground under my feet—like a freight train coming down the grade, very fast—and looked up to see a wall of water tumble around a bend and surge toward me.*
　　　　　　　　　　　　　　　　　　　　—Edward Abbey, desert naturalist, 1968

While it was Meadow Valley Wash that bore the brunt of the great flood of January 1, 1910, it was Clover Creek Canyon that the SPLA&SL badly wanted to abandon. Clover Creek Canyon is so narrow that a railroad in its depths must forever be vulnerable to flooding. Moreover, the maximum grade in Meadow Valley Wash is 3 miles of 1.50 percent between Elgin and Boyd, whereas Clover Creek has the stiffest grade between Cima and Salt Lake City, 3.5 miles ranging from 1.40 to 2.06 percent (uncompensated) against eastbounds between mileposts 471.2 and 474.7. While the Wash has plenty of curves, Clover Creek is positively tortuous: in the 7 miles between Minto and Islen the curves are practically continuous and are as tight as 10°33'.

After hiking through the surrounding mountains in early 1910, the SPLA&SL's engineers convinced management that an alternative to Clover Creek was wishful thinking. Reconciled to the inevitable, the SPLA&SL extended the High Line from Caliente into Clover Creek, as far as the west portal of Tunnel 13 (milepost 471.3). Above that point it had no choice but to accept the original elevation, or abandon the six 1890-built tunnels in favor of new tunnels. Four small line changes were made between Tunnel 13 and milepost 477.7 at Barclay to improve creek crossings.

BELOW, LEFT AND RIGHT: At 10:57 A.M. on March 17, 1992, the LAAP1-16 emerges from Tunnel 11 east of Caliente, as viewed from the top of Tunnel 12. About four minutes later its helper follows. These two tunnels through the legs of a hollow mesa consumed most of the money spent on the High Line in Clover Creek. The original line ran around the mesa on a narrow ledge of sand, no place for a permanent right-of-way. In 1927–28 the UP spent $720,000 to enlarge these tunnels, but so far CTC and big power have obviated any need for a second track.

In 1981 the UP began hauling trainloads of containers to and from Los Angeles for American President Lines (APL). In 1984, this became a double-stack train. In early 1986, APL gave the UP a ten-year contract for all of its business between Los Angeles and Chicago in return for a lower rate.

To lower its rate, the UP decided it could lengthen the double-stack trains to 140 platforms long (280 containers) and run them less frequently, saving on crews. There was just one problem: the UP had only seven places in the 620 miles between Yermo and Salt Lake City where one of these immense double-stack trains could clear the main! At the time the typical siding west of Caliente was around 5,600 feet long; east of Caliente they were typically 6,000 feet, all of them extended to this length during the 1942–48 CTC projects. They were adequate for almost anything except 8,600-foot double-stack trains. Very quickly, beginning in spring 1986, the UP extended 25 sidings on the LA&SL to 8,800 feet or longer, just enough space for 28 five-platform double-stack cars and 9 units. (This project should not be confused with the coal-train capacity program of 1981–82.) Roughly every third siding, about one every 20 miles, was extended: Spadra, Dunn, Sands, Dawes, the south siding at Cima, Ivanpah, and Calada, California; Erie, Wann, Garnet, Moapa, Hoya, Carp, Kyle, Boyd, Islen, and Crestline, Nevada; and Heist, West Milford, Cruz, Lynndyl, Jericho, Boulter, Faust, and Warner, Utah. Several of these sidings were lengthened just four years earlier; now the UP had to lengthen them again. The project wrapped up that fall; the first regular long double-stack, the APLA4-26, left Los Angeles on October 26.

These trains needed a helper. Originally, the Victorville helper came over to San Bernardino and pushed to Summit. Another helper called at Yermo ran ahead to Balch, coupled on and pushed to Cima, cut off and followed to Las Vegas, changed crews and ran ahead to Carp, coupled on and pushed to Crestline, and then ran light to either Milford or Las Vegas. This seemed like too much work, so in November 1986 the UP borrowed two Santa Fe SF30-C's with radio remote control and used them to control UP units on train LAAP2-11 from Los Angeles to Cheyenne, Wyoming, the remote units entrained 80 cars deep. Although successful in the sense that nothing came off the track, the UP decided it did not want specialized locomotives, and settled on a two-unit manned helper that coupled on at East Los Angeles and remained coupled to Milford, changing crews at Yermo and Las Vegas. In early 1993, however, the UP decided it was more economical to shorten these trains to 100 platforms and run them more frequently, eliminating what had been the nation's longest helper operation. *Two photographs, Jamie Schmid*

Late on a fall afternoon, October 18, 1988, the air is dead calm. At the east switch of Richmond, Clover Creek Canyon is silent. The birds are napping, waiting for evening, and the flies are holed up, the temperature already too cool for them. The only sound is from the signal relay box, where the CTC relays click on and off in ceaseless rhythm, sampling the code wires, vigilant for the code that will tell them to bring this signal to life, or to send current to the switch motor, and make it whir to life and reverse the switch. The only motion is the saw-toothed shadow of the canyon rim. Slowly, silently, it engulfs the canyon like spilled black ink. It creeps across the track, and climbs up the canyon's north wall, blotting out the shadow of the westward absolute signal.

On the through plate-girder bridges across Clover Creek, iron plates announce to ants in the wash, if they should ever tear their eyes away from their incessant commerce, that the American Bridge Company riveted these bridges together in 1911. These bridges have seen hand-fired 2-8-0s, oil-fired Challengers, the streamliner *City of Los Angeles* in several different versions, F-units, the Aerotrain, and long double-diesels. Hundreds of thousands of carloads of bawling sheep and stoic hogs and glum cattle swaying in unison to and fro have clattered over their decks, millions of tons of coal and steel and oranges and lumber have rumbled between their girders. For 77 years they have done their job, efficiently, perfectly, without complaint, asking only for a coat of aluminum paint every 20 years or so. If ants needed a monument to industry, orthodoxy, and durability, these bridges would be a suitable candidate.

Down at the west switch at Eccles, the canyon lines up with the rays of the dying sun. At 6:35 P.M. Tunnel 12 emits a deep rumble for a brief moment, then Dutch Flat suddenly reverberates with the guttural snarl of two GE diesels. Out of darkness and into the molten light of sunset races an east-bound piggyback train, a streamer of golden exhaust flying from its two locomotives, its three dozen trailers and containers wriggling slightly as they follow their motive power up the hill. In what seems like two heartbeats the train is gone. Its clamor echoes hollowly down the canyon in bits and snatches, until that too is gone, swallowed up in the dark desert canyon. Almost as an afterthought, the sun vanishes behind the Delamar Mountains five minutes later, saturating Clover Creek Canyon with the slate-gray light of evening. Above the canyon the first stars shine unblinking and bright in a breathtakingly transparent indigo sky.

Twenty-four days later, Tunnel 11 near Eccles glows with the headlights of a westbound coal train, about to poke its nose around the 4° curve at the west portal at 6:04 P.M. on November 11, 1988. One wonders what David Eccles of the Utah Construction Co., the prime contractor on the Leamington Cut-off, the SPLA&SL, the Western Pacific, dozens of other major railroad projects, and the namesake of this location, would think of this imposing double-track tunnel through pink-and-white banded rhyolite. Perhaps he would examine the way workmen had used boards to form its rippled concrete lining, or admire the spring of its arch, or puzzle why it has but one track when it was so clearly built for two. Overbuilt, he might mutter; waste of good concrete.

*Three photographs, Eric Blasko*

## CLOVER CREEK CANYON

*Where the rocks close in together, as in some of the cañons of our Southwest, the railway curves about them and finds its way often where one would hardly suppose a decent wagon road could be built.*
—John Bogart, state engineer of New York, 1890

From Farrier to Crestline the railroad gains 4,257 feet in altitude, allowing for the 1981–82 Crestline line change. In terms of a stiff, sustained climb, i.e., no major flat spots or down grades, and grades of more than 1.0 percent encountered, it is the third-tallest hill in the U.S. and Canada, after the west slopes of Southern Pacific's Donner Pass and Rio Grande's Tennessee Pass.

Until dieselization in 1947–48, all eastbound trains received helpers up the steeper part of this hill. The helpers ran west from Caliente to Leith, wyed, and backed 10 miles down to Carp (a wye was installed at Carp in 1944 to save time). Freight trains received at least one cut-in helper and passenger trains were double-headed. If the freight was particularly heavy, the helper

would meet it at Rox or Farrier. Water would be taken at Carp or Elgin, and again at Caliente, where a second helper would cut in ahead of the caboose while the crews changed. Then the train, sometimes with four engines, would blast out of Caliente for Crestline, stopping at Acoma for water. At Crestline the helpers cut out and either battled traffic to return light to Caliente or ran to Modena to help heavy westbounds up the 1.0 percent to Crestline. During World War II the UP stationed a pair of 1100-class S2's at Modena to help westbounds, because the water supply at Modena (Crestline had no water) could not keep up with the legions of thirsty 2-10-2's and 2-8-2's.

In "Promoted to the Right Side of the Cab" *(Trains, July 1958)*, LA&SL engineer Walter Thrall recalled that a Caliente helper assignment was a good job in 1944:

"I was assigned to Caliente for only two weeks, but I enjoyed every minute of it. How well I can remember the echo of the whistles through the canyon and the deep-throated barks of the exhausts. We would exceed running time when we were running light so that we could spend a few extra minutes in the friendly warmth of the open telegraph offices and enjoy a cup of

coffee with the girl operators. We would bring them the papers and the local news. Many a time the dispatcher would come on the wire: 'See anything of that helper engine yet?' We might have been there 4 or 5 minutes. She would reply, 'I think I see his headlight showing now.'

"Once in a while we would be run on through Caliente to Crestline if the Utah Division didn't have any rested crews. The wye at Crestline was, I believe, the coldest place I have ever been. Not only did Caliente have a good beanery in the depot but the town was accommodating. If we went to a movie there and happened to be called during the show, a typewritten note was projected at the bottom of the picture: ENGINEER THRALL YOU ARE CALLED FOR 10 P.M."

ABOVE LEFT: At 12:08 P.M. on November 11, 1988, an eastbound APL double-stack sweeps through the volcanic cliffs at Richmond. Out of sight is its two-unit SD40-2 helper, which is rated at 3,300 tons on this climb. The LA&SL rated its 2-10-2's at 1,132 tons, UP's 4-6-6-4's at 1,750 tons, and four F3's at 3,240 tons (assuming 50-ton cars) on this climb. Since the LA&SL's tonnage historically has run east to west there were few trains heading up Clover Creek after 1948 that four F3's or FA's could not

handle unassisted. Until 1953 one helper remained at Caliente, a TR5 cow-and-calf, to boost heavy eastbound perishable trains such as the UX (Utah Manifest) and CN (Colton Fruit) up to Crestline. Now once again there are no helpers here. *Eric Blasko*

ABOVE: At 9:42 A.M. on April 26, 1985, a westbound piggyback train squeals through a succession of 10° curves at Little Springs. After 1948, when Minto and Barclay were pulled out, Clover Creek Canyon had just four sidings in the 32 miles between east Caliente and west Crestline, sparse for slow, heavy-grade territory. In 1976 the UP created Little Springs, a 2,520-foot CTC siding which could not have been of much help. The UP reduced it to a business track after 1983, because in 1982 it had built a 5,812-foot siding at Richmond, and had relocated the main line at Eccles to cut off a curve at milepost 466.5, making the old main line a 15,105-foot siding (at a cost of $1.9 million). The UP probably built Richmond where it is instead of where the 4,947-foot siding at Minto used to be to avoid building two or more new bridges across Clover Creek. *Tim Zukas*

If measured by its speed limit, Clover Creek Canyon between mileposts 470.7 and 475.0 is the most tortuous place on the Union Pacific from Council Bluffs to Los Angeles, 1,814 miles. It is the only place other than in a terminal area where all trains are limited to 20 mph. This speed limit arises from Clover Creek's combination of a maximum grade of 2.06 percent with 14 curves of 10° or tighter. That is about as tight as curves ever get on Union Pacific's modern main lines.

According to the track chart the grade averages 1.8 percent uncompensated for 2.2 of these miles, which makes it steeper than the westward track between Wahsatch and Ogden, Utah, or the No. 3 Track west of Hermosa, Wyoming. In other words, if a train can make it up the hill to Crestline, it is good for any climb in the 1,350 miles from Crestline to Omaha.

AT LEFT: At 12:56 P.M. on April 30, 1985, Extra 3309 East snakes up Clover Creek Canyon at milepost 474 between Richmond and Islen, its three SD40-2's on a rare short stretch of tangent track, between Tunnels 15 and 16. The train is returning 91 empty Rio Grande and UP coal hoppers to Provo.

Starting in the background, this train is coiling through a left-hand 10°06' (maximum) curve, a 10° right-hand curve, and an 8° (maximum) left-hand curve, this last curve ending at the east portal of Tunnel 15. In 1987 and 1989 the UP installed concrete ties on most of the track between Richmond and Islen to help control gauge and alignment.

This rocky canyon seems altogether too twisted, too narrow, and too precarious for a standard-gauge railroad. If the LA&SL had never happened, and you came through Clover Creek in a jeep, the notion of 10,000-ton trains between these pinched walls would seem improbable. Yet the UP has run trains through this canyon since the summer of 1901, and without much change in the alignment the OSL&UN's engineers surveyed over a century

ago, in 1889. On the original UP main line across Wyoming there was elbow room to effect great changes in the alignment, but not in Clover Creek Canyon. It is probable that the slowest track on UP's Omaha to Los Angeles main line will retain this distinction well into the future. *Tim Zukas*

ABOVE LEFT: On the hot afternoon of March 21, 1985, the LAWST-20 (Los Angeles to Wood Street–Chicago Trailers), 44 loads, no empties, and 3,126 tons, roars out of Tunnel 13 east of Richmond, its brakeman riding the front platform. Out of Los Angeles at 11:27 P.M. on March 20, this train has so far averaged 32 mph, not bad considering the hills. *Eric Blasko*

ABOVE: At 3:20 P.M. on March 25, 1988, the motor-car indicator mounted on the intermediate signal at milepost 474 between Tunnels 15 and 16 rotates from the vertical to horizontal position, announcing that a westbound train is approaching. About 15 minutes later, the whine of a heavy train in dynamic braking can be heard bouncing off the canyon walls. At 3:41 P.M., the noise crescendoes and the SCYR (Salt Lake City to Yermo) pops out of Tunnel 16, its six units sucking hot desert air through their dynamic brake grids and blasting it, superhot and shimmering, out the top. The UP has made use of the extra room in Tunnel 15 to swing the track from one side to the other, reducing the curvature just a little. *Eric Blasko*

# CLOVER VALLEY

*I deeply regret the necessity for killing your Indian prisoners.
I fear it will make conciliations more difficult.*

—Letter from Southern Mission President Erastus Snow
to the Clover Valley and Meadow Valley settlements, 1864

Before there were white people in this country there were the people of the Fremont culture, who grew corn, beans, squash, and sunflowers in small irrigated plots alongside the creeks. In their leisure they decorated the rock with pictographs and petroglyphs of animals, people, and gods. These can be seen in Etna Cave near Etna; in Grapevine Canyon east of Boyd; and on a roadside boulder about a mile above Elgin. About 700 years ago the climate changed. Drought became permanent, and the precipitation pattern changed. Often a year's

worth of gentle rain was compressed into a few cloudbursts. The fields withered, and the Fremont Culture disappeared. In their place came the Southern Paiute, a loosely organized tribe of wandering hunters and gatherers.

During the 1850s and 1860s about 2,000 to 4,000 Mormon immigrants arrived annually in Utah. Soon there were more Mormons than the tillable land around Salt Lake City could support. Explorations by the Southern Mission in 1854 and 1858 established that Meadow Valley (Panaca after 1864) and Clover Valley were suitable places for farming. Clover Valley was described as "a pretty little valley of meadow land, containing 200 to 250 acres." There was good grazing in the mountains, and Clover Creek burbled through the valley.

In spring 1864 a dozen Mormon families arrived in Clover Valley, and began planting wheat and grazing cattle. The Paiutes could not resist helping themselves to crops and

cattle. Initial goodwill dissolved into low-level warfare. The small, isolated Clover Valley settlement was unsafe, so the Mormons left in 1866, returning in larger numbers three years later. A small community grew up in Clover Valley, called Barclay.

In time, too many cattle ate the range down to the roots. It eroded, and could no longer support so many cattle or people. In 1900, the census found 43 people living in this valley (but only 30 in Las Vegas!). Now there are perhaps a dozen.

BELOW LEFT: At 3:06 P.M. on May 1, 1985, an eastbound TOFC train curves through the graceful track at milepost 477 east of Islen. Until 1948, Barclay siding was in the long background tangent, amongst the green fields of Clover Valley. Ranchers still grow hay in this lush enclave. Their houses and barns are tucked into the

trees at the far end of the valley. They use the hay to supplement the forage their cattle obtain in these arid ranges during the summer months. Come fall, they will round up the cattle, load them into trucks, and ship them to feedlots for fattening. In the far distance at left, past the gray-green forested summits of the Clover Mountains, are the 10,000-foot peaks of Utah's Pine Valley Mountains. *Tim Zukas*

BELOW RIGHT: At 4:48 P.M. MST on March 25, 1988, westbound pig train CSLAZ (Canal Street–Chicago to Los Angeles) glides down the main at Islen, beneath volcanic tuff flushed with warm afternoon light. About 15 cars of hogs are on the head end, en route to the packing house in Los Angeles. *Eric Blasko*

ABOVE RIGHT: Steam engines did not so much steam from town to town as they did from water tank to water tank. A steam engine was a machine in perpetual need of a drink. There was only one regular water stop in Clover Creek Canyon, at milepost 485.3 above Acoma (there was an emergency supply at Big Springs), where the pumphouse still stood on May 1, 1985. Taking water was a laborious process on a mountain grade. Because it was impossible to spot helpers exactly under the spout, the train was cut ahead of each helper, and each pulled up to the tank with its portion of the train. After all had watered, the train was reassembled, an air test made, the flagman was whistled in from his station a mile to the rear, and all of this done without a radio. To the delight of officials, diesels put an end to this tedious process, which had to be repeated about once every 20 miles on a mountain grade. *Tim Zukas*

## CRESTLINE: THE TOP OF THE DESERT

*A [civil] engineer, once on a time, standing behind his instrument, was surrounded by a crowd of natives, anxious to know all about it. He explained his processes, using many learned words, and flattered himself that he had made a deep impression upon his hearers. At last, one old woman spoke up, with an expression of great contempt on her face, "Wall! If I knowed as much as you do, I'd quit ingineerin' and keep a grocery!"*
—Thomas Curtis Clarke, civil engineer, 1890

At Crestline the LA&SL stands on top of the desert, 5,962 feet above sea level. Look back, to the west, where the LA&SL spirals down 100 miles of rugged canyon to Moapa, to the bottom of a hole 4,400 feet below. West of Moapa the railroad plows forward through the Mojave Desert, across the crests and troughs of old mountains drowning in their own dirt, up and down like a clipper ship in geology's version of a bad storm. Between Crestline and Yermo, 330.5 miles, there are only about 15 miles of reasonably level track, scattered into 13 short sections.

Look forward, to the east, where the LA&SL sweeps down to the mountain-ringed floor of the Escalante Desert 800 feet below, then races across the flat deserts of the Great Basin toward Salt Lake City. Past Modena there will not be another grade of consequence until the climb to Boulter Summit is encountered on the other side of Lynndyl, 170 miles east of Crestline.

To the west is the Mojave Desert: a low, hot desert, stippled with creosote bush and Joshua-trees, the realm of the desert iguana, the desert kangaroo rat, and the desert tortoise. To the east is the Great Basin Desert: a high, cold desert, tufted with sagebrush, shadscale and grass, the realm of mule deer, the black-tailed jack rabbit, and the coyote. They are very different places.

Crestline is a momentary respite of gray-green foliage; here the mountains are just high enough to snag a little moisture from the prevailing westerly winds. The snow fosters a stubby forest of Utah and Rocky Mountain juniper, and single-leaf pinyon. The pinyon nuts, eaten raw or roasted, were a staple food of the Paiutes, also the juniper berries, eaten fresh or in cakes. Pinyon jays, wild turkeys, bears, deer, and packrats consume huge quantities of the nuts and berries.

ABOVE, LEFT AND RIGHT: The night of March 19, 1982, a fast-moving front bumps into the low mountains at Crestline. Before it can tear itself free and charge off to an appointment with more important mountains, it must pay a toll in snow. Morning dawns with a sky of cerulean blue. Lingering cottonball clouds from last night's storm hasten east to catch up to their brethren. The desert has turned white and lumpy, little lumps of sagebrush and big lumps of trees, all cloaked in life-sustaining snow. At 2:30 P.M., a unit coal train off the Utah Railway slogs west through the melting snow, the high-pitched cry of its turbochargers and the throbbing roar of its 16-645E3 engines piercing the clean mountain air with a perfection never heard at more mundane altitudes. Its wheels hiss through the reverse curves above the former siding at Lien, then screech through what was then the greatest curve on the Los Angeles & Salt Lake Railroad, the 10°02′ horseshoe at milepost 495.7. A few minutes later the bellow of the four SD40-2s becomes muffled as they roll over the top of the desert at Crestline. The muted roar continues until the train balances the summit, then dies off as the units change to dynamic braking for the 100-mile descent to Moapa.

As soon as the ground dried out in May 1982, crews unloaded their bulldozers, scrapers, off-road dump trucks, compactors, front-end loaders, rock drills, air compressors, pickup trucks, tool trailers, light poles, lube trucks, and a backhoe or two, most of it painted yellow, caked in mud, and dripping with gobs of red lithium lube, and proceeded to blast, rip, dig, scrape, haul, dump, compact, and generally make noise until that fall the UP had 3.2 miles of brand-new grade, and the tight curves that the desert had so grudgingly yielded to the OSL&UN's horse-powered Fresno scrapers in 1890 were handily bypassed with deep cuts and high fills. Crestline siding, which lapped over the summit so that engineers of the 2-10-2 era could balance their trains while the brakemen set retainers, was moved east onto a 1.0-percent grade, something which never would have been done in the steam era. The summit itself moved west about a quarter-mile and was lowered by about 20 feet, enabling the UP to shorten the line without increasing the compensated grade. Maximum curvature was reduced from 10°02′ to 1°25′, total curvature reduced by 506°45′ (one and three-eighths circles), and the main line was made 0.87 miles shorter, all for just $6,590,000. At about 11 A.M. on October 14, 1982, the CLS-13, the livestock train to Los Angeles, wound through the horseshoe. The track gangs quickly cut in the new line, and just before noon the SUPRV-13 was the first train over the new line. All very efficient, very modern, and for civil engineers and accountants, very exciting.
*Two photographs, Jamie Schmid*

## THE ESCALANTE DESERT

*Perhaps no portion of the great West today presents to the actual farmer, looking for a place in which to establish a home, so great an inducement as does that portion of the Escalante Valley in Utah known as the "Beryl District"... there is no better farming country in Western America.*
—Chas. E. Miller, UP Advertising Agent, August 1923

By about 1860 all of the good farmland along the Wasatch Front was taken up. Mormon leaders encouraged new émigrés to spread into the state's deserts, implying that the verdant farms along the Wasatch Front had likewise been useless desert until hardworking settlers had changed them into their present fertile state. Nothing could be further from the truth, but thousands of trusting settlers went forth and built new homesteads on the marginal lands where mountain met desert, "their little fields clustered like suckling shoats at creeks running out of canyons," in the words of one pioneer. It was, concluded geographer Richard H. Jackson, "testimonial to the willingness of settlers to accept the leaders' admonitions to seek out the oases and the Lord would modify the climate." Out in the broad alkaline valleys, where there was no flowing water, the Mormons made no attempt at cultivation.

In 1909, Utah Senator Reed Smoot induced Congress to double the size of homesteads under the 1862 act to 320 acres. Anyone could gain title to a half square mile of free land, provided they built a house and tilled the land. Thus was born the West's last great land rush. People from all walks of life rushed into the West's sagebrush deserts, convinced that hard work and scientific methods would create success where the Mormons had failed. Much of the impetus to farm Utah's Escalante and Sevier Deserts was created by the SPLA&SL and the UP, who renamed them the Escalante "Valley" and the Sevier "Valley." Numerous articles in *The Arrowhead*, a free magazine distributed by the Salt Lake Route until 1932, were devoted to the purported rich soils and abundant water of southwestern Utah. Photographs in *The Arrowhead* showed water rushing through irrigation works and successful farmers waist-deep in lush vegetation. In reality there was only enough water to irrigate small portions of the desert, and the photographs of "oceans of alfalfa in Utah's New Agricultural Empire" were often taken in a different state!

Few of the modern-day homesteaders took heed that this land was available only because no one had ever wanted it. Their doubts were assuaged by a trick played by nature in 1912–13, wet years when grass sprouted. There was water a few feet underground in these "valleys," but it flowed with fine sand that clogged pumps and pipes, and well-drilling and pumping were too expensive until the late 1940s. Once tapped, the aquifers were rapidly depleted. The desert could not tolerate dryland farming either; once the sagebrush was uprooted, the bone-dry topsoil promptly blew away.

Where there was enough mountain water to catch in dams and channel to fields, such as along the Sevier River at Delta, the Beaver River at Milford, and in the Pahvant Valley at Fillmore, fields could be brought to life. But the Escalante Desert was destitute of water and by the early 1930s the West's last pioneers had one by one given up and drifted off, never to return. They left behind a checkerboard of ruined land, a network of roads to nowhere, and tumble-down farmhouses.

ABOVE LEFT: On a cold morning, March 18, 1979, moist clouds bump across the Escalante Desert at Milford. Blackened with dirt thrown up from wet track, the Super Van stops at the depot for a quick crew change. In its heyday the Chicago-to-Los Angeles Super Van was hot, all piggyback and big fast power. The Alpha Beta trailers on the head end are destined for the supermarket chain's 11.5-acre warehouse at La Habra.

Milford was founded by cattlemen in 1873, and named for the place where a road to a stamp mill crossed the Beaver River: "mill ford" became Milford. Rails reached this outpost in 1880, and since that day Milford has been a railroad town. Because the westward ruling grade increases west of Milford from 0.8 percent to 1.0 percent, the UP typically marshaled excess tonnage at Milford until sufficient power could be found to haul it west. A 100-foot turntable installed in 1925 was the last major improvement to the 1905-built engine terminal, which disappeared with the end of steam in the early 1950s.

In 1923 Milford received its third depot (the first burned down on July 7, 1890), a 30-foot-by-197-foot depot/hotel that was the largest of the classic LA&SL Mission-style depots. This was not the easternmost example of this style on a Harriman railroad: the Utah Light & Railway Co., Salt Lake City's streetcar line (purchased by Harriman in 1906), built a Mission-style shop complex in Salt Lake City in 1908 in red brick instead of white stucco. Sometimes the Mission-style is erroneously called "Mission Revival"; Taco Bells are "Mission Revival," not the LA&SL's depots. The Mission style, a free adaptation of the Southwest's Franciscan missions, was California's counterpart to the Colonial Revival architecture which was then all the rage in the East. The UP tore down Milford's Mission-style depot in 1979, replacing it with a glass, steel, and concrete office building. *James Belmont*

BELOW LEFT: Up on the roof of the desert, Extra 3715 West howls through the horseshoe curve at Crestline on a late afternoon in May 1980. Nowhere do forests seem so green as where deserts surround them. *Dave Stanley*

ABOVE: In the 1920s the UP touted Beryl as the greatest farming country in the western U.S. Looking around from atop UP's well tower at Beryl on December 22, 1993, it is baffling that people fell for UP's tall tale. Where nothing can be seen but sagebrush and sand, an 84-unit coal train trudges west on the Escalante Desert's long tangents. From milepost 518 at Heist to 576 at Milford, there are just four curves.

This train and five more, loading on the Rio Grande at Skyline, Utah, have a hot date with a collier at the Port of Long Beach. In two days the UP will start shutting down most of its railroad for Christmas, but these coal trains will keep right on running. The mines always need empties, or they will drown in their own coal. There are never enough empties to satisfy the mines, so the railroads must get rid of the loads. The loads must not arrive at the dock too early, because it cannot store large quantities of coal, nor too late, because the colliers have their own load-empty cycle, stretching 5,000 miles across the Pacific Ocean. If anything stops for too long, such as for a holiday, this system begins to fall apart. *Mark Hemphill*

The West's mountains get the precipitation, the trees, the tourists, the resorts, the books of praise. The West's deserts get nothing. The deserts are overshadowed by the mountains in both a literal and a literary sense: each range casts a rain shadow over its downwind deserts, reducing them to a poverty of aridity: "will work for rain."

The storms brew up over the Pacific Ocean and head east. The clouds cavort for a few hours or a few days in the peaks of the Sierra Nevada, drench them in rain and snow, then sail over the Great Basin to bless their next beneficiary, the Wasatch Range. Often, the storms trail virgas beneath them as they cross the deserts—dark streamers of rain extending a few thousand feet below the clouds and evaporating before they ever touch the ground. The word comes from the Latin *virga*, as in "virgin." The virgas torment the thirsty deserts with rain that is ever so slightly out of reach. The Escalante and Sevier (pronounced "Severe") Deserts receive about nine inches of precipitation in an average

year. It sounds like a lot, but spread out over 365 days it amounts to about one-fortieth of an inch of water a day. What the deserts receive in usable water is actually much less. Most of this precipitation falls as snow during the winter, when it is too cold for plants to grow, and most of the snow does not melt but sublimates (passes directly from the solid state to the gaseous state without becoming a liquid) right back into the dry air. Very little soaks into the desert soil. The wonder is that *anything* grows here.

On October 11, 1993, a squall line skates across the Sevier Desert at Lynndyl, sprinkling a narrow path with holy water, then mischievously pummeling it with hail. On the warm ground the hail quickly melts. For a few minutes the normally odorless desert air is fragrant with rain and damp dust and wet sagebrush. For this vegetation and the animals that depend upon these plants, there will be sustenance for a few more days. For those plants outside the storm's narrow trace, there is nothing. As quickly as it arrived the storm moves on. The tawny light of late afternoon

rushes in beneath the clouds and gilds the damp sage. As a coal train waits at the switch to the Intermountain Power Project plant, a rainbow appears over the track. A minute later the light fails and the rainbow vanishes.

At sunset the next day, the YROG-11 (Yermo to Ogden) arrives at Van and heads into the siding to clear an important westbound. The YROG is at the bottom of the pecking order; it clears for everyone; but with four units and one hundred cars it cannot squeeze into the 5,997-foot siding. Its last two cars are out to foul the main. The YROG also has to pick-up a car from the Van house track, so the westbound has to cool its heels. At 6:30 P.M., its train back together, the YROG throttles up and begins to creep forward out of the siding. Outlined in the fading saffron light of the western sky are a train, a signal, a switch heater, and a pole line, main-line single-track railroading in the West reduced to its essential elements. *Two photographs, Jamie Schmid*

# THE LEAMINGTON CUT-OFF

*This was Harriman's formula: save millions by spending millions.*
—A. C. Kalmbach and David P. Morgan, 1949

The zenith of railroad construction took place between 1897, after the Panic of 1893 ended, and January 1, 1918, when the USRA took over the nation's railroads and most construction stopped. In these 20 years, the Western Pacific, Virginian, and Spokane, Portland & Seattle built low-grade super railroads through rough country, the Moffat Road, Milwaukee Road, and Clinchfield punched main lines through mountains believed impractical for standard-gauge rails only a decade before, and rich railroads such as the Pennsylvania, Santa Fe, SP, and UP threw practically their entire main line away and started over. Curves were straightened, sags leveled, hills chopped down, valleys bridged, and mountains tunneled through.

What made this happen—the fabulously expensive new lines, the extravagant grade-reducing cut-offs—was the trebling of ton-miles between 1890 and 1908 as America industrialized, and the utter inadequacy of the hand-fired 2-8-0. Train tonnages outstripped the capabilities of the human fireman. To stoke one of these hogs a fireman might be called upon to shovel 15 tons of coal in his workday; he could do no more. Locomotives were increasingly designed around the fireman. They could be built no larger without a second fireman; the only alternative on a stiff grade was to add two or three helpers. The only solution to skyrocketing operating costs was the low-grade cut-offs and the all-new super railroads.

After World War I new construction and massive realignments did not begin anew, except for some odds and ends that had not been taken care of before the war. Labor and materials had grown more expensive, and the locomotive builders met the challenge with mechanical stokers, which allowed larger fireboxes, larger boilers, larger cylinders, more drivers, and so forth, removing the fireman from their design equations. The stiff ruling grade, railroading's bête noire in 1900, no longer looked so worrisome by the mid-1920s.

On the LA&SL, the Leamington Cut-off from Salt Lake City to Lynndyl qualifies as super railroad. During his tour of the work during 1903 consulting engineer W. P. Hardesty was astonished by the amount of earth the Utah Construction Co. had moved to achieve super-railroad standards, observing that Harriman could have saved a lot of money on the cut-off by allowing a few short 1.0-to-2.0-percent grades.

LEFT: At 2:46 P.M. on October 13, 1986, the LAPC (Los Angeles to Pocatello, Idaho) rolls down the east slope of Boulter Summit, on the Leamington Cut-off just east of Lofgreen. The majestic snow-covered peak in the left background is Mount Timpanogos, 11,750 feet high, the highest peak in the Wasatch Range. To its right are Lightning Peak and Provo Peak. The city of Provo lies at their base. The Salt Lake & Western came through Five Mile Pass at far left, and ran across the face of the low foothills from left to right, joining the Leamington Cut-off near Boulter. *Jamie Schmid*

BELOW RIGHT: At 4:41 P.M. the next day, the LACSZ winds through the reverse curves at milepost 709.5 west of Lofgreen. Rare in 1995 is the single-level container train; double-stacks are king. Maximum curvature on the Leamington Cut-off is just 4°, and there are only six of them. Two of the six are right here. *Railway Age's* correspondent marveled upon his visit to the unfinished grade in winter 1902 that he "was shown an alignment which is

seemingly free from curves even with the solid mass of hills it passes through, over, and under." The 116.7-mile cut-off has a maximum grade of 0.8 percent. Deep cuts, tall fills, and broad curves in broken country are the dead giveaway of a low-grade super railroad. *Jamie Schmid*

ABOVE RIGHT: Behaving like you-know-what, hundreds of sheep cross over the LA&SL at milepost 710 just west of Lofgreen at 7:50 A.M. on May 5, 1990. The previous night the shepherds bedded down their flock among the pinyons and junipers at left. They let a westbound with stock cars climb by at 7:40 A.M., then quickly drove their flock over the rails. A few minutes later an eastbound dropped down from Boulter, missing the river of bleating wool by only a few minutes. *Scott Bontz*

## THE GREAT SALT LAKE BASIN

*Lake of paradoxes, in a country where water is life itself and land has little value without it, Great Salt Lake is an ironical joke of nature—water that is itself more desert than a desert.*
—Dale L. Morgan, historian, 1947

The Great Salt Lake is the puny remnant of an enormous freshwater lake that geologists call Lake Bonneville. Formed about 25,000 years ago during a period of heavy precipitation and glacial formation when lava plugged the route of the Bear River near Downey, Idaho, Lake Bonneville covered most of northwestern Utah and reached all the way south to Modena. The lake spread over some 19,800 square miles and at maximum was about 1,100 feet deep, depressing the earth's crust by as much as 200 feet. Wave action carved shorelines into the mountains. The highest horizontal line on the Wasatch Range above Salt Lake City is its ancient shoreline.

Lake Bonneville forced an outlet through the plug at Downey about 14,500 years ago, lowering the level of the lake about 350 feet. What is called the Provo shoreline formed. The second-highest line on the mountains, it is usually more prominent than the Bonneville shoreline. About 10,000 years ago, as the last Ice Age ended and the climate became arid, the lake dropped below its outlet and steadily shrank, leaving behind the Great Salt Lake, Utah Lake, and Sevier Lake. The Great Salt Lake is the largest of the three, but in comparison to Lake Bonneville it is a puddle in a parking lot. Utah Lake, refreshed by the Provo River and other streams, maintains a constant level. Sevier Lake is a playa, dry except in very wet years.

In 1850 Captain Howard Stansbury found the lake's level at 4,201 feet above sea level, with an average depth of 13 feet. In most of recorded history the lake's level has fluctuated between 4,191 and 4,212 feet above sea level, depending upon rainfall in the Wasatch Range—until 1983, when an unusual wet cycle raised the lake's level by 12 feet to its historic maximum of 4,217 feet. This was enough to flood SP's Lucin Cut-off and UP's former WP main line, and to come within a few feet of the Rio Grande and UP main lines along the eastern shore. Only at great expense were the UP and SP able to raise their main lines above the lake's briny grasp.

In 1963, when the Great Salt Lake was at its lowest level in recorded history, dissolved salts accounted for 28.5 percent by weight, making it nine times saltier than sea water. Because the lake is currently much larger due to above-normal precipitation, it is now about 13 percent salt by weight. The Great Salt Lake became salty because it has no outlet, whereas Utah Lake, which drains into the Great Salt Lake, remains freshwater. Extraction plants along the Great Salt Lake's shores concentrate the salts in evaporation ponds. Most of this is garden-variety table salt (20.3 percent by weight in 1956), along with magnesium chloride (2.9 percent), sodium sulfate (2.5 percent), potassium chloride (0.8 percent), calcium sulfate (0.1 percent), and other valuable trace metallic salts.

ABOVE LEFT: On May 16, 1992, an APLA double-stack train has just begun its climb out of the Great Salt Lake Basin as it passes the intermediate signals at milepost 758.5, on the Leamington Cut-off east of Erda. The contorted limestone strata of the Oquirrh Mountains behind the train give evidence of the inexorable forces that have alternately ripped apart, crammed together, and overturned

the earth's crust in central Utah's Sevier Thrust Belt. At the top of this grade the Leamington Cut-off passes through Stockton Bar, then dips into Rush Valley. At the other end of Rush Valley it climbs more than a thousand feet to Boulter Summit, a hilly gap between the East Tintic and the West Tintic Mountains, where the LA&SL reaches its ultimate high point, 6,061 feet above sea level. Then it descends through lonely Tintic Valley to Lynndyl, where it meets the former Utah Southern Railroad Extension coming south from Juab and Provo.

This long, supported grade at Erda begins at Lake Point and uses a succession of big fills and side hill cuts all the way to the top at the west end of the cut through the Stockton Bar, a total of 20 miles of 0.8-percent grade which gains 841 feet in altitude. The Bar, just north of Stockton, is an old shoreline feature of Lake Bonneville, and separates the Tooele Valley from the Rush Valley. It blocked the Utah Western in 1877 due to the narrow-gauge's inability to pay for an 800-foot tunnel. When the OSL surveyed the Leamington Cut-off in 1901 it planned on a 2,000-foot tunnel through the bar, but test pits revealed the bar to be composed entirely of gravel, support of which would have made a tunnel very expensive. Instead, subcontractor Flick & Johnson excavated 1.25 million cubic yards in a cut very large for its day, 3,700 feet long, 327 feet in maximum width, and 98 feet in maximum depth,

the work done entirely by two to three steam shovels working 20 hours a day for nine months. Perfected and greatly enlarged during the 1890s, steam shovels made possible the virtually impossible of two decades before, the economical excavation of huge cuts. Armies of Chinese and Irish have long been enshrined in railroad lore, yet the blacksmiths, inventors, and back-alley engineers who made steam shovels practical deserve equal credit for making possible the super railroads of the early 1900s.

ABOVE RIGHT: On July 18, 1992, the HKYR (Hinkle, Oregon, to Yermo) rounds the curve just east of Erda. Interstate 80 and UP's former Western Pacific main line to Oakland separate land from lake in the distance. Beyond them is Stansbury Island, a mountain range which is sometimes an island and sometimes not, depending upon the depth of the lake. Fifteen thousand years ago, most of the main line from Downey, Idaho, to Modena was under water. *Two photographs, James Belmont*

117

# SALT LAKE CITY

*Well, I prayed that He would lead us directly to the spot which He has done. For after searching, we can find no better.*
—Brigham Young picks the spot for the city, July 27, 1847

Brigham Young's railroad, the Utah Central, naturally received a choice location for its depot in Utah's capital city, just three blocks from Temple Square at the foot of South Temple Street. The OSL&UN built a larger wood-frame depot with gingerbread trim on this site during the 1880s. With the arrival of the SPLA&SL in 1905, Salt Lake City needed facilities suitable for transcontinental traffic, so in 1906 the OSL began work on an entirely new yard, engine terminal, and station at Salt Lake City. Unlike the small, squalid OSL depot, the new OSL and SPLA&SL Salt Lake City Union Station was of epic dimensions: 677 feet long, 70 feet wide, and 100 feet to the top of the roof trim. Its grand hall, or main waiting room, was 55 feet wide and 134 feet long, its barrel-vaulted ceiling arching 60 feet above the main floor. The structure was of masonry, concrete, and steel, finished on the exterior with pressed brick, finely tooled granite, and Sienna marble, and topped with a roof of dark-green slate and copper. Marble, tile, and scagliola (ornamental plasterwork) decorated the grand hall and public areas. Its designer, D. J. Patterson, architect for the Southern Pacific Railroad, used Second Empire styling for the $450,000 station. Enormous murals at either end of the grand hall depicted the arrival of the Mormons in the Great Salt Lake Desert in 1847 and the driving of the Golden Spike in 1869. Five splendid stained-glass windows on the west wall depicted major themes of the West: the buffalo, the Pony Express, the stagecoach, the mines, and at center, the transcontinental railroad. Many big city stations were muddled, poorly proportioned, grim, or just ugly; this station was beautiful. It opened in July 1909.

On May 1, 1971, Amtrak Day, passenger service disappeared from the three UP lines into Salt Lake City. The umbrella sheds were torn out in 1972 to make room for high-wide cars, and in April 1977 the UP moved most of its offices out of the station. When Amtrak reestablished passenger service over the LA&SL in 1979, the UP restored the station for Amtrak service. It lasted in this role until October 1986, when Amtrak moved three blocks south to the Rio Grande depot, leaving 25 UP employees rattling around in the aging station. Most of the station tracks were pulled out by July 1987. Early in 1989, the State of Utah asked the UP to donate the landmark structure to the state for preservation; having no further use for it, the UP gave it to the state later that year. It now serves as a cultural center and for other public functions that usually have little to do with transportation.

ABOVE: On August 4, 1977, Amtrak #25, the *Pioneer*, awaits its 10:15 P.M. departure for Seattle. The street side of UP's Salt Lake City station is wonderfully ornate, but the track side is quite barren of decoration. The five stained-glass windows of the grand hall can be seen above the train. Amtrak's timetable listed "coach service" for the *Pioneer*, a euphemism for a long night in a reclining seat. Promoted as a restoration of passenger service on UP's Northwestern District, the *Pioneer* was an exhumation, an air-conditioned version of the old accommodation train.
*Amtrak #25, David Lichtenberg; five windows, Mark Hemphill*

AT RIGHT: On November 14, 1992, the APSCOA departs Salt Lake City at Grant Tower. Utah's copper-topped capitol is in the distance. The APSCOA adds container tonnage at Salt Lake City before leaving for Oakland, California, on the former Western Pacific. Built in 1953, Grant Tower controlled the crossings of the LA&SL Freight Line to Los Angeles, Rio Grande's Salt Lake City-Ogden main line, and WP's main line to Rio Grande's Roper Yard and the D&RGW-WP Union Depot. (The WP, like the D&RGW a George Gould property, used D&RGW's Salt Lake City facilities.) In 1986 the Rio Grande added Grant Tower to its Denver dispatching consoles.

The WP main line crossed the LA&SL Freight Line at WP-UP Junction and paralleled the LA&SL to Smelter, where the WP continued west at lake level while the LA&SL turned south and began climbing. When the UP and WP began running the Overland Mail from Chicago to Oakland in 1972, they began sharing each other's CTC main lines from WP-UP Junction to Smelter. The WP also began sending many of its trains to UP's North Yard instead of to Roper Yard. After 1982, the trackage at Grant Tower was rearranged to extend UP's No. 1 and No. 2 Tracks from 5th North Street to WP-UP Junction. The APSCOA is swinging south from the former Freight Line to Los Angeles (at left), the No. 1 Track here, and entering the former WP main, the No. 2 Track here. A few cars back the train is using Rio Grande's main line (which enters Grant Tower at right), and beyond that the train is using the former OSL Salt Lake City wye. Somewhere underneath this mess is the grade of the Utah Western. *James Belmont*

Completion of the SPLA&SL in 1905, the rapid growth of Salt Lake City and Utah in general, and a great increase in freight and passenger traffic necessitated the construction of union OSL/SPLA&SL terminal facilities in 1906–07. A new yard, called North Yard, was built directly north of the old Utah Central yard and became the main blocking point for OSL trains to the east, north, and northwest. A new engine terminal at North Yard replaced the old roundhouse, which was torn down to make room for the new station. The facilities at North Yard included a 20-stall brick roundhouse with 75-foot turntable, boiler house and blacksmith shop, a 500-ton six-pocket coal trestle and steel water tank, and a car repair shop and five-track coach-cleaning yard.

The old yard was renamed South Yard and rearranged to handle local switching and transfer. Its facilities included eight through station tracks, a 660-foot-by-50-foot brick-and-steel freight house, a hide house "for handling green hides, beer kegs, junk, etc.," scales, and transfer platforms. A new viaduct carried Nouth Temple Street and the streetcars of E. H. Harriman's Utah Light & Railway Co. over South Yard. A manual interlocking was installed at 5th North Street, where North and South Yards connected and the main line crossed from the west side of North Yard to the east side of South Yard. A second manual interlocking protected the crossing of the SPLA&SL Passenger Line and the Rio Grande Western Freight Line at 9th South Street. The

crossings of the SPLA&SL Passenger Line and the RGW Passenger Line at 4th West Street, and the SPLA&SL Freight Line and the RGW main line west of the depot, remained stop-and-proceed. Including the station, the cost for the new union terminal was nearly $1.5 million.

Traffic continued to increase and locomotives became larger, so in 1914 the roundhouse received a 3-stall addition and a 100-foot pony-truss turntable. The freight house was extended by 233 feet in 1917. In 1924, seven more stalls were added, plus a 30,000-barrel oil tank for LA&SL locomotives. Seven stalls were lengthened in 1927; four 81-foot stalls became 110-foot stalls in 1928 as did four more in 1941. Servicing facilities were added for diesel switchers in 1942. By 1945, the roundhouse had grown like Topsy, having 32 stalls in five different lengths ranging from 85 feet to 117 feet. More-elaborate diesel-servicing facilities were added at the roundhouse in 1948 when the LA&SL dieselized. No longer needed, stalls 5 through 20 were demolished in 1950.

In 1938 the UP built new electric interlockings where the LA&SL Passenger Line crossed Rio Grande's Freight Line at 9th South Street and Rio Grande's Passenger Line at 5th West Street, replacing the mechanical interlocking at 9th South and a stop-and-proceed at 5th West. At the time the UP ran eight daily first-class passenger trains, the *City of Los Angeles* every third day,

nine daily gas-electric trips to Smelter, one local freight each way daily, and two eastbound freights daily over the Passenger Line. Today the Passenger Line is rarely used. In 1942 and 1944 the yard received 73,708 feet of new track to handle war traffic. In 1942 a new 2.7-mile double-track passenger main line was built along the east side of North Yard to eliminate the bottleneck at 5th North where the main line had crossed over to the west side of North Yard, and the old interlocking at 5th North was pulled out. These improvements helped to handle the UP's steadily increasing traffic. For example, on an average day in June 1953, 49 trains and 45 miscellaneous moves passed Grant Tower: 16 trains and 22 miscellaneous moves on the Rio Grande, 13 trains and 3 miscellaneous moves on the WP, and 20 trains and 20 miscellaneous moves on the UP.

In 1951 the UP demolished the remaining roundhouse stalls at North Yard, 1–4 and 21–32, and began building a large diesel and turbine shop in their place. Why Salt Lake City, 40 miles down a sidetrack from the Overland Route, was chosen for the shop instead of Ogden is a mystery. State and local politics may have played a part. The $6-million shop, built of reinforced concrete, glass block, and steel, formally opened on August 2, 1955. It featured a 270-ton overhead crane, perhaps the largest of its kind in the West, to lift entire gas-turbine locomotives. New sanding towers and service pits were installed south of the shop, alongside the old powerhouse. At full output, the shop force of 400 performed 20 heavy repairs a month, and UP's units made over 4,000 servicing stops at the Salt Lake City Diesel Shop each month. When completed it was the largest diesel shop in the U.S. It was the principal repair point for UP's gas turbines during their career, and handled diesel power from the whole system.

In 1973 a $3-million modernization replaced the original servicing tracks south of the shop with a new servicing facility west of the shop, and the shop's west wing was expanded with steel canopies to provide more shelter for running repairs and inspections. At present, Salt Lake City is UP's third-largest shop. Its 350 employees fuel and sand locomotives, make inspections and running repairs, change out main generators and traction motors, and staff the wheel shop. Car repair is now handled in a $500,000 "One-Spot" shop, a 114-by-200-foot steel canopy just north of the diesel shop. Completed in December 1972, the One-Spot repairs cars in assembly-line fashion.

Beginning in 1972 the WP began using North Yard for trains such as the Overland Mail, and its locomotives began pooling with the UP through Salt Lake City to North Platte. When the ICC approved the UP-WP-MP merger on December 22, 1982, the old Rio Grande-Western Pacific gateway closed completely, all WP trains going to North Yard. Heavy traffic on the former WP and LA&SL has now overwhelmed North Yard with some 65 to 70 trains daily. Penned in on all sides, the yard has nowhere to go. A new yard could logically be built on the waterlogged mud flats west of the city, but this would require extremely expensive subgrade improvements.

ABOVE LEFT: On a busy afternoon in Salt Lake City in August 1972, Extra 6943 West waits for a track in North Yard while Extra WP 3535 East, a WP run-through, highballs out of the yard en route to Ogden. In the background another DDA40X-led eastbound waits for a crew, and an NW2 drills cars into the yard. This was just after the WP-UP run-throughs began.

ABOVE RIGHT: After recrewing on a pretty afternoon in May 1975, four Centennials ease their Los Angeles to Ogden train past the diesel shop on the No. 1 Track. The UP built this double-track bypass around North Yard in 1942. At left background is the state capitol, at center is downtown Salt Lake City and the Mormon temple, and beyond the city is the snow-capped Wasatch Range, one of the world's tallest and most impressive fault scarps.
*Two photographs, Keith Ardinger*

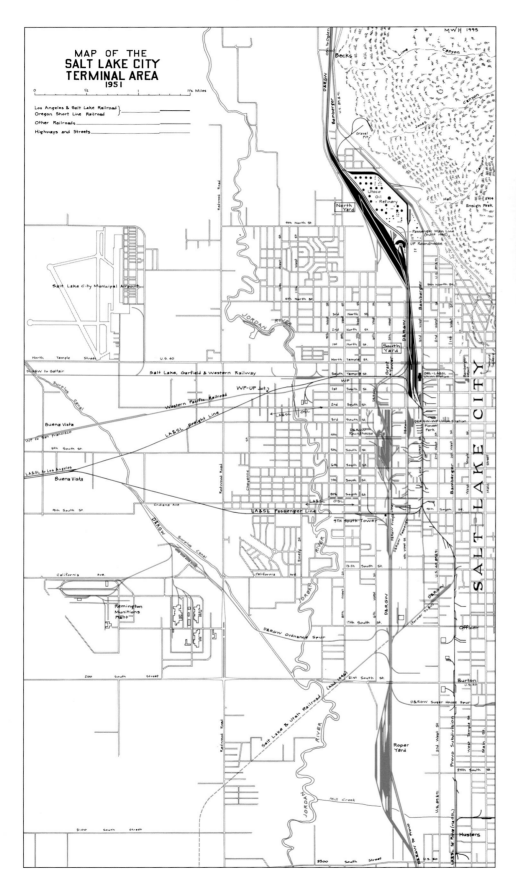

## The Provo Subdivision: Utah's Pittsburgh

*When Abraham Lincoln said, "Utah will yet become the treasure-house of the nation," he could hardly have realized that one day the state would have the largest open-pit mine in the world.*
—Leonard J. Arrington, historian of the Church of Jesus Christ of Latter-Day Saints, 1963

Bypassed by the Leamington Cut-off in 1903, the 134.1-mile Provo Subdivision has largely been forgotten by railroad history. Because the streamliners, fruit blocks, and stock trains all ran via the shorter, flatter, straighter, and faster cut-off, historians have often characterized the Provo Subdivision as a lengthy industrial spur or quaint branch line. That characterization is naive. Although the subdivision has always subsisted on local business, it is an extremely heavy local business to and from steel mills, smelters, sugar factories, chemical plants, and ancillary industries, plus coal from the Rio Grande and the Utah Railway at Provo, all in a concentration unparalleled in the Rocky Mountain West. This business put flesh on the LA&SL's scrawny bones.

By 1869–70 Utah's major metal deposits had all been discovered; what was needed was a railroad to make mining profitable. That was provided by the Utah Central and the Utah Southern. During the 1870s three large smelters began refining lead and silver ores at Murray. Utah's silver production exploded from 1,750 ounces in 1869 to 1.7 million ounces in 1871, and 4.4 million ounces in 1876. By 1876 Utah was producing 20 to 50 percent of the nation's lead, and 13 percent of its silver. By 1900 Murray and neighboring Midvale had become the West's smelting center, providing Utah's railroads a sizable business in coal, ore, and refined metals.

Refining of rich sulphide copper ores from Bingham Canyon began in 1899–1900 with the erection of the Highland Boy, Bingham Consolidated, and U.S. Smelting, Refining & Mining Co. smelters at Midvale. In 1904 the OSL built the 1.5-mile U.S. Smelter Spur (now the Dahl Spur) from Atwoods under the Rio Grande main line to reach all three. The location of these smelters is doubtless the reason that the division between the OSL and the SPLA&SL was made 13 miles south of Salt Lake City at Sandy instead of a more obvious place such as south Salt Lake City. Harriman was not going to share any more goodies with Clark than he had to.

The copper smelters emitted enormous quantities of sulfur-and arsenic-containing smoke, which poisoned livestock and devastated crops in the valley. The affected farmers successfully sued the smelters for damages, forcing them by 1908 to either close down or install bag houses to capture the fumes. By using bag houses, American Smelting & Refining Co. (ASARCO) ran its Murray smelter until 1950, and U.S. Smelting ran its Midvale smelter until June 1958 and its adjacent concentrator into the late 1960s. The Highland Boy and Bingham Consolidated smelters closed. In 1906 Utah Copper Co. and Boston Consolidated Mining Co. each built a huge copper concentrator at Magna to process low-grade porphyry copper ores from

Bingham Canyon, their concentrates traveling a short distance to ASARCO's huge new copper smelter at Garfield. Utah Copper absorbed Boston Consolidated in 1910, remodeled Boston Consolidated's Arthur concentrator, and enlarged its own Magna concentrator, to process 18,000 tons of ore a day. By 1943 this had increased to over 100,000 tons a day. International Smelting & Refining Co. (an Anaconda subsidiary) built a 4,000-ton-per-day lead-zinc-copper smelter at Tooele in 1909–15, and Combined Metals Reduction Co. opened a 1,000-ton-per-day lead-zinc concentrator at Bauer in 1925. These concentrators and smelters furnished a business to the LA&SL that for many years dwarfed its transcontinental business.

Utah Copper's Bingham Canyon operations grew so fast that in 1917 the LA&SL and WP had to relocate their main lines between Smelter and Buena Vista to make room for the Magna and Arthur concentrators' tailings pond. Kennecott Copper, which absorbed Utah Copper in 1941, purchased ASARCO's Garfield Smelter in 1959. Bingham Canyon is still the nation's largest copper mine.

Closure of the Bauer concentrator in 1958, the Tooele smelter in 1972, and Anaconda's Carr Fork Project above Tooele in 1982 (which killed the Tooele Valley Railway) made Kennecott's Garfield Smelter the last big smelter in Utah. It is still a big shipper, producing over 700 tons of copper daily (16.4 percent of the U.S. total in 1983), plus 350,000 ounces of gold, 2.5 million ounces of silver, and 8 million pounds of molybdenum annually. The sulfur that once poisoned farms is recovered from the stack and made into about 1,000 tons of sulfuric acid daily. More sulfuric acid is manufactured in the U.S. than any other industrial chemical, 73.6 billion

pounds in 1986; about 60 percent is used to make fertilizer from phosphate rock, the rest for automotive batteries, petroleum production and refining, steel making, etc. Conveniently for the UP, several large phosphate fertilizer plants are located in southern Idaho, and another at Garfield.

ABOVE LEFT: During October 1973, the helper on the Provo Turn runs through the intersection of 3rd West and 3rd South Streets, past the Rio Grande-Western Pacific Salt Lake City Union Depot. The GP30 is loafing here, but will be called upon at Murray for help up to Mount Summit. At Provo the turn will drop its cars, put its caboose on a train already assembled by the Provo yard switcher, and high-ball back to Salt Lake City with the same crew.

ABOVE: The Passenger Line to Los Angeles and the Provo Subdivision are combined as they leave UP's Salt Lake City Union Station. Two blocks south of the station they swing onto (old) 3rd West Street, and run down the middle of the street for seven blocks. Just north of 9th South Street the Passenger Line turns west for Los Angeles and the Provo Subdivision swings southeast onto private right-of-way. During May 1972, new leaves sprout from the box elders in Pioneer Park as a Provo Turn rolls south (railroad west) on 3rd West Street behind five SD24's, "not exceeding 12 mph." The UP station can be seen in the background. *Two photographs, Keith Ardinger*

In the great scheme the Rio Grande was dwarfed by the UP, except between Provo and Salt Lake City where the Rio Grande ran a main line and the UP a secondary line. The difference between the two lines was striking. Where UP's Provo Sub trains struggled over Mount Summit, a mile to the west Rio Grande's fast freights glided through Jordan Narrows on a water-level line. The Rio Grande double-tracked between Salt Lake City and Midvale in 1903 and between Provo and Geneva in 1944, and put in CTC from Provo to Midvale in 1929 (a very early CTC installation) and from Midvale to Roper in 1937. The UP, by comparison, did not add a single block signal to the Provo Subdivision until it installed 6.0 miles of CTC between Provo and Geneva in 1951.

The two railroads seldom missed a chance to tweak each other. In 1923 when the LA&SL built the Ironton Spur across Rio Grande's main line to reach Columbia Steel's new blast furnace, the Rio Grande made it build an interlocking at the crossing. In 1923 Ironton was the only place a Rio Grande train saw anything other than a train-order signal in 623 miles from Salt Lake City to Pueblo, Colorado—which probably amused the Rio Grande.

In 1983 the Great Salt Lake began rising to its highest level in recorded history, with no end in sight. Rio Grande's Salt Lake City to Ogden main line, closer to the lake than UP's, started to sink into the mud and waves commenced to lap onto its embankment. Rio Grande trains

began detouring over the UP. The Rio Grande had a flatter, faster route between Salt Lake City and Provo, so a swap was arranged. On July 6, 1985, in exchange for trackage rights between Salt Lake City and Ogden, the Rio Grande granted the UP trackage rights over its 6th Subdivision, Utah Division, from milepost 700.6 in Provo to milepost 743.5 (13th South Street) in Salt Lake City. About 2.5 miles of Rio Grande and UP main line from 13th South Street to Grant Tower were combined as joint double track. After this date the UP kept the Provo Subdivision in service to reach local customers between Salt Lake City and Provo, but as much as possible UP's through trains and the iron-ore trains from Minnesota to Geneva began using the Rio Grande main line.

Worsening congestion along Utah's Interstate 15 corridor made the Utah Transit Authority investigate rail alternatives in the 1990s. On March 31, 1993, the authority purchased UP's Provo Subdivision from milepost P-775.19, the Utah County line at Mount, to milepost P-798.84, its connection with the Passenger Line in Salt Lake City, as a right-of-way for a proposed light rail line. Also on March 31, the Salt Lake City Southern Railroad, a RailTex short line, leased the same segment (which includes the Dahl Spur) for freight operation. Light rail may happen someday, though Salt Lake County's voters recently turned down a sales tax intended to fund its construction. In the meantime, the Salt Lake City Southern has doubled

the business the UP had on this track to about 160 cars a month. Utah Transit Authority also has an option to purchase the Provo Subdivision from Mount to Lindon, just south (railroad west) of Pleasant Grove.

AT LEFT: On February 24, 1978, UP's Provo Turn has stabbed two Rio Grande trains at Lakota Crossing. For some reason the eastbound UP could not get a signal at the interlocking, so the head brakeman walked down to the box and punched the button, but nothing happened except reds on Rio Grande's two-track main line. Apparently he was unaware of the instructions, to the effect of "if any of these push-buttons is operated, all signals at the plant are placed on Stop immediately." About 15 minutes later two Rio Grande hotshots showed up and had to stop. Eventually Rio Grande's dispatcher straightened out the mess by giving the UP train a Permissive Card, and now the UP brakeman climbs aboard as the engineer revs up his SD45 and two DD35's.

Lakota Crossing was an eternal pain. Originally all trains came to a stop before proceeding. When the Rio Grande installed CTC from Provo to Midvale in 1929, the crossing was left out, because the Utah Public Utilities Commission refused to allow automatic interlockings unless they included derails! The Rio Grande finally succeeded in installing a GRS interlocking at Lakota in September 1931, but the diamond was limited to 25 mph because of the frog's sharp angle: 8°20'. Movable-point frogs installed in March 1943 eliminated the speed restriction, at the price of maintenance. An extra complication was the circuitry allowing UP and Rio Grande trains to switch in the vicinity of the crossing without tripping it. In December 1985, just after the UP began using its Rio Grande trackage rights, the Rio Grande ripped out the crossing and installed switches from the UP onto the Rio Grande, much to the relief of all concerned. *Doug Harrop*

ABOVE: The UP leased two SD38's from the McCloud River Railroad from April 1988 through May 1989 to help out during a system power shortage. On July 9, 1988, they are on the LUF51, the Provo Turn, climbing the south (railroad west) side of Mount Summit at milepost P-772.8, about two and a half miles from the top. The two UP units are no help; they are dead-in-tow, en route to the Salt Lake City shop. By 1988 a train over Mount was rare in the extreme; the reason for this one was a maintenance window on Rio Grande's main line that afternoon. *James Belmont*

AT RIGHT, TWO PHOTOGRAPHS: On a crisp morning, October 7, 1974, the 100-car MIGW (Minntac, Minnesota, to Geneva Ore) blasts out of Draper on the 1.14 percent to Mount, exhaust pluming into the autumn air. Five of UP's eight SD40X's (and a U30C) are on the MIGW, which was a regular assignment for the SD40X's. The 3040 is helping. The Geneva ore-train helper operation was one big reason the UP wanted onto Rio Grande's main line. *Kenneth Ardinger*

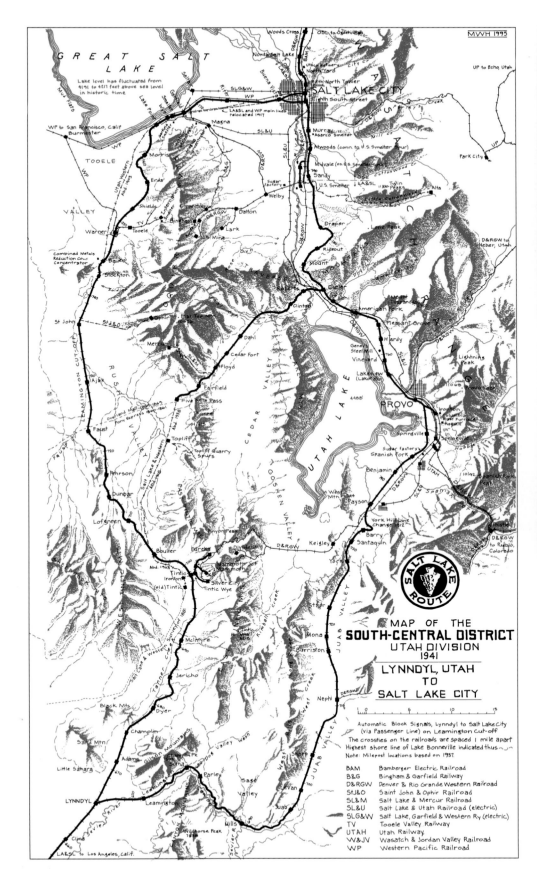

MAP OF THE
**SOUTH-CENTRAL DISTRICT**
UTAH DIVISION
1941
**LYNNDYL, UTAH**
TO
**SALT LAKE CITY**

Automatic Block Signals, Lynndyl to Salt Lake City
(via Passenger Line) on Leamington Cut-off
The crossties on the railroads are spaced 1 mile apart
Highest shore line of Lake Bonneville indicated thus▨
Note: Milepost locations based on 1937.

| | |
|---|---|
| BAM | Bamberger Electric Railroad |
| B&G | Bingham & Garfield Railway |
| D&RGW | Denver & Rio Grande Western Railroad |
| StJ&O | Saint John & Ophir Railroad |
| SL&M | Salt Lake & Mercur Railroad |
| SL&U | Salt Lake & Utah Railroad (electric) |
| SLG&W | Salt Lake, Garfield & Western Ry (electric) |
| TV | Tooele Valley Railway |
| UTAH | Utah Railway |
| W&JV | Wasatch & Jordan Valley Railroad |
| WP | Western Pacific Railroad |

Mining and smelting were by no means the only industries to set roots along the Wasatch Front. The Provo Woolen Mills operated from 1869 through 1932, and Utah's vegetable and dairy farms supported many canning and evaporated-milk plants. By 1914 Utah ranked fifth in the U.S. in production of canned goods, most of which were shipped by rail. In 1891 the first successful beet sugar factory in the Intermountain West opened at Lehi, on a site served by the OSL&UN and Rio Grande Western. Its success spawned more sugar factories throughout Utah, all requiring round-the-clock rail service during the fall beet campaigns, and consuming large quantities of coal and lime. By 1915 Utah was the third largest sugar-producing state in the U.S. Other sugar factories served by the LA&SL, and their dates of operation, were at Payson, 1913–25; Spanish Fork, 1916–42 (via trackage rights on the Rio Grande from Springville); and Delta, 1917–24. The Lehi plant closed in 1939; large-scale sugar-beet farming ceased in Utah in 1979.

During and after World War II, Utah's skilled labor, inexpensive land, and status as a rail hub brought the military to central Utah. Military facilities expanded or opened during the war included Ogden Arsenal; Utah General Depot (near Ogden), the largest quartermaster depot in the U.S.; Hill Field south of Ogden; a U.S. Navy supply depot at Clearfield; the Tooele Army Depot; and a Remington ammunition plant in Salt Lake City. The Geneva steel plant was built as a war plant (more about Geneva later). Sperry Rand Corp., Marquardt Corp., and Thiokol Chemical came to Utah in 1956–57, where they joined Hercules Powder in building missile components.

ABOVE LEFT: At 6:25 P.M. on September 21, 1992, the afternoon Provo switch engine ambles railroad east along Pacific Drive in American Fork with lumber loads, scrap gons, and a single covered hopper for local customers. These towns are built on gravel washed out of the mountains by melting glaciers. The sediments run about 13,000 feet deep in Utah Valley, but Utah Lake itself is no more than 18 feet deep. The end of through freights over Point of the Mountain (Mount Summit) in 1985 created the need for local service between Geneva and Cutler performed by UP's Provo switch crew; previously, the road freights did this work. *David P. Oroszi*

BELOW LEFT: On May 9, 1993, the giant OMIGV (Ore, Minntac, Minnesota, to Geneva) train slowly backs its 107 loads of taconite pellets across the scale at the south end of Geneva Steel's A Yard. This train typically ran three or more times weekly until August 21, 1994, when SP took over the contract. Behind the train is Lone Peak, an 11,523-foot intrusion of Tertiary granite into very old Precambrian rocks, which accounts for its atypically jagged ridges. At left are Geneva Steel's three blast furnaces. Geneva Steel's recently installed air-pollution control equipment has greatly reduced smog in the Utah Valley; for a view of what the valley's air used to look like, see the photograph at Lakota on the previous page. *James Belmont*

ABOVE: Extra 2528 East rolls through the undulating farmland between the towns of American Fork and Lehi on October 27, 1985, about a month before the end of through freight service via Mount. The town of American Fork, settled in 1850, is in the background; Mount Timpanogos is at left. In 1873 the Mormon men of these towns built this line for the good of their church and communities.

Extra 2528 East is a junk manifest from Milford, with loaded cement hoppers billed to Utah Cement's transload spur near Murray, five miles south (railroad west) of Salt Lake City. Eastbounds on the Provo Sub in the mid-1980s often had a block of these cars at the head end, which were picked up at Ash Grove Cement at Martmar. Built in the early 1980s by Martin-Marietta Cement to supply cement to the huge Intermountain Power Project at Lynndyl, Martmar now ships cement via the UP to Salt Lake City, Las Vegas, and Los Angeles. *James Belmont*

From 1905 through World War II, Utah was the smelting capital of the U.S., if not the world: in 1919, the Salt Lake Valley produced 4.45 million tons of copper, lead, zinc, silver, and gold. Converted into 50-ton boxcar loads, every day that year Utah's railroads had to haul away 244 boxcars loaded with metal. Thousands of carloads of ore, coal, and coke went into the smelters and concentrators every day. (This wealth came at a price; for several years now UP and Rio Grande have hauled "dirty dirt" trains from the smelter sites at Murray and Midvale to dumps at East Carbon City and Grassy Mountain, Utah.)

After 1950 the smelter traffic began to dwindle, except for Kennecott. But the Provo Subdivision became more important to the UP than ever. Steel, iron ore, and coal traffic to Geneva made up for the smelters, and in 1980 unprecedented tonnages of coal began pouring out of Spanish Fork Canyon on the Rio Grande and the Utah Railway, most of it inter-changed to the UP at Provo for forwarding to southern California. For a century the dark territory from Provo to Lynndyl seldom had more than 4 to 6 trains a day. In 1980 it suddenly it had 16 or more. When the huge Intermountain Power Project (IPP) at Lynndyl started up in 1986, it alone demanded 2 trains daily. In 1982–83, UP spent $9.8 million to install CTC between Provo and Lynndyl, with controlled sidings at Payson, Starr, Nephi, Sharp, Juab, and Parley. By the mid-1980s UP had relaid most of the subdivision west of Provo with second-hand 133-pound continuous welded rail. Today about 50,000 tons of coal roll west from Provo every day. Coal is not as glamorous as the main line's expedited fruit blocks, stock trains, or double-stacks, but in terms of tonnage the "secondary" Provo Subdivision has always been the tail that wagged the dog.

ABOVE: At 8:15 P.M. on May 29, 1993, an 84-car CUWIP coal train emerges from dark shadows in Leamington Canyon and heads into the setting sun at milepost P-668, two miles east of Lynndyl. For the last 45 minutes, this train has been winding downgrade in the canyon; now its two SD60's and two DASH 8-40C's throttle up for one last effort, 1.5 miles of 1.0 percent up into Lynndyl. The CUWIP will tie up the main line for only a few minutes before leaving on the 8.9-mile IPP spur, which leads to the middle-of-nowhere Intermountain Power Project. Intermountain painted the lower halves of its aluminum IPPX cars black because of unloading difficulties during the winter, when wet coal freezes in transit. Sunlight absorbed by the black paint usually produces just enough warmth to keep the coal from freezing to the sides of the cars. This train loaded at Wildcat, on the Utah Railway. *Dave Gayer*

ABOVE RIGHT: Late on April 9, 1990, an IPP coal load roars underneath Rio Grande's Tintic Branch at milepost P-735.76, just west of Payson. The Tintic Branch serves a quarry that supplies Geneva Steel with limestone and dolomite. At left is Provo Peak, 11,068 feet tall and 6,500 feet higher than the Utah Valley floor. Its summit ridge arcs southeast into Corral Mountain.

This overpass marks the beginning of York Hill, 8.5 miles of 1.0 percent (compensated) that takes the Provo Subdivision over the divide between the Utah Valley and the Juab Valley. As built by the Utah Southern in 1875, the track just went straight up the hill on 5 miles of 1.5 percent. A 1913 line change between the D&RGW overpass and current milepost P-727.2 reduced the grade with a horseshoe curve on the east side of the valley. The 6° curve turns through 163°39', but since it is buried in apple orchards it is difficult to recognize its presence except from the air. York siding, now gone, was at the top of its namesake hill, where the Utah Southern ran out of rails in 1875. *Tom Moungovan*

BELOW RIGHT: A cold night at Provo, January 26, 1978, finds a collection of UP's lesser power idling in front of the joint LA&SL–Utah Railway locomotive shop, built in 1921. A mostly vacant shell by this time, it was torn down in September 1981. In UP's SD40-2 era Provo was the dustbin for some of its oddball power. TR5's, GP20's, GP30's, SD24's, DD35's, SD45's, A-units and B-units—sooner or later they all came to Provo to stumble through their last miles.

When the Utah Railway opened for business on July 1, 1914, it became in effect UP's extension into Utah's Wasatch Plateau coalfield. The LA&SL and the Utah Railway jointly owned 2,000 "Utah Coal Route" drop-bottom coal gondolas, built a joint yard in Provo in 1917, and opened a joint shop in Provo in 1921. The Utah's 2-10-2's, 2-8-8-0's and cabooses were built to UP designs. The preponderance of the Utah's coal has always gone to the UP at Provo. Nevertheless, the UP has never had any ownership stake in the Utah Railway, which was built and owned by the U.S. Smelting, Refining & Mining Co. The Utah Railway is now a subsidiary of Arava Natural Resources, a descendant of U.S. Smelting. The interchange relationship between the Utah and the UP at Provo has always been very close, yet much of the coal the Rio Grande brings to Provo goes to the UP as well. Also, the Provo depot was a Rio Grande and Salt Lake Route union depot from September 1, 1909, until it was dismantled in October 1986. *James Belmont*

## UTAH CENTRAL: OGDEN TO SALT LAKE CITY

*Don't forget brethren, it is the kingdom we are laboring for, and that the building of the [Utah Central] railroad is one of the greatest achievements ever accomplished by the Latter-Day Saints.*
—John W. Young, December 28, 1869

By 1906 the 35-year-old Utah Central line from Ogden to Salt Lake City could no longer handle the business funneled to it by the newly completed SPLA&SL and the OSL, so the OSL began to completely rebuild and double-track it. That spring the OSL began building the 4.29-mile Sandy Ridge Cut-off, which replaced 4.24 miles of old main line between Ogden and Roy. The cut-off, opened for traffic on December 10, 1906, entered the Ogden terminal via a new bridge over the Weber River, so the connection was named Bridge Junction. The old line was used as a second main track until December 29, 1915, when the OSL downgraded it to become the Evona Branch.

In 1908 OSL began installing double-track from North Yard in Salt Lake City to Ogden, completing 7.5 miles to Woods Cross in 1909. Also in 1909, the OSL installed ABS between Salt Lake City and Bridge Junction via the Sand Ridge Cut-off, using US&S Style B lower-quadrant, two-arm semaphores. Working eastward from Woods Cross, the OSL completed 5.71 miles of second track in 1910; 6.79 miles in 1911; 5.38 miles in 1912; and 15.20 miles to Bridge Junction in 1913, using an almost all-new alignment between Farmington and Roy. The Shepard Lane Line Change of 1911 eased curves north of Farmington where the Utah Central

had wound around an alluvial fan that extends from the Wasatch into the Great Salt Lake. Another 6-mile line change removed the main line from the business districts of Layton and Clearfield. The two-arm semaphores were respaced in 1938 for increased stopping distances, and were replaced with color-lights during the late 1940s. In 1974–75 the UP upgraded the double-track ABS to CTC.

Prior to World War II, UP's principal customers between Utah's two largest cities were sugar-beet factories at Layton and West Ogden. Since World War II, its principal customers have been the largest petroleum refining complex in the intermountain West. At present, Amoco at Salt Lake City and Chevron at North Salt Lake each refine 45,000 barrels of crude a day, Flying J at North Salt Lake refines 15,000 barrels daily, and Phillips 66 at Woods Cross refines 20,000 barrels daily. The Amoco refinery was built by Utah Oil Refining Co. (later Utah Oil Co., or Utoco) in 1909. Utoco relied upon crude oil delivered by the UP in tank cars until it built a pipeline to Wyoming oil fields in 1939. Utoco's Vico oil and Pep 88 gasoline were distributed by rail throughout Utah and Idaho. The Woods Cross refinery dates to 1932 and the Chevron and Flying J refineries to 1948–49. In 1948 all four refineries began receiving most of their crude by pipeline from the Rangely Field at Rangely, Colorado. While the UP had lost the crude-oil haul, it was not a total loss, since the UP owned 76 percent of the Rangely Field. Discovered in 1945, UP's share of Rangely's production zoomed to 3.6 million barrels in 1951, but faded to 2 million barrels by 1962. The UP sold its share of the Rangely Field for $62 million in 1963. The UP still has large stakes in western Wyoming and northeastern Utah oil fields.

Utah is usually thought of as a coal state, not an oil state, but since 1960 its oil fields and its refineries have usually produced more Btu's of energy than Utah's coal mines. The UP is usually thought of as a railroad, not an oil company, but since World War II its oil and gas wells have contributed from one-fourth to one-half of the company's net income.

ABOVE LEFT: On July 4, 1992, the OAAP (Oakland to Chicago APL) gains speed as it leaves Salt Lake City. At far left is UP's Salt Lake City TOFC ramp. The COFC ramp, built in 1964 as an auto ramp, is just beyond I-15 in the background. Autos are now handled at a large ramp built at Clearfield in 1985. At right is Rio Grande's Salt Lake City–Ogden main line and Chevron's refinery. Rio Grande's trains to and from Ogden enter the UP main line at North Salt Lake Crossover, just to the right of this photograph; Rio Grande locals continue to Woods Cross to switch Phillips 66. The distant, dirty scar seen through the refinery stacks is part of Kennecott Copper's Bingham Canyon Mine. UP's customers in the Salt Lake City area currently receive or ship approximately 140,000 carloads annually–some 400 carloads a day. *James Belmont*

BELOW LEFT: At 7:00 A.M. on July 3, 1978, GP20 486 and SD7 455 head railroad-east at LA&SL milepost 806, just south of Clearfield, after switching the refineries and other industries between Salt Lake City and Ogden. The OSL's ex-Utah Central mileposts began at Ogden and counted upward to Salt Lake City, continuing to meet the LA&SL at Sandy and at the Jordan River west of Salt Lake City. In the late 1970s, LA&SL mileposts replaced them. The Freight Line mileposts now continue east to Ogden Wye, milepost 817.2, erasing one more trace of the Utah Central. At the same time the Provo Sub milepost numbers received a "P" prefix. *Bruce Barrett*

ABOVE: As evening shadows lengthen on August 15, 1976, the 14,000-ton Atlantic City ore train pulls slowly out of Ogden en route to Geneva behind one-year-old U30C's. Bridge Junction is below the white Sperry Division of General Mills flour mill in the background. The sandy cut in the background was the namesake of the Sandy Ridge Cut-off. *Keith Ardinger*

## THE OGDEN UNION RAILWAY & DEPOT CO.

*A couple of months ago the eye, in glancing over the depot grounds, saw a dreary, swampy flat with a few rickety frame buildings erroneously called "depot," and a hole in the ground where a depot really should stand. Now these shanties are hidden from view by the beautiful structure being reared in front of them, about a block nearer the city.*
— *Ogden Standard,* January 1889

Big things happened at Ogden, where the Union Pacific and the Southern Pacific exchanged dozens of trains every day on the Overland Route. The UP and SP laid out Ogden to speed the east-west transfer, leaving the OSL to enter and leave Ogden almost as an afterthought via tangled crossovers at Bridge Junction at one end and at Cecil Junction at the other.

Neither the Union Pacific nor the Central Pacific wanted to connect in the wilderness at Promontory. The real question was whether to fix the junction at the Mormon town of Ogden or the Gentile town of Corinne. Ogden was the junction with the Utah Central; Corinne was the jumping-off point for Montana's mining camps. Brigham Young sweetened the pot for Ogden by giving the UP and CP 131 acres of land at Ogden free of charge. Young, perhaps the most intelligent and farseeing leader the West has ever seen, included a proviso that the land be used for a joint terminal or given back, which guaranteed that the UP and CP could not take

the land and later move their terminal to Corinne without penalty. Corinne's shameless boosterism was to no avail, but to create an appearance of impartiality, the UP and CP agreed to build a joint terminal known as Junction City 5 miles west of Ogden. An act of Congress confirmed this location on May 6, 1870. In November 1869 the UP sold its 47.5 miles of track from Promontory to Junction City to the CP. While the two railroads drew up plans for a terminal at Junction City, they unofficially created a terminal at Ogden. To get around Congress, the UP leased the 5.0 miles of track from Ogden to Junction City to the CP for 999 years (the SP still has about 0.81 miles of first main track and 0.16 miles of second main track at Cecil Junction leased from the UP).

By 1874 Junction City was a dying idea; neither railroad was about to build an expensive new terminal on this mud flat. The Utah Central and Utah Northern connections at Ogden made the decision final. But neither could the UP and CP agree how to go about improving the ramshackle facilities at Ogden. In September 1886 UP's patrician president, Charles Francis Adams, could not bear this any longer, and ordered work to begin on a new Ogden depot. An excavation was dug and a foundation laid, then work stopped while Adams browbeat the CP into forming the jointly owned Ogden Union Railway & Depot Co., the UP and CP signing the papers on September 19, 1888. The UP and CP gave the OUR&D title to the 131 acres of jointly owned depot grounds they had received from Brigham Young, and resumed

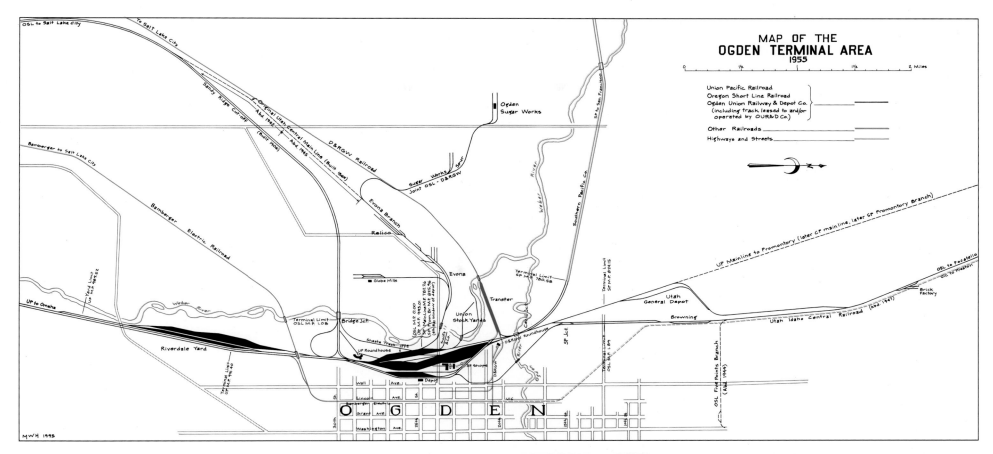

MAP OF THE
**OGDEN TERMINAL AREA**
1955

Union Pacific Railroad
Oregon Short Line Railroad
Ogden Union Railway & Depot Co.
(including track leased to and/or
operated by OUR&D Co.)

Other Railroads
Highways and Streets

building the new red sandstone-and-brick depot the next month. The depot opened on July 31, 1889. Thereafter the OUR&D operated the yard and depot, but each road retained its own engine facilities and supplied switch engines to OUR&D. Junction City, Corinne, and the lineage of the 131 acres underneath the yard were all forgotten.

The UP began switching the yard under contract to OUR&D in the mid-1960s, and in March 1968 the OUR&D clerks signed an agreement that sent them to either the SP or UP. The OUR&D is still in existence, however, and still contracts switching at Ogden to the UP. After the UP-MP-WP merger of 1982, the historic UP-SP transfer at Ogden virtually disappeared. Bitter competitors ever since, the UP and SP would very much like to get out of their marriage at Ogden, but thanks to Brigham Young no divorce is possible. If the UP and SP ever cease using Ogden as a joint terminal, i.e., if the OUR&D is dissolved, the 131 acres underneath what is now one of UP's principal yards reverts to the descendants of the nine Mormon families who held title to it when Brigham Young gave it to the Central Pacific and Union Pacific in January 1869!

LEFT: In 1927, the UP built a new engine facility at Ogden including a 20-stall brick roundhouse, 100-foot turntable, 350-ton coaling station, and brick machine shop. A 135-foot turntable was installed in 1941 and 9 stalls in the roundhouse were extended in 1942 to accommodate the 4-8-8-4's that the UP had just begun running on the Wasatch grade east of Ogden. On August 26, 1960, steam has been gone from Ogden's roundhouse less than two years. In place of 800s, 3900s, and 4000s are solid sets of one-year-old SD24's and one-month-old GP20's still wearing their original 700-series numbers. These were UP's only EMDs with the panoramic one-piece windshields, another nice-to-have feature soon abolished in pursuit of economy.

RIGHT: On November 21, 1962, five new GP30's wait with their eastbound train for a crew. The location is the east end of East Yard, now called Riverdale Yard, built in 1953–54 to block eastbound traffic off the SP (the Main Yard was rearranged to handle westbound traffic). *Two photographs, W. A. Gibson, Sr. (collection of W. A. Gibson, Jr.)*

## Montana Main Line: Ogden to McCammon

*It must be remembered that a cheaply constructed line can be rebuilt, but with a badly located line nothing can be done except to abandon it entirely.* —Thomas Curtis Clarke, civil engineer, 1890

The Utah & Northern from Ogden to Butte, Montana, as completed in 1881, was a classic Jay Gould gold-rush railroad: really cheap, inadequate the day it was built, a 416-mile narrow-gauge abomination. The daily first-class passenger of 1883 wheeled over the road to Butte in 26 hours and 10 minutes, averaging 17 mph. In 1889 the OSL&UN had had enough, and began building a new standard-gauge line between Ogden and McCammon on a practically all-new grade. The Mormon farmers who built the Utah Northern had laid a winding track over Collinston

Divide between Dewey and Mendon on 2.2-percent grades to save money. The OSL&UN bypassed this hill with an expensive new low-grade line from Dewey to Oxford running through Bear River Canyon, a narrow slit between the Wellsville Mountains and Gunsight Peak. From Oxford to McCammon the OSL&UN built an all-new grade adjacent to the old. The standard-gauge main was cut in on October 1, 1890, reducing the ruling grade westward to McCammon to 0.70 percent, and eastward to Ogden to 0.67 percent.

This line fed many cars of livestock and lumber to southern California, as well as ore to Utah's smelters. During the fall sugar-beet campaign traffic got quite heavy. The OSL installed ABS from Ogden to Cache Junction in 1913, using US&S Style B two-position lower-quadrant semaphores wired on the overlap principle. The OSL extended the ABS from Cache Junction to McCammon in 1917–18, but instead of the usual US&S Style B semaphores competitor GRS supplied similar Type 2A semaphores. In 1948–49 the UP spent $1.5 million to lengthen sidings

and replace the oil-lamp semaphores with US&S Style P-3 color-light signals wired on the APB principle. Track Warrant Control has since replaced train orders.

Since the 1950s the UP has made few major changes to what is now part of the Cheyenne Service Unit. It is now laid with second-hand 115-pound and 133-pound continuous welded rail. The southbound livestock redballs are long gone, but the tonnage balance is still tilted south. Usually two trains each way daily suffice to haul the line's mostly carload business: lumber, potatoes, grain, and fertilizer south; and coal, merchandise, and chemicals north. There was also at one time a once-weekly "K" Line double-stack from Los Angeles to Portland, Oregon.

LEFT: The HKYR (Hinkle, Oregon, to Yermo) edges through the 12 mph curves of Bear River Canyon at milepost 49 between Cache Junction and Wheelon, nearing the west end of the canyon at 7:30 P.M. on June 25, 1990. Ten-degree curves and falling rock make this the slowest stretch of main line on the entire South-Central District, outside of a terminal or town. The track is pinned onto the face of Wellsville Mountain. Laboriously fitted stone retaining walls support the track where the mountain is too sheer for a ledge. Steel trestles at mileposts 45.04 and 45.89 span gulches too deep for retaining walls. *Scott Bontz*

ABOVE: Late on the afternoon of November 13, 1992, the jack-of-all-trades PCSC (Pocatello to Salt Lake City) sails through the sag at milepost 89 of the Ogden Subdivision. Although the 62-car PCSC has traveled only 45 miles since setting out from Pocatello early this morning, its crew are about to go dead, because the train was called upon to spread ballast en route. After a meet with the YRPC (Yermo to Pocatello) at Swan Lake, the PCSC will be recrewed at Cache Junction. The iron-stained basalt ramparts at right are what remains of the volcanic plug that blocked the Bear River, turning it south into the Great Salt Lake Valley and forming Lake Bonneville. The lake pushed through these cliffs about 14,500 years ago. A catastrophic flood lasting for about a year lowered the level of this inland sea by about 350 feet, and incidentally eliminated a great deal of animal and plant life in the Snake and Columbia River Basins. This gap is called Red Rock Pass. *Dave Gayer*

RIGHT: The morning sun on June 16, 1993, dispels the shadows in the Bear River Canyon at Cutler Reservoir just in time for a northbound freight to walk through the 12 mph zone north of Wheelon. Tunnel 15, sometimes called the Bear River Tunnel, is in the background shadows, and beyond that the end of the canyon. Cutler Dam supplies 30,000 kW of hydroelectric power to owner Utah Power & Light and stores irrigation water. Wheelon was named for J. C. Wheelon, superintendent of the Bear River Water Company, a Utah Sugar Co. subsidiary. *Doug Harrop*

# THE CACHE VALLEY: UTAH'S HEARTLAND

*The coming of the railroad, for the Mormon Country as for all the West, marks the end of an era.*
—Dale L. Morgan, historian, 1947

The Cache Valley is quintessential Mormon country. Never overrun by mining or heavy industry or big cities, it remains steadfastly a farming, grazing, and dairying valley. Settled by Mormons in 1859, for the next two decades the Cache Valley was often a terrible place to live. No one knew anything about dry farming, and the harvests were often so poor that farmers had to abandon their fields and move out. The Mormon families banded together to build irrigation dams and canals, but periodic invasions of grasshoppers between 1860 and 1879 wiped out as much as half of the valley's crops. Bitter cold winters and deep snow killed stock, early and late frosts killed crops, too much heat dried up the ditches, and too much rain tore apart the fragile irrigation works. It was not like television's sugar-coated farm families, where every Indian uprising or tornado is resolved in less than an hour with homilies and happy faces.

Railroad construction and mining in Utah, Idaho, and Montana brought the first prosperity the Cache Valley had ever seen: a hog purchased here for $36 could be sold to hungry Montana miners for $600. Many farmers worked on the grades of the Union Pacific, Central Pacific, and Utah Northern, making more money in a week than they could in an entire summer of dry farming. Construction of the Utah Northern into the valley in 1870–71 allowed the valley's wheat, butter, and eggs to travel to markets as far away as San Francisco. The perfection of dry-farming techniques in the 1880s increased wheat production from 235,000 bushels in 1880 to 1,500,000 in 1910. Income from cash crops, dairy products, cattle, and railroad grading financed more irrigation projects. Orchards were planted, and dairy cattle increased to 16,000 by 1910. Railroads made much of this prosperity possible, but it was a mixed blessing. Before the railroad Utah was an island surrounded by difficult seas, its fortunes rising and falling according only to nature, the skill of its farmers, and the wisdom of its leaders. After the railroad Utah was just a waystation on the international economic system, which cared not a whit for family or church or community, only the ability of Utah's farmers, miners, and workers to produce at a lower cost.

In the 1890s Cache Valley farmers began specializing in sugar beets, because they made more money per acre of land than any other crop. They shipped the beets by rail to the Ogden and Lehi factories; since freight charges amounted to about one-fourth of the $4 a ton the farmers were paid for the beets, in 1900 David Eccles incorporated the Logan Sugar Co. and the next year completed a 600-ton (daily capacity of sliced beets) sugar factory just south of Logan. The factory doubled in size by 1906, processing about 35,000 tons of beets during the intense fall beet campaign. Farther north, Lewiston Sugar Co. completed a factory at Lewiston in 1905. Both companies were brought into the Amalgamated Sugar Co. by 1904. High sugar prices during World War I inspired the construction of an independent factory at Cornish, and an Amalgamated factory at Smithfield, both opening in 1917. The collapse of sugar prices after the war closed these factories in 1919. Franklin County Sugar Co. built the last new factory in the Cache Valley, at Whitney in 1922. The obsolete Logan factory closed in 1926 because there were not enough beets grown in the valley to supply it and Amalgamated's modernized Lewiston factory.

In a good beet harvest, the OSL might carry 4,000 fifty-ton carloads of beets to Lewiston and Whitney (which explains why three different routes across the valley were necessary) and about 800 boxcars loaded with 100-pound bags of sugar out of the valley, very good business for 68 miles of branch-line trackage. The sugar factories also consumed a sizable tonnage of coal and limestone. After World War II the valley's sugar beet business became less profitable every year. The Whitney factory closed in 1962, Lewiston in 1972, and beet growing ceased in 1979. The business that had defined Cache Valley railroading for nearly 80 years was finished.

Beets were not the whole story, however. There were also Carnation Milk's evaporated-milk plants, and several large fruit and vegetable canneries, these products moving by rail throughout the U.S. After World War II the availability of refrigeration enabled people to switch to fresh milk and vegetables, and frozen foods, curtailing the need for evaporated milk and canned goods. What was once the West's largest pea cannery at Smithfield now just makes tin cans. UP's outbound business at present includes wheat, inedible beef tallow, and empty tin cans; inbound business includes plastic pellets to a plant on Lewiston Sugar Spur and cardboard to Preston.

LEFT: On August 3, 1993, the Cache Valley Local passes one of the many small dairies in the Cache Valley, just south of Richmond. Six miles away on the other side of the valley lies the main line from Ogden to McCammon. The valley got its name from French trappers who cached beaver pelts here in the 1820s. *James Belmont*

BELOW: On June 25, 1990, the Cache Valley Local has tied up for the evening at Logan. At the time, the local started at Cache Junction on Monday mornings, with a unit set out by a northbound train, and spent the rest of the week working to Preston and Cache Junction on alternate days, returning each evening to Logan. On Fridays it returned its unit to Cache Junction, where a southbound train picked it up and took it to Salt Lake City for servicing. The Logan depot closed on January 13, 1986. The section gang used it until 1994, when it was sold. *Richard Kundert*

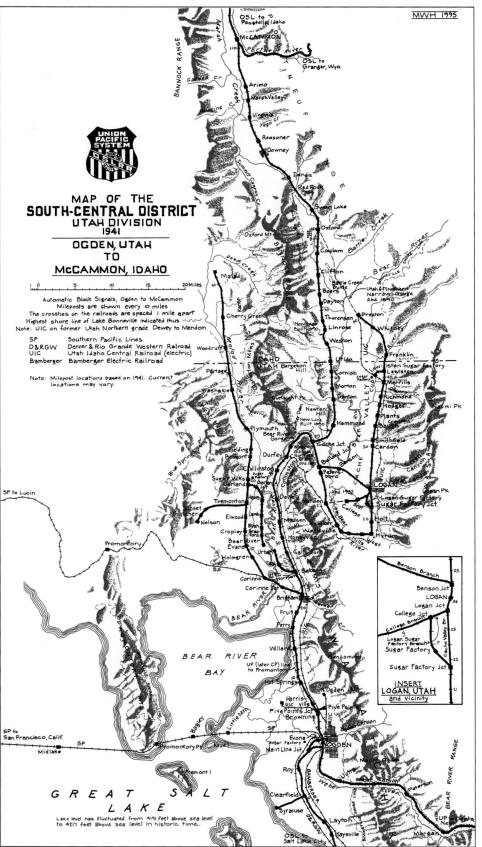

MAP OF THE
**SOUTH-CENTRAL DISTRICT**
UTAH DIVISION
1941
OGDEN, UTAH
TO
McCAMMON, IDAHO

# THE MALAD BRANCH

*The Church was successful in its endeavor to benefit the people and save this industry.*

—Charles W. Nibley, Presiding Bishop of the Mormon Church, 1916

Construction of a diversion dam on the Bear River just east of the Cache Divide and a large canal to carry the water into the Bear River Valley in 1889–90 made it possible to plant large acreages of thirsty sugar beets in the Bear River Valley by 1900. In 1901 the Utah Sugar Co. purchased the water project, began building a new 600-ton sugar factory at Garland, and the OSL built the Malad Valley Railroad to haul beets and sugar. The Amalgamated Sugar Co. built a sugar factory at Brigham City in 1916, closed it in 1920, then sold it to Utah–Idaho, which operated it sporadically until 1937. The OSL built numerous spurs, branches, and side tracks to load and ship beets to these factories, and to minimize time-consuming wagon hauls.

After 1901 Utah–Idaho Sugar and Amalgamated Sugar came under the control of American Sugar Refining Co. (ASR), "the Sugar Trust," which dominated sugar just as E. H. Harriman dominated railroads and Rockefeller dominated oil.

In 1914, under pressure from government trust-busters and imported cane sugar, ASR began thinking about closing its Utah beet factories. This raised a specter of widespread bankruptcy in Utah's agricultural communities, as Utah's once-diversified farmers and banks had invested very heavily in the expensive irrigation works required for extensive cultivation of sugar beets, as well as in the factories themselves, and could not have switched to less-profitable crops without going under. In May 1914 the Mormon church bought Utah–Idaho and Amalgamated from ASR. Critics of the church who claim it played too large a role in Utah's economy conveniently overlook this episode, when the church very likely saved many Utah farmers, banks, and merchants, Mormon and Gentile alike, from bankruptcy. The church operated both companies in unison until 1930, when it sold Amalgamated, and eventually its active role in Utah–Idaho's management diminished as well.

Utah-Idaho's Garland factory was very successful, and was enlarged to 2,500 tons daily capacity of sliced beets by 1965, a year when it consumed 173,000 tons of beets and produced 45,000 tons of sugar, much of this moving by rail. By 1979, however, beet sugar had lost so much of its market to cane sugar and corn sweeteners that the Garland factory closed for good, bringing UP's Utah sugar-beet traffic to a close.

ABOVE: On the evening of August 3, 1993, the Malad Local leaves Nucor Steel's modern mini-mill at Plymouth with loads of new steel. Nucor built the $4.5-million mill in 1979. The every-day-but-Sunday Malad Local hauls scrap to Nucor and old freight cars to the David Joseph Co. scrapyard next door, which cuts them up for Nucor. Once a week the local continues to Malad to pick up wheat, and once a week it drops off spent space-shuttle booster-rocket sections at Corinne for refueling. Thiokol's Brigham City plant, 20 miles west of Corinne, builds the solid-fuel booster rockets for the space shuttle. The 166-ton fueled booster sections are shipped by rail from Corinne to the Kennedy Space Center for final assembly. The first sections left Corinne in 1979. The beet-loading tracks that once sprouted from the Malad Branch like leaves from a corn stalk are all gone; now there is not a single siding or spur between Nucor and Malad, 20 miles.

ABOVE RIGHT: As a farmer works his fields and sheep graze on August 31, 1993, a 34-car Malad Local runs up the branch just south of the former siding of Elwood. The GP15-1 was used on a trial basis that week. It was a little light for the job; a steady diet of GP38's and GP39-2's has been the power of choice in recent years, replacing SD40's and SD40-2's.

Beyond the track are the Bear River's aimless meanders, then the imposing Wellsville Mountains, which separate the Bear River

and Cache Valleys. This range is an extension of the Wasatch Range, mountains uplifted several thousand feet along a 200-mile-long fault that remains very active to this day.

In the "old" days the country branch line had a variety of small customers: the feed mill, the lumber yard, the team track, the propane dealer, the grain elevator, and maybe a lumber mill or a chicken farm or a quarry. On the modern UP, branch lines of the one-great-big-plant variety or the big-city-industrial-district variety are all that remain. The Cache Valley Branch, with no truly large customers, will likely depart the system very soon. Nucor and Thiokol may make the difference for the Malad Branch, however.

BELOW RIGHT: On April 19, 1992, yearling Herefords graze in a field across the track from UP's Brigham City station. A former OSL station, it used locally cut stone for its walls and a carpenter's nightmare for a roof. It was the last old station in the state of Utah still owned by the UP. After its agency closed on January 13, 1986, the Malad Local crews used the station for an office and the section gang stored tools and supplies in its baggage room. The Golden Spike National Historic Site purchased the station on February 1, 1994, and hopes to use it for tourist trains, if and when the site is able to relay rail on 28 miles of the original Union Pacific (later Central Pacific, later still SP) grade from Promontory to Corinne. *Three photographs, James Belmont*

ABOVE: *Wm. (Hank) Mills (collection of Martha Mills)*　INSET: *Fred Matthews*

# PART III

# TOURIST TRAINS

## *Passenger Service on the South-Central District*

On the South-Central District, the Union Pacific fielded a complex and changing array of streamliners such as the *City of Los Angeles, City of St. Louis,* and the modern *Challenger* of 1954, luxurious heavyweights such as the *Los Angeles Limited,* pure tourist trains such as the prewar *The Challenger* and the summer-only *Park Special,* coach-only mail trains such as the *California Fast Mail,* accommodation trains such as the *Pony Express, Pacific Limited,* and *Butte Special,* traditional first-class trains such as the *Utahn* and *Transcontinental,* and the shorthaul *City of Las Vegas.* There were also the usual branch-line motor cars and mixed trains, which lost most of their business to autos by the 1930s. Until 1968, however, you could ride a combination car (later a caboose) on the regular Cache Valley and Malad Branch locals, and ride the caboose on the daily freight between Salt Lake City and Provo.

The Santa Fe (and to a lesser degree the SP) put up ferocious competition between the Midwest and Los Angeles. The UP-Santa Fe rivalry in no small way influenced the rapid development of lightweight streamlined trains and diesel-electric motive power in the 1930s, and forced both railroads to continually improve the quality of their service. Often the two roads matched each other's schedule to the minute, each other's price to the cent, and each other's service to the last fork in the diner. The winners of this battle were the passengers, who by the mid-1950s enjoyed service unsurpassed in quality and value whichever road they chose.

On May 15, 1936, the streamliner era on the South-Central District began with the departure from Los Angeles of the M-10002, the first *City of Los Angeles.* Its designers gave it an aerodynamic profile, and styled it with modern, understated elegance inside and out. Its extra fare and limited capacity–84 Pullman and 86 coach seats–made it an exclusive train for sophisticated people in search of a travel experience. Previously, UP's passenger service on the South-Central District had been rather uninspiring; now the UP had a train that could compete with Santa Fe's best. Five times monthly the *City of Los Angeles* "sailed" from Chicago and Los Angeles, arriving in the other city 39 hours 45 minutes later, at least 19 hours faster than UP's heavyweight *Los Angeles Limited.*

Nineteen months later the UP doubled its number of monthly sailings with the arrival of a second *City of Los Angeles,* consisting of E2's LA-1, 2 and 3, and 14 cars. Unlike the earlier custom streamliners, the second *City of Los Angeles* used separate locomotives and cars that could be switched in or out of trainsets. As the streamliner concept proved out, the UP began to cascade its earliest trainsets onto less-demanding runs, replacing them with new, improved, and enlarged trainsets. A remodeled M-10004, formerly the *City of San Francisco,* bumped the M-10002 on August 18, 1938. It featured an unusual porthole-windowed observation-lounge car called *Copper King,* an obscure reference to Senator William Clark. It traveled the LA&SL only until July 1941 when a new train powered by E2's LA-4, 5 and 6 replaced the M-10004 trainset.

After World War II, on June 2, 1946, the *City of Los Angeles* resumed its 39-hour 45-minute schedule. On May 14, 1947, the *City of Los Angeles* offered daily service for the first time, using four trainsets filled out with modernized heavyweight cars. By 1950 the UP had enough equipment on hand for five all-streamlined trainsets, and added dome diners and dome observations to the *City of Los Angeles* in 1955.

Tourists were at least as important on the South-Central District as businessmen. Here again the UP and Santa Fe scrapped for business with special packages. The UP offered tours to the Utah parks, Las Vegas, and even Boulder Dam when it was under construction, and ran through Pullmans to Cedar City (until 1958). Believing that better service might capture more tourists, the UP split the *Los Angeles Limited* in two on July 11, 1935. The first section reverted to an all-Pullman train. The second section became a high-quality tourist train, which on August 21 received its own name: *The Challenger.* The UP reserved at least one of *The Challenger's* air-conditioned coaches for women and children, provided low-cost tourist sleepers, porters in the coaches, and three meals for just 90 cents a day, eliminated the petty charges for drinking cups, pillows, and blankets, and most important, put passengers' needs first. Then the UP had another good idea, and on August 23, 1935, it added stewardess service, hiring young women who were registered nurses. Families liked *The Challenger* so much that it had about 300 passengers each way daily by 1937, and often more than 50 children were on board. *The Challenger* received modernized heavyweight cars in 1936, and began receiving new streamlined cars in 1938, testament to its success. The Santa Fe, of course, promptly created the similar *Scout.*

Despite its success, *The Challenger* had no place in UP's postwar scheme. UP's new president, George Ashby, wanted to operate only first-class trains on the long routes. In March 1947, he announced that UP would eliminate its tourist sleepers (and thus its tourist trains). "With the elimination of tourist cars, passengers will have their choice between Union Pacific streamliner service and modern coaches, and standard sleeping cars in regular trains," said Ashby. *Trains* magazine scarcely veiled its dismay that the UP now had nothing to offer "people who do not care to sit up on the three night transcontinental trains and yet cannot afford full first class." *The Challenger* disappeared on May 14, 1947, its place taken by the first-class *Utahn,* which in turn was replaced by the streamliner *City of St. Louis* on April 29, 1951. On January 10, 1954, the UP admitted its mistake and inaugurated a new all-coach, all-streamliner *Challenger,* trains 107 and 108, and dropped the heavyweight *Pony Express.* Like its earlier version, the new *Challenger* was low in cost and high in amenities–few tourist trains had dome coaches.

It was too late. Tourists now preferred the family station wagon to the train. A 1957 survey found that only 6.1 percent of Utah's tourists arrived by train. Beginning in 1956 the UP combined the *Challenger* with the *City of Los Angeles* from September 15 to June 1. After September 15, 1960, it became a second section of the *City of Los Angeles* on the infrequent occasions it ran separately, as was the case on July 11, 1964, when heavy holiday traffic justified an all-coach second #104 *Challenger,* its 19 cars and four E-units wrapping completely around Sullivan's Curve on Cajon Pass. Six years later, business was so thin that two people could find solitude in a dome car on the *City of Los Angeles.* On May 1, 1971, when the last westbound *City of Los Angeles* arrived in Los Angeles UP passenger service on the South-Central District ended.

# LIMITED LIFE

*Whilst behind the lacquered doors with heavy brass locks*
*The millionaires sleep.*          —Valéry Larbaud

If you had gathered all of the South-Central District's first-class passenger trains circa 1949 side by side—the *Utahn*, the *Pony Express*, the *Los Angeles Limited*, and the *City of Los Angeles*—you would not have needed train numbers to tell them apart. *The City of Los Angeles*, trains 103 and 104, would have had the best power, EMD E6's or new E7's, and nothing but new streamlined cars from ACF and Pullman-Standard. No head-end business to sully this train, only a single baggage car which you would imagine to be groaning with steamer trunks and a bird cage or two.

Step next to the *Los Angeles Limited*, trains 1 and 2. You would find PA's or Erie-builts on the point, an indication that the UP was not quite as concerned that it absolutely, positively, arrive on time. The *Limited* was by no means a second-rate train, however. Prior to World War II it was an all-Pullman train. In 1949 it had six sleepers plus a seventh during the summer from Chicago to Cedar City, with

two through sleepers to New York City—one via the New York Central, the other via the Pennsylvania Railroad—and a third through sleeper to Minneapolis–St. Paul via the Chicago & North Western. Its club-lounge car featured a barber, valet, and radio. You pictured the *Limited* as a train redolent of cigar smoke, with dark-green upholstery and stuffy service. The conversations of its patrons would be about lumber futures and coal strikes, rarely baseball scores. You imagined dinnertime to be a serious affair, the pages of the *Los Angeles Times* and *The Salt Lake Tribune* competing for table space with the china and silver, six waiters in white jackets moving quickly and silently among 48 men in gray flannel suits.

Last you come to the *Utahn*, trains 3 and 4, and the *Pony Express*, trains 37 and 38. You could guess at a glance that these were the trains employees rode on passes. Like the *Los Angeles Limited* they did not rate the new EMD power nor a solid streamlined consist, and unlike the *Limited* they were heavy with head-end business and made up mostly of coaches. You would glumly resign yourself to a night of fitful dozes punctuated by a succession of hasty stops at indistinguishable desert hamlets. In 1949 the UP catered to all classes. The proletariat had the *Utahn* and the *Pony Express*, the bourgeoisie the *Los Angeles Limited,* and for plutocrats nothing less than the luxe *City of Los Angeles* would do.

AT LEFT: The *Utahn*, trains 3 and 4, succeeded the first *Challenger* on May 14, 1947, carrying coaches, two sleepers, and the through mail and express. During the summer it also carried a Chicago–Cedar City and a Cedar City–Los Angeles sleeper for tourists visiting the Utah parks. Beginning as a heavyweight train, it accumulated streamlined cars as more became available. On October 30, 1950, #3 glides down Cajon Pass behind three Erie-builts, just west of the former station of Gish. Its mail and express cars are dressed either in UP's conservative two-tone gray or the Pullman green of a bygone era. Originally a Cheyenne, Wyoming, to Los Angeles train, the UP extended the *Utahn* to Omaha by November 1948. The UP dropped the train and its tongue-twister name on April 29, 1951, when it extended the streamliner *City of St. Louis* west to Los Angeles from its previous terminus at Ogden. In 1949, the *Utahn* left Los Angeles at 11 A.M., arriving Salt Lake City at 5:10 the next morning. The similarly equipped *Pony Express* left Los Angeles at 7:30 P.M., arriving Salt Lake City at 5:00 the next evening, its schedule slower than the *Utahn* because it served the flag stops.
*Frank J. Peterson (collection of Alan Miller)*

ABOVE RIGHT: The grand dame of LA&SL passenger service was not the *City of Los Angeles*, a brash newcomer for starlets and their sycophants, but trains 1 and 2, the *Los Angeles Limited*. Established as a 68-hour all-Pullman Chicago-Los Angeles train on December 17, 1905, the year the Salt Lake Route opened for service, the *Limited* survived the Great Depression and World War II, but could not weather the new postwar order. Once it filled a necessary gap between the extra-fare *City of Los Angeles* and the regular-fare *Utahn* and *Pony Express*, but as airlines siphoned off the business travel it ran out of clientele. On October 8, 1950, #1 races up the east side of Cajon Pass near Thorn. On January 10, 1954, the upstart all-coach *Challenger* replaced its out-of-date parent, the *Los Angeles Limited*. *Frank J. Peterson (collection of Alan Miller)*

BELOW RIGHT: On a sunny day in the late 1940s, F-M H20-44 1367 helps three F-M Erie-builts on train #4, the eastbound *Utahn*, as two early-day railfans take in the view. The *Utahn* has just turned the corner at Cajon, where the 1912-built eastward track leaves the bottom of the valley and begins winding through the gnarled slopes towards Summit. The double signal head gave an aspect of red over yellow if the block ahead was occupied, allowing fast uphill trains to keep moving when they caught up to a sluggish freight in the block ahead.

Hard as it is to imagine, the diesel-locomotive business had winners and losers long before the last steam locomotive trundled off to a scrap yard, long before most railroads rostered a single freight diesel, and long before most mechanical officers were convinced that diesels were not a toy-shop novelty. One can make the case that EMD won the right to dieselize America the day its FT demonstrator 103 rolled out of La Grange. After that, the diesel makers at Schenectady, Eddystone, Beloit, and Lima were always too late. EMD had grabbed the crest of the technological wave, and scramble as they might, EMD's competitors could never catch up.

In the beginning, it looked as if Fairbanks-Morse and not EMD had the inside track at the UP, because the UP gave F-M the nod for its first diesel-electric freight locomotive, a 6,000-hp A-B-A Erie-built, delivered in December 1945 with 68:19 gearing for freight service. This was F-M's first road diesel; its success was crucial if F-M was to get a share of the locomotive business. But when the UP sent the Erie-built out on the road, it immediately ran into big trouble. F-M's opposed-piston (OP) engine developed significantly more horsepower per cubic inch of displacement than competing designs, so it had to dissipate more waste heat into its cooling system and exhaust. The OP engine had worked brilliantly in submarines where the intake air was dense and humid, and where there was a virtually infinite supply of sea water for cooling. But at 4,194 feet on the top of Cima Hill on a 105° July day, the OP had to rely upon thin, hot dry air for its heat sink. F-M had upped the rating of its OP engine 11.8 percent from its submarine rating to achieve 2,000 horsepower at the generator in a single unit. Coupled with the limitations of a locomotive-cooling system that relied upon hot air blown through radiators instead of cool water pumped through heat exchangers, F-M's designers had asked too much from the OP's piston crowns: they could not conduct heat to their oil cooling spray fast enough, and they began to fly apart with disastrous consequences for the OP engine. F-M's last locomotive manager, Robert Aldag, Jr., stated UP's response succinctly: "The UP people were not pleased."

On May 5, 1946, the UP re-geared the Erie-builts for 102-mph passenger service, hoping they would do better there than they had in freight service. Although F-M managed to convince the UP to buy six more A-units and four more B-units in 1947–48, F-M's window of opportunity had slammed shut. Until more E-units arrived from EMD, the UP pooled its 13 Erie-builts with the also unsatisfactory Alco PA/PB's on secondary trains such as the *Utahn*, *City of St. Louis*, and *Los Angeles Limited*. In 1955 the UP re-geared the Erie-builts for freight service and sent them to the Northwestern District, where they lasted until 1961.
*Ralph Lettelier (collection of Alan Miller)*

## CITY OF LAS VEGAS

*Here comes Tomorrow—FAST! To help railroads solve the problem of a $700 million yearly loss in passenger service, Electro-Motive engineers have designed and built a new lightweight train that promises to revolutionize travel by rail.* —General Motors, 1956

Passenger traffic peaked on the UP in 1952, then inexorably decayed. In hindsight it was a plunge the UP was powerless to arrest, but in the mid-1950s that inevitability was not yet clear. The UP thought it had only to find the right combination of service, technology, and price to reclaim passengers from airplanes and autos. In 1956 GM thought it had the answer: the Aerotrain. In one bright shining package GM wedded automotive

technology, assembly-line production, off-the-shelf components, its legendary market savvy, and the flanged wheel, a combination that looked unbeatable. Its appearance was revolutionary: Space Age, Train-O-Rama. Actually the Aerotrain was totally unsuited to rail travel, but remembering that GM had just revolutionized railroads with diesel-electrics, it seemed plausible they were about to do it again.

Cautiously, the UP leased one of GM's Aerotrains for six months, placing it in daily turnaround service between Los Angeles and Las Vegas on December 18, 1956, as the *City of Las Vegas*, trains 115 and 116. Would people choose an Aerotrain over an aeroplane for their trip to the casinos?

ABOVE: On December 22, 1956, on its fifth eastbound trip, the Aerotrain slows for its stop at East Los Angeles, one of four stops it made in the Los Angeles Basin to gather up gamblers. *John E. Shaw, Jr.*

ABOVE RIGHT: GM's designers apparently failed to imagine that someone might want to use its dandy Aerotrain on mountain grades. The train weighed only about 300 tons loaded; nevertheless, its 1,200-hp 12-567C engine—the same power plant EMD put into a switch engine—was weak in light of the train's 100-mph gearing. A GP9 helper on Cajon Pass and Cima Hill ensured that hillbillies in a Model T would not embarrass the bantam train. On December 23, 1956, a GP9 tugs the Aerotrain up Cajon Pass near Pine Lodge. It turned out that lack of power was just one of the Aerotrain's problems. Its Howdy Podner club-lounge and Chuck Wagon buffet were clever but too cramped. The undersized

air-conditioning plant became an insoluble problem. Despite an airbag suspension, the train rode like it had square wheels. Its cars, which were modified GMC bus bodies, creaked, quivered, and made a terrific racket except when standing still. The UP extended the lease through the summer while GM looked for solutions. There were none, and UP gladly gave the train back to GM on September 15, 1957. *John E. Shaw, Jr.*

BELOW RIGHT: The Aerotrain had managed to hold out to the UP the hope that a special train between Los Angeles and Las Vegas might recapture passengers, though in its busiest months it handled only about 180 cash fares per trip, hardly denting the market. To replace the Aerotrain, the UP assembled a conventional consist of one or two E-units, several coaches, a former *City of Denver* club-lounge, and a lunch counter-cafe car for food service. This also allowed the UP to match the consist to demand, which the fixed Aerotrain consist did not allow.

The new *City of Las Vegas* took over on September 15, 1957. It was comfortable and competent, but had no novelty value; passengers lost interest, and the UP reduced its winter schedule to triweekly on January 19, 1958. In June 1962 the UP changed the train's name to *Las Vegas Holiday Special*, in a last-ditch effort to capture package and charter business. On May 9, 1965, now biweekly train 116 winds through Cajon Pass near Summit, at milepost 57.5X on the eastward track. The train then cost $20 round trip vs. $22.86 on a Western Airlines DC6B. A seven-hour train could not compete with a one-hour plane or a five-hour drive, and the UP discontinued trains 115 and 116 on August 7, 1967.
*Chard Walker*

## DESERT LIFELINE

*We went everywhere on trains–ten miles to a whistle-stop to visit farming relatives, or twenty-five miles to the county seat, where adult members of the party transacted some business or other and the young ones attended a silent movie.*
—Western writer Dee Brown, 1987

The glamorous limiteds, the backwoods mixed trains, the stainless-steel fleets–these are the trains that seduce railroad historians. Unnoticed and unsung are the often nameless main-line mail and accommodation trains. But to the people of the rural West, they were the only trains that counted. These trains stopped at their towns, delivered their mail, and picked up the milk. Until roads were improved, the mail and accommodation trains were the lifeline for the West.

On the LA&SL, the UP shuffled local service onto its least important trains. Before World War II, Chicago–Los Angeles trains 14 and 21, the *Pacific Limited*, did most of this work. Through mail rode the *California Fast Mail*, trains 5 and 6, on a schedule of 19 hours 5 minute from Los Angeles to Salt Lake City that was second only to the 14-hour 54-minute schedule of the *City of Los Angeles*. After 1941 the UP dropped the *Fast Mail* on the LA&SL and gave its mail to the *Pacific Limited*. Beginning on June 2, 1946, the *Pacific Limited* ceased running to Los Angeles and new Denver–Los Angeles trains 37 and 38, the *Pony Express*, provided local and mail service on the LA&SL. After the UP discontinued the *Pony Express* in April 1954, the local work went to the *City of St. Louis*. But when burdened with local stops the *City of St. Louis* had trouble meeting its schedule, so in October 1955 the UP extended trains 5 and 6, the Omaha–Ogden *Mail & Express*, to Los Angeles. Trains 5 and 6 outlived all their betters on the LA&SL except the *City of Los Angeles*, persisting even after losing their RPO on January 27, 1967, until they quietly disappeared in fall 1969.

BELOW: Early on a January 1968 morning #6 curves through the barren hummocks at Apex, on time for its 6 P.M. arrival in Salt Lake City. *Wm. (Hank) Mills (collection of Martha Mills)*

Left: On a hot evening in September 1969, one of the last runs of #5 coasts into Las Vegas past the Mint Hotel, with two coaches, more than enough for its few passengers. Built in 1957 by Milton Prell, a Los Angeles jeweler alleged to have mob connections, the Mint was one of the first high-rise hotels in Las Vegas. *Emery Gulash*

Below: In better days, during October 1962, a UP fuel truck tops off the four E-units on #5 at Salt Lake City while the roundhouse forces correct a minor mechanical problem. Unlike the streamliners, trains 5 and 6 were daylight trains on the LA&SL. *T. J. Donahue*

# The Last Streamliner

*California, and specifically Los Angeles, was the true incubator of the modern service station, a standard structure with huge signs.*
　　　　　　　　　　　　　　　　　　　　　　　　—Daniel Yergin, oil historian

In 1945 the passenger train was marked for death, but soothsayers cast bones and predicted a glowing future. In 1955 the passenger train was fatally wounded, but doctors predicted a swift recovery. In 1965 the passenger train was comatose, and everyone pointed fingers. Who was to blame?

It was not railroad executives. They had hardly comported themselves with grace and aplomb as the rail passenger business disintegrated, and many had scrambled to be the first to dump their trains, but they could scarcely hold a gun to the public's head and make them ride trains. Nor was it the public. They wanted speed, comfort, safety, price, and convenience. All of these they received from the airline and the automobile, not all in equal measure to the passenger train, but in an aggregation the passenger train could never hope to match. Nor was it labor. They too wanted the good suburban life; they too wanted to be first-class citizens like the passengers they served. (And airlines, auto manufacturers, and truckers also had powerful unions.) Nor did the blame lie with government, who gave the people what they demanded. The people demanded subsidized airports and superhighways, and the government indulged them, just as it had subsidized railroads with land grants and construction financing a century before when the people had demanded that. No, the passenger train was killed by oil.

*Oil?*

More specifically, cheap oil. Up through World War II the U.S. had a coal-based economy. Coal made the Industrial Revolution happen. (Imagine the trains and factories of a World War I America fueled by wood.) But at the end of World War II cheap oil toppled King Coal from his throne, a coup d'état hardly noticed at the time, yet it was possibly the single greatest technological event since the invention of the steam locomotive. Cheap oil flooded the world after World War II. It came from the Middle East, from Venezuela, from West Texas, and even from

LEFT: The *City of Los Angeles* connected with air-conditioned, streamlined UP buses at East Los Angeles. The bus service dated to the opening of the station in 1929; it replaced UP's local train service in the Los Angeles Basin, with service to all the suburbs (and tourist attractions such as Disneyland when it opened). One bus route ran north to Pasadena and Glendale, a second southeast to Anaheim and Orange, and a third due south to Long Beach and San Pedro, duplicating UP's principal branch lines. Curiously, the streamlining which revolutionized industrial design in railroads, automobiles, and airplanes in the 1930s and 1940s had no counterpart at Disneyland. Walt reached into the past and future for his themes, and found most of his inspiration for his portrayal of an America that never was at the Chicago Railroad Fair of 1948, but it is striking that he never borrowed from the streamline era. Disney built a Tomorrowland, a Fantasyland, a Frontierland, an Adventureland, and an ersatz turn-of-the-century Main Street without crime, foreclosures, immigrants, mud, or horse manure—but no Streamlinerland. Disneyland's Autopia ride, where everyone slowly tailgates another automobile on a pointless road and breathes stinking exhaust, provided Disney's vision of modern transportation. Perhaps Disney was more prophetic than he himself imagined. *Buses, Alan Miller; UP emblem, Bob Todten*

UP's wells in Wilmington. Cheap oil changed the world. And unlike coal, it did not disappear at the whim of John L. Lewis and the United Mine Workers of America. It was also much cleaner, more versatile, and easier to handle.

In real prices gasoline steadily got cheaper from 1945 to 1970. Demand doubled, tripled, quadrupled. Oil's response to the demand, in seeming contradiction to economic sense, was to become cheaper! Oil is cheaper now than it has ever been in history. Cheap oil made the automobile accessible to everyone. Cheap oil got fuel-guzzling jet aircraft off the ground. Cheap oil made diesels extremely attractive versus both coal and oil-burning steam engines, because of the diesel's much greater thermal efficiency. In New York Central's comparison of 4-8-4s and E-units in 1946, the E-units beat the 4-8-4s cold on fuel cost (if not on total cost): 28 cents per mile for a pair of 2,000-hp E-units versus 41 cents per mile for a 4-8-4. Cheap oil slew steam, then it stalked the passenger train.

In the 1960s a generation grew up that had never ridden on a train. Once the sound of a lonesome steam whistle at night evoked America; now the auto evoked America. Europe may have fine paintings, we crowed, but we have more cars! America rearranged its cities and towns to focus on expressways, parking lots, shopping malls, and drive-through burger stands, as once it had focused its cities and towns on the railroad station. By 1971 depots were yawning tombs where winos stared at the floor. The action now took place on the Strip—the main highway through town.

*Passenger trains?*

They were a frumpy relic. Born by coal, killed by oil.

AT LEFT: On April 30, 1971, the final eastbound *City of Los Angeles* rolls into East Los Angeles, its funeral attended by reporters, railfans, and perhaps a few who remembered the first *City of Los Angeles* of 1936 as a symbol of hope and returning prosperity when America seemed to be permanently mired in depression's gloom. This photograph shows a culture in transition: a colorful, happy diversity of pantsuits, miniskirts, sports slacks, and one blue polyester plaid jacket. Today almost everyone here, regardless of age, sex, race, or economic status, would be dressed in an identical uniform of jeans, T-shirt, and tennis shoes. In 1971 jeans were for kids, carpenters, and convicts.

Forlorn in the sprawling modernity is the ivy-draped East Los Angeles depot. Already it was an artifact from an ancient, mythical city, a city of orange groves and cowboy matinees, Harold Lloyd and Mary Pickford. The depot's architecture, Spanish Eclectic, was old hat the day it opened in 1929. A new architectural infatuation was sweeping Los Angeles, Art Deco and Art Moderne. Yet in a few years those styles were also obsolete. As soon as the city found a style it threw it away, remaking itself every decade in its fruitless search for an identity. It is no surprise that the automobile, Hollywood's symbol for rootlessness, became synonymous with Los Angeles and the southern California suburban culture, instead of buildings, which were too fixed in place and too permanent.

In 1971 the big signs of big oil loom in the fume-filled sky: Chevron, Union 76, and Shell. The skies are now turned a poisonous brown, the orange groves bulldozed for suburbs, the suburbs bifurcated by freeways, and the peaceful desert evenings obliterated by the ceaseless din of automobiles in the City of Commerce and Industry. *Alan Miller*

ABOVE: *Frank J. Peterson (collection of Alan Miller)*    INSET: *Keith Ardinger*

# PART IV
# LONG HAULS

## *Freight Traffic on the South-Central District*

The critics of the SPLA&SL's route were correct—there was little traffic for it to haul. It could not turn a profit until 1913. The SPLA&SL had a dearth of local business except at either end, where it had to compete with interurbans and steam roads. The SPLA&SL lacked feeders in California; although the UP and SP were ostensibly allied until split apart by the Supreme Court on December 2, 1912, the SP preferred to haul its freight as far east as possible rather than give it to the SPLA&SL at Colton. Later, the "Santa Margarita Agreement" of February 6, 1923, required the SP (until 1966) to haul all its traffic originating north of Santa Margarita and Caliente, California, to the UP at Ogden, and its traffic originating in southern California to El Paso, Texas, regardless of final destination. This left nothing for the LA&SL. The SPLA&SL had the longest route to Los Angeles: in 1962 a car moving from Chicago to Los Angeles traveled 2,299 miles on the UP (via the Milwaukee east of Council Bluffs, Iowa); 2,253 miles on the SP (via the Rock Island east of Tucumcari, New Mexico); and 2,113 miles on the Santa Fe (via Amarillo, Texas). The SPLA&SL had the slowest and most mountainous route to Los Angeles: in 1994 the UP rated 280 of the 785 miles from Salt Lake City to Los Angeles at speeds slower than 45 mph. Although Los Angeles consumed huge tonnages of lumber, cement, steel, and grain, ships had most of this business (particularly after completion of the Panama Canal in 1914) because ships cost much less to operate than railroads. In 1911 ships could deliver Australian coal to Los Angeles cheaper than the SPLA&SL could deliver Utah coal!

But mostly the problem was geography, which had not favored the Salt Lake Route. Lacking water, most of the land along its route was unsuitable for farming. Without farming, there were no towns. Without towns, there was no market. Without a market, there was no industry. Without industry, farms, or towns, a railroad has nothing to haul. True, the West is rich in minerals, but without industry or centers of population nearby, mineral deposits often have no real value.

The SPLA&SL in 1908 was very much a frontier railroad, having 2.89 freight ton-miles for every passenger-mile (statistics are for revenue traffic), while the UP proper had 7.14 ton-miles for every passenger-mile. In 1908 the SPLA&SL accounted for a mere 5.58 percent of the UP system's ton-miles and 12.42 percent of its passenger miles, and had nearly the same tonnage density as UP's little granger road St. Joseph & Grand Island. Subtract the heavy business in coal, coke, and ore between Provo and Salt Lake City and it would appear that the SPLA&SL had little long-haul freight. Generally two to three short freights each way daily sufficed between Los Angeles and Salt Lake City.

Twenty years later UP's system ton-miles had grown 249.75 percent but its passenger-miles had declined 2.15 percent (Model T's had annihilated local passenger traffic). The LA&SL did much better; between 1908 and 1928 its ton-miles grew an impressive 358.38 percent and its passenger-miles bucked the trend and grew 38.91 percent. Much of the LA&SL's growth had to do with Los Angeles's growth. Thanks to Los Angeles the LA&SL also did better than the UP system during the Depression, losing 24 percent of its ton-miles between 1929 and 1935 versus 29 percent for the system. Yet in 1935 the LA&SL still accounted for only 9.84 percent of the system's ton-miles.

In the 1940s the LA&SL finally started to look like a good idea. War traffic provided a taste of the big time, and steel mills built in Utah and California in 1942–44 supplied the LA&SL with its first truly heavy long-haul traffic. After the war, main-line traffic stabilized at about five trains each way daily. They were longer, heavier trains thanks to dieselization in 1947–48, and faster too, exemplified by the Day Live Stock, UP's first roller-bearing fast livestock train. California's aggressive truckers forced the UP to establish its first piggyback operation, between Los Angeles and Las Vegas in 1953. SD24's in 1959 provided the muscle to eliminate helpers on the LA&SL—the "We Can Handle It" slogan on the cab of SD24 448 was no idle boast.

In the 1970s the Pacific Rim exploded with economic activity. The UP began hauling trainloads of grain, potash, soda ash, and coal to Los Angeles for export to Pacific Rim countries. Imported manufactured goods began flooding into the Ports of Los Angeles and Long Beach, making them the two largest container ports in the U.S. by 1994.

Today, the LA&SL's main line has reached respectability. It now averages 10 to 11 freights each way daily, many of which are heavier than five trains of 1908.

Nevertheless, geography has not been vanquished. Don't be fooled by the artificial oases; water is still in short supply. The desert still begins at the steps of the Mormon Tabernacle in Salt Lake City and ends at the ocean docks at San Pedro. The UP must still work harder than the Santa Fe to haul freight to and from Los Angeles. In 1975, for example, the UP routinely gave hotshots LAX and VAN four 6900s each and limited them to 3,500 tons to compete with the Santa Fe.

The desert is now emptier than it was in the 1920s. Miners' camps, trading posts, the homesteads of hopeful farmers—all abandoned to the wind and sun. There is no mistaking that this is an outland. This is where you half expect to stumble across the bleached bones, desiccated boots, and tattered clothes of an unfortunate prospector.

Geography is still law on the desert and water is its court. Water controls the biochemistry of the desert's flora and fauna, and passes judgment on the efforts of man. Water pinned the Fremont culture of A.D. 1000 to the banks of the rivers, defeated Coronado's search for the seven cities of Cibola, and bound the Mormons to fields nurtured by mountain freshets. Geography dictated that the LA&SL would zigzag around mountains and cut across basins to lessen its cost of construction. Water and grades demanded that UP's first freight diesels go to the LA&SL: 28 four-unit, 6,000-hp FA/FB and F3 sets acquired in 1947 and 1948. On October 30, 1950, four centuries after Coronado's conquistadores rode proudly into the desert, Extra 1603 West charges out of Frost, its bright yellow paint glittery in the afternoon sun, its crisp white flags held high in the blue desert sky. But Alco had underestimated the desert. On the LA&SL's long grades the Alcos ran hot, and after a while they did not run at all. They retreated in ignominy to the temperate climate and flat track of UP's Eastern District. Like the conquistadores on their quest for gold and glory, the Alcos were a splendid sight as they strode across the desert. Like the conquistadores, they quietly staggered from the desert in defeat, and were never seen there again.

## BAD WATER

*"This would be good country," a tourist says to me, "if only you had some water."*
— Edward Abbey, Utah park ranger, 1958

The growth of Los Angeles during the 1920s from a city of only regional importance into a sprawling metropolis began to provide the Salt Lake Route's hoped-for heavy traffic. A good measure of the LA&SL's traffic growth is the increase in the capacity of its road locomotive fleet from 5.5 million pounds tractive effort in 1917 to 9.1 million pounds in 1929. The SPLA&SL's initial fleet was a motley assortment of small locomotives bought new or inherited from the Los Angeles Terminal and the Oregon Short Line. New road power purchased during construction or shortly after completion included six 4-6-0's, four 4-4-2's, and twenty-six speedy 4-6-2's for passenger service, and eighty-four heavy 2-8-0's for road freight and helper service. As traffic grew between 1907 and 1917, the Salt Lake Route added five 4-6-2's and nine 2-8-2's, and three 2-8-0's from the Las Vegas & Tonopah. Between 1917 and 1929, however, real growth occurred. During these 12 years the LA&SL added fifteen 2-8-2's, thirty hefty 2-10-2's, and ten three-cylinder 4-10-2's to its freight and helper pools, retaining sixty-nine of its eighty-seven heavy 2-8-0's. The LA&SL sped up its longer, heavier passenger trains with twenty lanky 4-8-2's, retaining twenty-three of its thirty-one 4-6-2's.

Initially the SPLA&SL used coal as far west as Las Vegas, but by 1914 it had replaced coal with cheap California fuel oil on its entire route, except between Salt Lake City and Provo. It found a use for the surplus coaling tower at Lynndyl to store the aggregate it used to make concrete fence posts (for the right-of-way fences that protected much of the Salt Lake Route from marauding cows). The OSL used coal between Salt Lake City, Ogden, and Pocatello.

Always vexing was the water problem. There was little water to be had out in the desert, and what the Salt Lake Route pumped out of the sand or piped to trackside from mountain springs was generally alkaline and full of dissolved minerals, anathema to locomotive boilers which dreamed of pure, sweet water. Water treatment plants were a stopgap; diesels were the solution.

ABOVE: The draft horse of the LA&SL west of Crestline during the steam era was the 2-10-2. Thirty of these 184-ton engines lumbered over the LA&SL's desolate main line for 25 years until superseded by diesels. Raw-boned, big-boilered, and powerful, they could do just about anything except boil bad water or run for their life. They were very hard on track even at moderate speeds, so the UP installed disc main drivers on many of them in the late 1930s to reduce pounding. On October 8, 1950, the 5515 helps a westbound extra out of Frost, its rich, oily exhaust besmirching the four shiny Alcos on its drawbar. Only 23 years separates the 5515's construction from the Alcos' construction—not much, considering that the same number of years separates UP's first SD40-2's from its most recent SD60M's.

ABOVE LEFT: The 5515, its flanks grayed by alkaline water and glaring sun, pushes behind the steel caboose of a westbound at Lugo, on the east slope of Cajon Pass, on October 30, 1950. Its large tender carries 18,000 gallons of water and 6,010 of oil, which it could consume in a depressingly short amount of time when working up a mountain grade. Eleven UP 2-10-2's worked on Cajon Pass in 1950-51, then departed for the last time when new EMD cow-and-calf helpers arrived.

BELOW LEFT: Twenty beautiful 4-8-2's were once the queens of the LA&SL, splendidly dressed in two-tone gray, made up with white pinstripes and bejeweled with chrome-plated cylinder heads. By 1950 they had been humbled to helper service, Cinderellas in a scullery. On June 18, 1950, the 7859 is momentarily framed in the bristly needle-like leaves of a Joshua tree as it highballs out of Victorville towards Cajon Pass. Alas, instead of fine Pullmans on its drawbar, there are just Alcos and grimy freight cars. At Summit the 7859 will cut off and slink back to Victorville. For steam on the LA&SL, the clock had struck midnight, and unlike fairy tales, there was no happily ever after.
*Three photos, Frank J. Peterson (collection of Alan Miller)*

# Dieselization

*Union Pacific participated in no small way in the development of the diesel locomotive about ten years ago and as yet has not accepted it.*

—UP President George F. Ashby writes to UP's Executive Committee, October 23, 1946

Unlike most western roads, which enthusiastically embraced EMD's FT, the UP was uninterested. To William M. Jeffers, UP's president during World War II, there was something immoral about coupling together four FT's to do the same work as one mighty Big Boy; he thought F-M's Erie-built superior because it packed 6,000 hp into three units instead of the FT's 5,400 hp into four. Eventually the UP purchased plenty of four-unit EMD F3's and Alco FA/FB's, yet Jeffers's hankering for big locomotives remained embedded in UP's culture, finding its next expression in massive gas turbines and double-diesels.

During World War II the Santa Fe solved its similar operational problems with FTs. The UP could have done likewise, but the LA&SL was not UP's most important line. UP's vision remained locked on the critical Council Bluffs to Ogden main line, where company coal was cheap and better water more plentiful. Not until October 1946, two years after the UP took delivery of its last new steam locomotives, did new president George Ashby stun UP's board with his proposal for what was then the largest-ever order for diesel locomotives.

In December 1946 the UP ordered the power to dieselize the South-Central District: twenty-eight 6,000-hp freight sets; two 6,000-hp and five 4,500-hp passenger sets; twenty-five 1,000-hp switch engines; and four 2,000-hp helper engines. The UP intended that this $22-million, 162-unit diesel order would dieselize the main line and tributary branch lines between Salt Lake City and Los Angeles (but not Salt Lake City to Provo).

Why dieselize the South-Central District, and not Wyoming? The decision had to do with basics: water, fuel, and tonnage ratings. The South-Central District lacked good water, though the UP had this problem under control, as evidenced by its ability to run 4-8-2's from Los Angeles to Salt Lake City without change, albeit at some cost. Fuel was another matter. The postwar epidemic of coal miners' strikes, the high cost of oil per ton-mile relative to coal, and a fear of oil shortages as the U.S. became a net oil importer gave the diesel's greater thermal efficiency more urgency. The FT on its nationwide tour of 1940 averaged 49 percent less fuel cost per ton-mile than the modern steam locomotives to which it was compared. Lastly, diesels were better suited to the long grades on the South-Central District because of their higher tractive effort at drag-freight speeds. Once the UP realized an F3 set would haul 5,080 tons unassisted all the way from Salt Lake City to Victorville (versus 3,350 tons for a Challenger), would cost half as much to fuel per ton-mile, would run past all of the water and most of the fuel stops, and did not need a daily boiler wash, there was no decision left to make—steam was history.

ABOVE LEFT: Train #202, the eastbound *Los Angeles Limited*, has met a small delay at Hesperia on July 24, 1949. A westbound freight has derailed, kinking the rail in the eastward main. The engineer and fireman peer anxiously from freight F3A 1428 while repair crews walk them by. At the time, UP train #2 was numbered 202 between Riverside and Yermo to avoid confusion with Santa Fe's numbered trains.
*Chard Walker*

BELOW LEFT: On May 5, 1949, an eastbound behind a four-unit FA/FB set growls past Colton Tower. The UP rated a four-unit F3 set at 3,700 tons between Victorville and Summit, whereas it rated an equivalent FA/FB set at 4,200 tons. Advantage, Alco. However, locomotives do not exist in the ethereal realm of a tonnage table, but out in a dirty desert, and there the Alcos died, victims of a hastily designed 244 engine with exhaust manifolds that burned up and marginal main bearings, and prone to internal fuel leaks leading to lube-oil dilution and catastrophic engine explosions. Since a dead FA has a negative tonnage rating, a set that lost a unit went from being able to shoulder 4,200 tons up Cajon's east side to only 3,030 tons. And for every dollar the UP spent to maintain an EMD F3 it spent a dollar fifty on an Alco FA. By 1954 the UP had banished the Alcos to the mild grades of the Eastern District. *Chard Walker*

ABOVE: During October 1948, a westbound extra freight behind new A-B-A F3's stops at Summit. The brakemen walk the cartops, setting retainers for the 3.0-percent descent to Cajon station and the engineer goes for a stroll. The F3's found success on the LA&SL, but only lasted there until GP9's arrived in 1954–55.
*Frank J. Peterson (collection of Alan Miller)*

## Steam's Last Runs

*Actually the diesels came so fast that it was hard to believe a complete transition had taken place ...our railroad had indeed changed, almost overnight.* —Walter Thrall, LA&SL engineer, November 1958

By fall 1948 enough EMDs, Alcos, and F-Ms were on hand to dieselize the South-Central District west of Salt Lake City and Provo (except for the Harbor Belt Line), the last regular train behind steam running east during December 1948. However, the UP had only enough diesels on hand to accommodate normal traffic levels. In June 1950 the heavy passenger loads for a Shriners' convention in Los Angeles required the UP to temporarily dispatch 4-8-2's 7019 and 7859 to Cajon Pass for helper service. Two weeks later, a distant war—North Korea's sudden invasion of South Korea—caught the LA&SL short on power. General Walton Walker's undermanned Eighth Army needed help fast to avoid being driven into the sea by the rapidly advancing North Koreans, and within days of the June 25 invasion the LA&SL was besieged by troop trains and military freight for the Korean Theater. The UP quickly sent up to ten oil-burning 2-8-2's, 2-10-2's, and 4-10-2's to join the two 4-8-2's in helper service as well as on the five-to-six-days-weekly Leon Turn from San Bernardino to Oro Grande.

In Utah, UP's 2-8-8-0's worked in turnaround service from Salt Lake City to Provo until 1953. With the arrival of large numbers of GP9s in 1954, steam operation between Salt Lake City, Ogden, and Pocatello, Idaho, became sporadic, with its last run out of Pocatello on April 30, 1956. Then it was over.

AT LEFT, THREE PHOTOGRAPHS: On June 5, 1956, heavy oil-burning 2-8-2 2726 rests disconsolately beneath the Ogden coaling tower, awaiting its trip to the scrapyard. Built for the OSL in 1913, traded to the LA&SL in 1918, and retired in August 1956, it had probably outlived most of the men who had built it. Over at the Ogden roundhouse the same summer afternoon, light MacArthur 1924 holds its own with the FA on the adjacent garden track in bulk, if not in tractive effort. The 1911-built 2-8-2 certainly outlasted the Alco diesel, serving the UP for 46 years before its December 1957 retirement. The FA managed only 17 years of service. On November 28, 1955, oil-burning Challenger 3716 lays over in an incongruous location, UP's brand-new Salt Lake City Diesel Shop.
*Ralph Gochnour*

AT RIGHT: A little dirty but still regal in two-tone gray, 4-8-2 7019 awaits a helper assignment at Victorville on June 11, 1950. It had just arrived to supplement UP's F-M H20-44 helpers with a busy month of Shriners' specials. When more steam showed up later that month, they chased the hapless H20-44's into secondary assignments.
*Chard Walker*

BELOW: When OSL 2-10-2 5317 left San Bernardino on October 24, 1951, and ran light to Salt Lake City, regular use of steam on the LA&SL main line ceased. Subsequent moves were special moves, such as when 4-12-2 9000 came west for permanent display at the Los Angeles County Fairgrounds in Pomona. At 7:30 A.M. on May 3, 1956, the long locomotive prepares to leave Yermo cab hop for Pomona. Everyone watched closely when it inched around the 10° curves on Cajon Pass. *John Hungerford (collection of Tom Moungovan)*

## LOOKING FOR THE RIGHT POWER ON CAJON PASS

*High Tonnages...and high ambient temperatures are taken in stride by the Union Pacific's 2000 hp. locomotives working the sand dusted local freight branches.*

—Fairbanks-Morse puts a good spin on its H20-44's in *Railway Age*, July 1952

The debacle of 1946, when Fairbanks-Morse's prototype Erie-built fell down on the UP, cost F-M any chance at UP's orders for road freight power when it dieselized the South-Central District in 1947–48. Yet it is not surprising that F-M was not entirely shut out, given UP's opinions about what locomotives should look like. When UP's mechanical men saw F-M's 2,000-hp demonstrator H20-44 at the 1947 Atlantic City show they saw the diesel-electric version of the heavy 2-10-2's they had used in helper service on the South-Central District. The UP purchased the demonstrator on the spot and ordered ten more. The H20-44's, numbered DS1360–70, entered helper service later that year on Cajon Pass and Cima Hill, and later handled road locals out of San Bernardino.

Although F-M's advertisements made the H20-44's sound powerful, they had difficulties on Cajon. An H20-44 was supposed to take 1,500 tons from Victorville to Summit but could only handle 1,300 tons, compared to 1,625 tons for a 2-10-2. When traffic got heavy in the summer of 1950 steam had its last laugh, taking over the Cajon Pass helper assignments.

Exacerbating the F-M's problems was their utter lack of flexibility. The UP had looked at its diesel-locomotive needs in steam-locomotive terms, so the H20-44's were missing such fundamentals as multiple-unit connections and dynamic brakes. If a train was too heavy for one F-M helper then two had to be called, each with its own crew. Although the UP added both features to some of the H20-44's they still had relatively stiff maintenance requirements and poor reliability.

In March 1951 UP ordered eight 2,400-hp TR5 cow-and-calf sets from EMD to replace the six 2-10-2's and two 4-8-2's then assigned to Cajon Pass. EMD's TR5 was two SW9's semi-permanently coupled together, the cabless calf controlled by its mother cow. On delivery in September and October 1951 the UP assigned six TR5 sets to switching, transfer, and helper service at San Bernardino, eliminating steam from the California Division main line, and the other two to Kelso for service on Cima Hill. During 1952–53 one of the TR5's worked in helper service out of Caliente as well. The TR5s displaced the remaining F-M H20-44's from the South-Central District; by 1953 all had been reassigned to the Northwestern District.

ABOVE LEFT: On the morning of January 12, 1949, H20-44 DS1365 pauses in deep snow at Summit, bound for Oro Grande as the Leon Turn. Caboose 3392 bears LA&SL sublettering.

BELOW LEFT: On August 30, 1948, H20-44 DS1366 sits in oil-splattered disgrace at Alray while Santa Fe's eastbound *El Capitan* swings by. While helping the eastbound *Los Angeles Limited* the 1366 suffered a crankcase explosion, an all-too-typical occurrence in the late 1940s for UP's F-Ms.

NEAR LEFT: Dynamic brake-equipped TR5 set 1874/1874B assists eastbound train #210, the *City of St. Louis*, at Sullivan's Curve on January 5, 1954.

ABOVE: While a westbound freight pauses at Highland Junction on July 11, 1950 to turn down retainers, helpers begin collecting behind it, first Santa Fe FT 110, then UP H20-44's DS1364 and DS1360. On the eastward main, Santa Fe 2-10-2s 3843 and 3844 dig in to lift an eastbound up Cajon Pass.
*Four photographs, Chard Walker*

While more powerful and reliable than the F-Ms, the cow-and-calf sets were just moderately successful as helper engines. First, they rode hard, because of their switcher trucks. Second, the UP, learning little from the F-Ms, did not order the TR5s with multiple-unit connections, making each set an independent unit requiring its own engine crew. Third, they went through brake shoes quickly and suffered wheel overheating on the descents from Summit and Cima because of their small wheels and no dynamic brakes. (This had never been a problem for steam engines because they distributed their braking energy over much greater wheel mass). In 1952–53 the UP added dynamic braking to the cows only; the dynamic brakes, however, required a careful touch UP's engineers did not always have. By 1956, after too many incidents of overloading and subsequent grid burnout, UP disconnected them. By then UP had found more appropriate switching jobs for its TR5s, and replaced them in helper service on Cajon Pass and Cima Hill with GP9s until it abolished these jobs altogether in 1959.

# Jet Power

*Imagine a B-52 revving up in your backyard.*
—Mel Patrick, railroad photographer

One would think gas turbines would have been the ideal locomotives for the South-Central District. They had tons of power, good for the South-Central's long grades, and were best suited to long runs in empty country, which very much describes the South-Central District. But they were not an ideal locomotive for the South-Central District, and visited it only infrequently. Interestingly, the UP had the South-Central District in mind when it purchased its gas turbines.

In November 1948 General Electric completed 4,500-hp gas turbine 101, the first such locomotive in North America. After successful road tests in early 1949, GE painted the 267-ton behemoth as UP-50. The 50 arrived on the UP in July 1949, and spent the next 21 months testing on the UP system, some of this time on the LA&SL, both in road service and in Cajon Pass helper service. Convinced of the 50's viability, on March 19, 1951, the UP ordered 10 improved turbines. GE delivered the first in January 1952. But instead of assigning the turbines to the South-Central District as intended, the UP ran them between Ogden and Green River, Wyoming. The UP ordered 15 more in December 1953; though these were likewise intended for the South-Central District, they also rarely strayed west

of Ogden. Similarly, when the UP ordered 15 of the 8,500-hp (later upgraded to 10,000 hp) "Big Blow" turbines on November 30, 1955, it intended that they and 30 more would replace most diesel power on road freights on the South-Central District. Yet this too never came to pass.

On the South-Central District the turbines ran into several problems. Their ear-splitting howl resulted in ordinances against their nighttime operation through several Los Angeles suburbs. This alone seems an insufficient reason to ban them from the LA&SL; one supposes they could have ended their westbound run at Yermo. The turbines suffered a horsepower loss in thin air at high altitudes and in hot weather, and dusty air in the deserts eroded their turbine blades, though this was not unexpected—and the supposition that these factors made the turbines unsuitable for the LA&SL overlooks the facts that the UP main line between Ogden and Cheyenne, Wyoming, has a higher average altitude than the LA&SL, is quite hot in the summer, and being very windy is often very dusty. No, the problem with the turbines on the LA&SL was their inability to cope with the LA&SL's long, steep ruling grades.

Buried in the statistics for the 4,500-hp gas turbines was their tractive effort: 105,000 pounds at minimum continuous speed (MCS), 12.9 mph. Four F3's, by comparison, put out 130,000 pounds tractive effort at MCS, and four GP9's 160,000 pounds. The turbines also had less dynamic braking

effort. One turbine could not do the same job as four F-units or four GP9's on the LA&SL, unless the UP chose to operate shorter trains (or use more helpers) and use more crews to haul the same tonnage. Moreover, the turbines became slippery as speed dropped to MCS and their engineers had to sand almost continuously on grades of 1.0 percent or steeper, the airborne grit doing nothing to reduce blade erosion (or wheel and rail wear). True, the "Big Blows" were over twice as powerful as the 4,500-hp turbines, but by the time they arrived, SD24's were on the property. A half-century earlier E. H. Harriman decided the LA&SL would have steep grades, a decision which still had major implications: the turbines would run between Council Bluffs and Ogden, where the grades were much lighter.

ABOVE LEFT: On August 16, 1962, Big Blow 29 howls up the east side of Cajon Pass at milepost 54, leading two SD24's and a westbound freight towards Los Angeles. At San Bernardino the 29's engineer will kill his turbine, relying on the two SD24's to roll his train through the Los Angeles Basin to East Yard, just as he has relied upon them to provide the necessary oomph on the LA&SL's grueling mountain grades. "The UP ran turbines into southern California for four months through the summer of 1962, and I spent a lot of weekends chasing them. I was driving a '62 Rambler, the last car I owned without air conditioning."
*Gordon Glattenberg*

ABOVE RIGHT: On February 24, 1950, the 50 prepares to leave Victorville for Cajon Pass, its fedora-hatted engineer peering impatiently from the cab while the train crew talks. The caboose, used by representatives from GE and UP's mechanical department, accompanied the 50 during its 21-month stay on the UP.
*Chard Walker*

BELOW RIGHT: Leaving a smear of oily exhaust, the 50 heads down the 3.0-percent westward track on Cajon Pass on March 22, 1950. The 50 made numerous trips between East Yard and Las Vegas between August 1949 and March 1950. The next visit of a gas turbine to the South-Central District was in May 1953, when the 57 came west for propane-fuel experiments. The 57 made 99 round trips between East Yard and Las Vegas until January 3, 1954, when the experiment ended. The experiment sought to reduce turbine-blade erosion by burning clean propane instead of relatively dirty residual oil. The test was successful in reducing blade erosion, but propane was too expensive compared to residual oil (which cost as little as five cents a gallon) to justify conversion.
*Chard Walker*

ABOVE: Following the propane experiments, the next visit of a gas turbine to Los Angeles was in 1958, when the 61 made a single round trip. On November 19 the 61 returns east at Ono in the company of two GP9's. Although residual oil cost half as much per gallon as diesel fuel, the turbines burned twice as many gallons per horsepower of output as UP's diesels, so there was no advantage there. The turbines' insatiable appetite for fuel and maintenance made them at best the equivalent of diesels in cost per ton-mile.
*Chard Walker*

## STANDARD POWER

*The Geep is, to coin a phrase, everyman's unit.* —David P. Morgan, 1954

As far as Omaha was concerned, most of the time the LA&SL was out of sight and out of mind. Omaha's usual response to a problem on the LA&SL was swift, sweeping change, much as a mother ignores children playing in the back yard until the noise level becomes too loud or too quiet, then rushes out to lay down the law, right or wrong. An example of Omaha's policy towards the LA&SL was its crash dieselization program in 1947–48, which replaced a water problem with a maintenance problem. What the LA&SL needed was a run-till-it-drops diesel that could handle a redball one day, a local the next. That diesel was not F-Ms or Alcos but the GP9, probably the best diesel ever built. EMD supplied hundreds of them to the UP beginning in 1954. Five years later EMD souped up its 567D engine, put it in a six-axle package, and produced the SD24. Here was a simple, standard solution for the LA&SL: versatile GP9's and powerful SD24's. Together they ran the LA&SL for over a decade without complaint, while Omaha fretted over the Wyoming Division.

ABOVE LEFT: At Summit, Santa Fe's signalmen rigged up simple signals east and west of the depot to alert train and engine crews wanting to cross over to turn engines on the wye or make reverse moves of an approaching train. Each was a piece of sheet metal which rotated 90° on its horizontal axis when a train drew near, revealing the word TRAIN to anyone at Summit. On April 16, 1966, the TRAIN sign at West Summit announces the arrival of SD24 408 and its eastbound train. The SD24's were the right package for the LA&SL main line: big horsepower for speed across the flats and six motors for long hikes up its mountain grades. *John E. Shaw, Jr.*

BELOW LEFT: On October 17, 1966, Extra 177 West runs the wrong way on the eastward track at Sullivan's Curve due to a derailment on the westward track just above Cajon station. Ten years earlier, a set of five GP9's on an LA&SL road freight was typical. Within a few years this would become an uncommon sight as bigger, newer SD40's and SD40-2's took over. *Chard Walker*

ABOVE RIGHT: On a sweltering afternoon, July 23, 1966, 101-car Extra 413 East slogs out of the Los Angeles Basin at Devore behind five SD24's, a Colton pick-up of PFE reefers on the head end. Generally the SD24's shuttled back and forth over UP's heavy-grade territory between Los Angeles and Green River, Wyoming. East of Green River was turbine territory. *J. W. Swanberg*

BELOW RIGHT: On March 3, 1956, Extra 172 East, the Leon Turn, stops on the eastward main at Summit. The Leon Turn hauled limestone and fuel oil east to Southwestern Portland Cement at Leon and Riverside Cement at Oro Grande, then returned to Los Angeles with bulk cement in covered hoppers and bagged cement in boxcars. With the departure of the FA/FB's in 1954, and the F3's in 1955, in 1956 GP9's were standard power on LA&SL freights. *John E. Shaw, Jr.*

## THE DAY LIVE STOCK

*Effective from Salt Lake City Thursday March 13 it will be arranged to handle livestock through to Los Angeles without stops for water and feed.* —UP Vice-President of Operations P. J. Lynch, 1947

Before World War II, livestock flowed from west to east. The western meat packing industry only supplied local markets. Los Angeles did not have one major packing house until 1921. In 1920 the LA&SL's livestock business was inconsequential, averaging 4.2 total carloads daily (the UP proper hauled 62.5 loads daily in 1920). But as Los Angeles grew, so did the LA&SL's livestock business to Los Angeles, to 18.3 carloads per day in 1929, and 27.6 per day in 1939; nevertheless, the principal flow of livestock was still eastward. Up to one million head of cattle and two million sheep funneled into the Ogden and Salt Lake Union Stock Yards yearly, arriving from Idaho and Montana on the OSL, northern California and Nevada on the SP and WP, and Utah and southern Nevada on the LA&SL. Some were slaughtered by Cudahy in North Salt Lake and Swift & Co. in Ogden, but most were reloaded after resting and forwarded to Midwestern packing houses.

In 1946–47 the traditional eastward flow of livestock through Utah reversed direction. Freed of wartime rationing, Californians demanded meat. By 1946 the LA&SL's average daily stock car count to Los Angeles had increased to 65.8 cars; however, the LA&SL was losing market share to truckers because its service was too slow. Train #299, the Night Live Stock, the LA&SL's fastest stock train, required 56 hours from Salt Lake City to Los Angeles, including a 10-hour stop at Las Vegas, where the livestock was fed, watered, and rested in pens (fed-

eral law restricts livestock to no more than 36 continuous hours in a car). Las Vegas's pens were also overtaxed by the increased business. With CTC nearing completion, and diesels on order, the UP decided it could run #299 from Salt Lake City to Los Angeles in under 36 hours. Test trains proved the concept, though the first, which left Salt Lake City on March 14, 1947, had to rest its stock in the pens at San Bernardino when it ran short on time. On March 21, 1947, #299 began running on a 32-hour schedule as the Day Live Stock (DLS), because it left Salt Lake City in daylight, whereas the Night Live Stock left at night. The DLS was a success; the Las Vegas pens closed by May 1947 and were torn down that fall.

Although the test trains reportedly used diesels (type unknown; UP's first F3's arrived on May 30, 1947), steam, probably 4-6-6-4's, hauled the DLS until June, when F3's and FAs/FB's arrived on the South-Central District. By fall 1947, the UP supplied 300 "Livestock Dispatch" stock cars to the DLS, reconditioned for high-speed service with Timken roller bearings and new draft gear, springs, snubbers, steel wheels, and steel roofs if not so equipped. The UP painted their sides Armour yellow with red lettering to draw attention to the DLS, and their roofs and ends aluminum to reflect sunlight and help keep the livestock cool. Most were double-deck, able to carry cattle on the lower level and sheep and hogs on both levels. By September 1950 the UP had 1,000 Livestock Dispatch cars in service at a cost of $5,032 each versus $4,695 for ordinary stock cars. (It should be noted that UP's Livestock Dispatch cars roamed system-wide, and by no means were they purely DLS cars, nor did the DLS use purely Livestock Dispatch cars.)

The DLS was assembled at North Yard in Salt Lake City. Its sheep and cattle mostly came from Idaho and Montana, via

the SLX (Salt Lake Manifest), BUS (Butte Utah Stock), and PSX (Pocatello–South Manifest), which connected at Salt Lake City or at Ogden via a transfer arriving Salt Lake City two hours ahead of departure. Its hogs (up to 1.5 million a year in the 1950s) and some cattle were collected after resting at Laramie, Wyoming, by the ADP (Advance Denver Pacific) and the CLS (Coast Live Stock). All DLS livestock rested at Ogden or Salt Lake City. The UP blocked the DLS with a Santa Fe Barstow set-out (for the San Joaquin Valley); a Santa Fe San Bernardino set-out (for San Diego); an SP Colton set-out; and five blocks for Los Angeles (one for the Santa Fe).

From September through December the DLS often ran in two to three 65- to 75-car sections; during the other three months priority fill was added to a maximum length of 85 cars at Salt Lake City. Some calves and sheep were backhauled from California. At 12:30 P.M. (as of April 1950) the DLS left Salt Lake City, paused at Las Vegas for a 45-minute inspection at 1:00 A.M., and arrived Los Angeles at 3:30 P.M., 28 hours later. Fast by freight standards, with rights over all other freights, the DLS averaged 28 mph—not comparable to the *City of Los Angeles*, which averaged 55 mph westbound, nor even to the workhorse *Pony Express,* which averaged 35 mph (as of 1949), but vastly better than the old Night Live Stock.

Despite the success of the DLS, during the 1960s UP's livestock business shrank. Better highways and trucks allowed packing houses to decentralize into the countryside adjacent to the feedlots, because it is cheaper to haul meat than the whole live animal. Truckers grabbed most of the longhaul meat business by hauling unregulated produce from California in refrigerated trailers and backhauling packaged meat and swinging carcasses. The Ogden Union Livestock Yards closed on

January 31, 1971, as did the Swift & Co. packing house. By the mid-1970s UP's livestock business had dwindled to just one customer, Clougherty Packing Co. in Los Angeles, which received hogs from the Midwest (the West, lacking a large corn crop, has always looked to the Midwest for its supply of hogs). To retain Clougherty's business, the UP spent $1.2 million in 1976 to renovate 270 triple-deck hog cars and eliminated the rest stop at Salt Lake City by installing watering troughs inside the cars to allow in-car feeding and watering. To water the hogs and keep them cool in the summer the UP built a hog drenching and watering station at Dry Lake, Nevada; to keep the hogs warm in the winter the UP installed operable steel shutters on the cars' sides. These improvements allow the UP to haul hogs 1,800 miles without unloading. Accordingly, Salt

Lake City Union Stockyards closed in 1976, its last employee moving to Dry Lake to run the drenching and watering station.

The Day Live Stock and the Council Bluffs–Salt Lake City Coast Live Stock were merged into the California Live Stock by 1964. The California Live Stock was abolished in 1985. For a time the hogs went west on the CSLAZ (Canal Street-Chicago to Los Angeles Trailers). Now they take the NPLAGE (North Platte to Los Angeles GE), which hauls an average of ten stock cars daily (each with 200–230 hogs) along with General Electric appliances. It is the West's last regular livestock haul.

FAR LEFT: On November 13, 1949, the DLS whines down Cajon Pass east of Pine Lodge. Five of UP's shiny new Livestock Dispatch cars are visible, but most are older friction-bearing cars from the Rio Grande, Burlington, and UP. *Chard Walker*

NEAR LEFT: On March 15, 1984, the California Live Stock stops at Dry Lake while the hogs are watered, then drenched as it pulls out. Depending upon temperature, the hogs are drenched from one to four times. *Two photographs, John Lucas*

ABOVE: On March 23, 1988, the CSLAZ twists through Rainbow Canyon east of Elgin with 17 cars of hogs. This is the location of the original station of Elgin, which was moved west to a more secure location after the 1910 flood. *Eric Blasko*

## UTAH'S OTHER COAL ROAD: THE LA&SL

*Coal is the bed rock upon which that system has got to be built, and until we find just where the bed rock is, and how far it extends, I should not advise doing anything more.*

–UP president Charles Francis Adams discusses a railroad from Salt Lake City to Los Angeles, 1889

Originally, Utah's coal came from UP's company mines in Wyoming, but as soon as the Rio Grande opened its line over Soldier Summit, high-quality coal from the 4-to-30-foot thick seams in Utah's Book Cliffs and Wasatch Plateau Fields displaced most Wyoming coal from Utah markets. Book Cliffs and Wasatch Plateau coal averages 12,400 BTU per pound, 7 percent ash, 7 percent moisture, and 0.5 percent or less sulfur content. High in energy and clean-burning, it is some of the best steam coal in the U.S., and a very desirable utility fuel. Certain Book Cliffs coals are also suitable for coking. Nevertheless, because Utah's coal all comes from underground mines it is expensive to mine, and because it is 800

miles from Los Angeles and farther still from midwestern power plants, it has a limited market outside of the far West. The UP profits from long hauls of Utah coal, but those long hauls often make Utah coal too costly to haul.

Coal, not citrus fruit, has been the South-Central District's mainstay. In 1920 coal averaged ninety-one 50-ton carloads daily on the LA&SL, ten times the LA&SL's average daily tonnage of citrus fruit that year and one-third of its total tonnage. Most of the coal hauled by the LA&SL in 1920 originated on the Utah Railway and the Rio Grande and reached the LA&SL at Provo. (This pattern continues to present; beginning in 1970 large tonnages of Colorado coal began moving to the LA&SL at Provo.) In the 1920s and 1930s most of this coal fueled smelters and sugar beet factories in Utah, Nevada, Idaho, and Montana, and heated homes, schools and businesses in Utah and Idaho. Until the 1940s very little coal went to Los Angeles because there was plenty of cheap oil and natural gas in southern California. The Great Depression cut Utah's coal production in half. World War II restored prosperity to Utah's coal mines only briefly, as after the war railroads dieselized and many industries and homes converted to cleaner (and often cheaper) oil and natural gas. If not for the steel industry, most of Utah's coal mines would have closed by 1960.

In mid-1942 the LA&SL began hauling 1,500 to 2,000 tons daily of metallurgical coal from the Rio Grande at Provo to the Santa Fe at Barstow for delivery to Kaiser Steel's coke ovens at Fontana, California. This coal came from Utah Fuel Co.'s Sunnyside No. 2 Mine at Sunnyside, Utah. Kaiser purchased Utah Fuel Co. in 1950 and greatly enlarged the Sunnyside, its output increasing to about 1.1 million tpy (tons per year) by 1960, or about forty-three 70-ton carloads per day. This accounted for about 82 percent of Kaiser's coal requirements, and as much as one-eighth of the LA&SL's daily tonnage. Kaiser blended its Sunnyside coal with low- and medium-volatile Oklahoma, Arkansas, and Colorado coal, because by itself Sunnyside's high-volatile coal makes rather poor blast furnace coke. Kaiser opened a unit train load-out at Sunnyside in December 1968. The 84-car Sunnyside unit train, symboled KUW/KUE (Kaiser Unit West/East), handled an average of 8,500 tons in its 100-ton rotary-dump "Coal Liner" cars each trip, running on a scheduled 96-hour, 1,612-mile turnaround. UP and Rio Grande each contributed two SD45s to the train. The Kaiser train actually needed as little as 77 hours for the round trip. This plus a second train using ordinary 100-ton hoppers (later replaced by more UP Coal Liners) moved about 1.1 million tpy to Fontana from 1968 until 1983. This was UP's first unit coal train.

U.S. Steel's Geneva Works at Geneva also received most of its coking coal from Utah and Colorado mines, all of it via the Rio Grande. Geneva Steel, which has owned the mill since 1987, now uses mostly eastern U.S. coking coal. On occasion the UP has hauled some eastern coal to Geneva, but Rio Grande hauls most of it because it has a better backhaul.

In 1965 large quantities of steam coal began moving down the LA&SL when Nevada Power started up Unit 1 at its Reid Gardner Plant at Moapa. Unit 2 followed in 1968, Unit 3 in 1976, and Unit 4 in 1983. This 580-MW (megawatt) power plant burns 2.1 million tpy at full load, or two hundred and fifty 84-car unit trains. Most of this coal has come from mines that load on the Rio Grande at Acco, Utah, U.S. Fuel's King Mine at Hiawatha, Utah (now closed), and Plateau Mining's Star Point Mine at Wattis, Utah, the latter two mines located on the Utah Railway. UP's Acco-Moapa trains are currently symboled CDAMA and its Wattis-Moapa trains CUPMA.

One major Utah coal mine, the Sufco No. 1, loads out on the UP. Sufco, formerly Southern Utah Fuel Co., opened its No. 1 Mine in Convulsion Canyon east of Salina in 1941, producing small quantities until the late 1960s. In December 1973 Coastal States Gas purchased Sufco, and enlarged its output to 2.6 million tpy at present. In the 1970s Sufco loaded most of its coal into 70-ton cars on Rio Grande's Marysvale Branch at Salina, a 30-mile truck haul from the mine. Some coal was trucked 80 miles to the UP at Sharp, where the loading facilities consisted of a front-end loader which could manage to fill fifty 100-ton cars in eight hours. In 1979 Sufco built a modern 2,500 tons per hour loadout at Sharp; after the Rio Grande abandoned its Marysvale Branch following the April 1983 mud slide at Thistle, this became Sufco's principal loadout.

In 1977 Sufco began shipping 400,000 tpy to Kennecott's 117.5-MW power plant at Magna, this business ending in June 1983 when Kennecott began buying its electricity from Utah Power & Light. Sufco's second large contract was for 500,000 tpy to Salt River Project's Coronado Plant at St. Johns, Arizona, whose 350-MW Unit 1 went on line in February 1980. This coal moved beginning in 1979, in a single 84-car trainset symboled SRUW/SRUE (Salt River Unit West/East) via UP to Barstow and Santa Fe to St. Johns, 1,165 rail miles, using pooled UP and Santa Fe power. This train made a round trip every six days until December 31, 1984, when the contract went to Pittsburg & Midway's McKinley Mine near Gallup, New Mexico, mostly because McKinley is only 94 rail miles from St. Johns.

In late 1981 Sierra Pacific Power Co.'s Valmy Station Unit 1 at Valmy, Nevada went on line. Sufco was the sole supplier to Valmy, under a 22-year, 850,000 tpy contract, until Valmy's Unit 2 went on line in June 1985. At that time the Black Butte Mine in south-central Wyoming began shipping a similar quantity. Each mine currently sends about one hundred 84-car trains a year to Valmy's twin 250-MW units, symboled CSRVY from Sharp and CBBVY from Black Butte.

In 1984 Sufco began shipping 200,000 tpy to the 100-MW Cool Water Coal Gasification Program at Daggett, a joint venture of Southern California Edison and Texaco. Work began in 1978 on this $300 million plant, which started up on May 7, 1984. In this process coal is pulverized, mixed 60/40 with water, combined with 99.5 percent pure oxygen, and injected at high pressure into a gasifier to produce a synthetic gas. The gas is burned in a turbine to generate electricity with reduced emissions and water use compared to a conventional coal-fired power plant. Daggett used about twenty-four 84-car trains a year until it closed due to high operating costs.

Western cement plants fueled by oil and natural gas hastily converted to coal after the 1973 OPEC oil embargo. At present there are 10 operating cement plants in California, served variously by UP, Santa Fe, and SP. This often determines whether their coal comes from Utah and Colorado, or New Mexico. The UP has hauled coal to California Portland Cement Co. at Colton, Southwestern Portland Cement Co. at Victorville, and Riverside Cement Co. at Crestmore and Oro Grande. Only Victorville and

ABOVE: In September 1969, UP's only unit coal train (according to the UP, at least) was the Kaiser Unit West. An extra Kaiser train, using three SD45's instead of four, and a 65-car consist of ordinary UP 100-ton hoppers instead of the Coal Liner rotary-dump gondolas, struggles west out of Las Vegas, fouling the blue desert sky with exhaust. The hiss of open sanders on the 1.0 percent is lost in the hammer of turbocharged 20-cylinder engines. The brakeman peers back from the second unit, wondering, perhaps, if this is extra-heavy coal. *Emery Gulash*

AT LEFT: On April 6, 1977, snowcapped Mount Timpanogos ramps skyward above Provo. A roundhouse man inspects the SD45s on the KUW (Kaiser Unit West) before it leaves for California. Some of these SD45's, such as Rio Grande 5336, lived most of their lives on the Kaiser train. UP's LA&SL unit trains used four SD40's, SD40-2's, SD45's, U30C's, or C30-7's (in almost any combination) until the late 1980s. All four had to work for these 11,000-ton trains to make it up the long 1.0-percent westward grades beyond Milford at 11 to 12 mph. (UP rates its SD40-2's for 3,200 tons on 1.0 percent.) Now, the UP often puts three of its big new SD60's and DASH 8-40C's on the same unit coal trains. Their advanced wheel-adhesion electronics allow a three-for-four unit reduction, but again, all units must work to make it up the 1.0-percent grades, and there is no improvement in speed, either. Locomotives may get bigger and better, but the urge to load them to their drag limit never seems to change. *James Belmont*

Oro Grande remain regular UP coal customers. Crestmore converted back to natural gas in 1993 to make white cement—coal ash gives cement its characteristic gray color. These plants consume from 50,000 to 150,000 tpy. Often this coal does not move in unit trains but is broken into 21- or 42-car blocks at Provo and sent west on regular freights. Ash Grove Cement at Martmar and other Utah cement plants typically receive their coal by truck.

In August 1978, the Intermountain Power Agency (IPA), a consortium of 26 Utah municipal utilities, 6 rural electric authorities, 5 California utilities, and the Los Angeles Dept. of Water & Power (the majority partner), selected a site eight miles west of Lynndyl for its 3,000-MW Intermountain Power Project (IPP). Lynndyl, 171 miles away from the nearest large Utah mine, was IPA's fourth-choice site. IPA's first choice, turned down for environmental reasons, was a mine-mouth plant on southern Utah's Kaiparowits Plateau. The UP has plans for 200 miles of branch line to access this coal, should anyone ever need it, and if environmental objections to mining development on the plateau can be resolved.

IPA began spending $5.5 billion to build twin 750-MW Units 1 and 2 at Lynndyl in 1980, postponing Units 3 and 4 because of slower-than-anticipated growth in demand. On June 17, 1985 IPP's first train arrived (from the Pinnacle Mine's loadout at Wildcat, Utah) to start building a 1-million-ton coal stockpile. Unit 1 went on line in July 1986 and Unit 2 in July 1987.

At present, Coastal's Skyline Mine at Skyline, Utah (on the Rio Grande) generally sends one 84-car train a day to the IPP, symboled CSKIP on the UP. A second train loads at various mines on the Utah Railway and Rio Grande, and sometimes at Sharp. The IPP burns about 4.4 to 5.0 million tpy, or about 525-595 84-car trainloads per year, giving employment to about 1,200 coal miners. Southern California receives about 75 percent of IPP's electricity.

Since the 1960s Japan, Korea, and Taiwan have imported large tonnages of coal because they have little or no domestic energy resources. Australia presently has most of this market because its coal is usually surface mined and close to tidewater, making it very inexpensive. The U.S., Canada, South Africa, China, and Russia fight for the rest of the market. The U.S. coal is the most expensive coal delivered in Japan, as much as $20 per ton more than Australian coal, because it is the most distant

from tidewater. Most U.S. coal exported to the Far East is low-volatile, high-fluidity Appalachian coal essential to making good blast furnace coke.

At various times in the late 1940s and early 1950s small shipments of Utah and Colorado metallurgical and steam coal were exported via Los Angeles, but this business was sporadic. In 1980, strikes closed many Australian mines and the price of Australian coal shot up 30 percent. Panicked buyers in Japan, Korea, and Taiwan turned to the U.S., purchasing four million extra tons of U.S. metallurgical and steam coal in 1980. Since East Coast coal ports and Appalachian mines could not quickly gear up to meet all of the demand, Far East buyers bought 1.2 million tons of western coal in 1980 and five million tons in 1981—compared to zero tons in 1979! The first big western metallurgical coal export order, 50,000 tons hauled by six trains, went to Long Beach in April 1980. The first export steam coal moved from the Plateau Mine via the Utah Railway and the UP to Japanese cement and power plants in late 1980. Most of the major mines in Utah and Colorado got in on the bonanza. By May 1981 over 40 coal trains a month were running to Los Angeles. Because Los Angeles and Long Beach are the only West Coast coal ports capable of fully loading deep-draft colliers (Stockton and Sacramento are too shallow), they handled 98 percent of this coal.

Some analysts predicted that exports plus new western power plants would drive Utah's coal production from 13 million tpy in 1980 to 30 million tpy by 1990. Excited by these predictions, railroads, coal companies, and West Coast ports invested several hundred million dollars to increase capacity in 1981–82. The UP spent $31 million on its Utah and California Divisions. Reports warning that West Coast exports would cease as soon as the Australian strike ended were ignored, even though in 1980 U.S. coal averaged $46 per ton delivered in Japan (western coal was higher), versus $36 per ton for strike-inflated Australian coal. In 1982 Australia's strikes ended; export orders from the West collapsed by June. While Japanese steam coal imports rose 11.8 percent in 1982, the U.S. share dropped by 40.4 percent, and its share of Japanese metallurgical coal imports dropped by 16.6 percent. In 1982, western export coal orders were halved to 2.5 million tons, and many Utah and Colorado mines closed that year or greatly reduced pro-

duction. Utah's coal exports plummeted from 3.5 million tons (417 trains) in 1982 to 625,000 tons (77 trains) in 1985. Utah's mines sliced employment from 5,151 in 1982 to 2,796 in 1984, and 10 of 24 coal mines closed by 1984. UP's South-Central District capacity improvement projects of 1981–82 were superfluous by fall 1983. (Had the boom lasted, more improvements were on UP's wish list, including a second main track between Cima and Elora, 6.7 miles.)

In 1988 West Coast coal exports began to recover, helped by the falling dollar and cutthroat price-slashing by coal mines and railroads. In 1994, about ten million tons of Utah and Colorado coal moved out of Provo and down the LA&SL, half of this to Lynndyl, the rest to Moapa, southern California's cement plants, and to export, plus about 800,000 tons from Sharp to Valmy. But come another oil panic, or another disruption in Australia's coalfields, and out West it might be 1980 all over again. Or is it 1880? Some things never change in the West, including the cycle of mining boom and bust.

ABOVE: Under a sky of azure serenity, an 84-car export coal train sweeps west through the Devil's Playground just west of Kerens in May 1981. The 84-car limit was set by the Rio Grande to accommodate its curves and grades on Soldier Summit, though this size also works well on the LA&SL. During late October 1986, the UP experimented with 105-car, 13,800-ton coal trains on the LA&SL, using five to six 3,000-hp units. A large number of pulled drawbars resulted, ending the experiment. Four 3,000-hp units are normal for these 84-car trains, but this one has a double set for reasons unknown. Since this date the UP has planted rows of tamarisk (salt cedar) trees on both sides of the track between Kelso and Crucero to control drifting sand. *Don Jocelyn*

# Iron Mines and Steel Mills

*Geneva...is the new decade's answer to the gloomy '30s, when all but the most optimistic American conceded that the expansion was over and the frontiers closed.* —*Life* magazine, November 25, 1946

In 1850 Mormon colonists moving south discovered "a hill of richest iron ore" at Iron Springs—the outcroppings of a 400 million ton iron ore deposit. In its quest to achieve economic self-sufficiency, the church established an iron works at Cedar City the next year. On September 30, 1852, they tapped their furnace and the first pig iron produced west of the Mississippi ran out. The Iron Mission persevered in the face of isolation, drought, and floods, but could not surmount technical problems and a lack of capital, and gave up in 1858 after producing 25 tons of pig iron. Another iron works, established in 1869 at Iron City (25 miles southwest of Cedar City) produced about 30 tons a month. It failed by the late 1870s, because of lack of money and distance from markets. The Mormon Church gave up. The iron ore had to wait for a better day.

In 1921 Columbia Steel Corp., a small West Coast steel maker, decided to produce its own pig iron. To minimize transportation costs on its raw materials, Columbia built a 350-ton (daily capacity) blast furnace and 33 by-product coke ovens (later increased to 56) at Ironton, a site just south of Provo served by both the LA&SL and the Rio Grande. The blast furnace was blown-in on April 30, 1924, and poured its first iron the next day, making Columbia the first integrated steel maker in the Far West. Columbia shipped its iron pigs to its open-hearth furnaces at Portland, Oregon, and Pittsburg and Torrance, California, where they were converted to steel and rolled into shapes. Some of the pigs went to Pacific States Cast Iron Pipe Co., which built a plant at Ironton in 1926 to make about 10,000 tons of pipe a year. Ironton's coal came from the company's Columbia Mine near Sunnyside, its limestone from the Keigley Quarry west of Provo, via the Rio Grande, and its iron ore, approximately 231,000 tons per year, from its open-pit mine at Iron Springs, via the LA&SL. U.S. Steel Corp. acquired Columbia Steel in 1930.

In early 1941, as war appeared imminent, the U.S. government observed that the West was lacking in steel-making capacity, particularly the steel plate needed to build the cargo ships necessary to support a trans-Pacific war. If the Panama Canal was blocked with sunken ships, steel would have to be shipped overland by rail, which would be very expensive. Much of the steel then used on the West Coast came from Bethlehem Steel's mammoth Sparrows Point mill near Baltimore, and was hauled to Los Angeles in company-owned ships for about $6 per ton. The comparable rail rate from Gary, Indiana was about $20 per ton. Thus in May 1941 the U.S. Government's Defense Plant Corp. decided to build a new steel plant at Geneva, just north of Provo, to supply steel plate and structural shapes to West Coast shipyards. The DPC chose this site for its proximity to Utah's large iron ore, coking coal, and limestone reserves, because it had plenty of water (over 200 million gallons a day were needed) and a skilled local labor force, and because main line railroads fanned out from Provo to all of the West Coast's principal cities. Often it is claimed that the Geneva site was chosen for its safety from enemy attack, but this was a trivial concern of Geneva's planners. This claim imagines a military capacity Japan never had.

Geneva, when completed, had 252 by-product coke ovens, three 1,110-ton daily capacity blast furnaces with an annual capacity of 1,150,000 tons of pig iron, nine 225-ton open-hearth furnaces, a 45-inch slabbing and blooming mill, a 132-inch (wide) plate mill with an annual capacity of 700,000 tons, and a 26-inch structural mill with an annual capacity of 250,000 tons. To supply additional pig iron, the government brought an idle 600-ton blast furnace from Joliet, Illinois, to Ironton, where it was blown-in on July 1, 1943, and built 300 beehive coke ovens at Sunnyside. Because of wartime material and labor shortages, and due to Geneva's sheer size (it was then the 11th largest steel plant in the U.S.), blast furnace No. 1 was not blown-in until January 3, 1944. The first steel was tapped from the open hearth furnaces on February 3, 1944, and the first plate rolled on March 22. With Germany's surrender on May 7, 1945 and Japan's on August 14, the need for Geneva diminished, and by November 12 the government reduced Geneva to hot stand-by basis. Geneva had produced 676,447 tons of plate and 144,280 tons of shapes, nearly all shipped to the West Coast.

U.S. Steel purchased the $200 million plant from the government for $47.5 million on June 19, 1946. The government sold the "Old Joliet" blast furnace at Ironton and its 300 beehive coke ovens at Sunnyside to Kaiser-Frazer Parts Corp. in May 1949. Kaiser operated its Ironton furnace until May 1950, shipping its pigs to the Midwest. In May 1951 U.S. Steel leased Kaiser's furnace. It operated the Ironton furnaces during periods of peak production to supply molten iron via hot-metal trains to Geneva's open-hearth furnaces. In April 1962 U.S. Steel blew out Ironton's blast furnaces for the last time.

Steel making at Geneva resumed in July 1946. On January 1, 1953 the Geneva Steel Co. and the Columbia Steel Co. became U.S. Steel's Columbia–Geneva Steel Division, which operated the Ironton, Geneva, Torrance, and Pittsburg plants, and the Utah coal, iron ore, and limestone mines. As built Geneva was unsuitable for peacetime, having an emphasis on heavy steel plate, so U.S. Steel invested $75 million to convert, upgrade, and enlarge Geneva, adding a hot-rolled coil mill in 1950, a tenth open-hearth fur-

nace in 1952, a hot-rolled sheet mill in 1953, and an $8-million welded steel pipe mill in 1955. By 1957 Geneva was producing over two million tons of steel ingots per year. Pacific States Cast Iron Pipe at Provo also expanded and modernized, producing about 100,000 tons of cast iron pressure pipe a year by 1950, most of this shipped by rail throughout the West and to export at Los Angeles.

The southern Utah iron ore mines dramatically expanded their output during the war, to nearly two million tons in 1945. CF&I began working its southern Utah reserves in 1943, shipping up to 50,000 tons a month from the Duncan Mine to its blast furnaces at Minnequa, Colorado (just south of Pueblo) via the UP and Rio Grande. After the war CF&I opened the Blowout and Comstock Mines, which provided about half of its iron ore needs. The Blowout closed in 1969; Comstock shipped to Pueblo until 1982 on unit train MNQA. The southern Utah mines shipped large quantities of iron ore to Kaiser Steel at Fontana, California, from 1943 into the late 1950s, and to the Port of Long Beach in the 1950s to be loaded on ships to eastern steel mills and to Japan. U.S. Steel opened the Desert Mound Mine in 1950 to supplement its mine at Iron Mountain and closed Iron Springs in the mid-1950s after exhausting its reserves.

During the 1950s these mines shipped up to 4.8 million tons a year over the LA&SL, some 200 to 300 cars daily—a huge tonnage for a railroad that 30 years before did not haul that many total cars in a day! The UP dieselized the Iron Mountain Branch in 1943, using a single NW2 stationed at Iron Mountain working three shifts. The road trains on the Cedar City Branch were dieselized with three-unit sets of FA/FB's and F3's in 1947–48. As of 1949, one or two daily trains made a turn from Milford to Iron Mountain, exchanging 90 empty unassigned UP hoppers for a similar number of loads. More power was added at Milford for the run to Provo, where the ore trains were either broken up and switched to Geneva, Ironton, or the Rio Grande, or kept intact for Geneva. UP's 3500-class 2-8-8-0's worked in turn-around service out of Salt Lake City. Westbound they delivered steel empties to Geneva, and pulled coal, coke, and ore empties for delivery to Provo. Eastbound they hauled coal, coke, and ore loads from Provo to Geneva and set them out for Geneva to run through its rotary dumpers, and pulled carloads of finished steel and forwarded them to Salt Lake City. The UP enlarged the Provo, Iron Mountain, and Lynndyl yards in 1942, Lund and Iron Mountain yards in 1947, Lund again in 1950, and relocated two miles of track at Iron Mountain in 1951 to handle this heavy traffic.

Almost all of Geneva's hot-rolled coil and sheet went to the finishing mills at Pittsburg via the SP and WP, for conversion to high-quality cold-reduced sheet steel and tin plate. Geneva depended upon Pittsburg to absorb most of its steel, there being little direct market for Geneva's products in the West. Geneva met about one-fourth of the West's steel needs during the 1950s.

In 1940 Henry J. Kaiser decided to build freighters and small warships on the West Coast. However, no mill would guarantee him sufficient tonnages of steel plate. No problem: he would build his own, wangling a $100 million loan from the Defense Plant Corp. in February 1942. Kaiser wanted to build his mill at Los Angeles Harbor, but the DPC was fearful of Japanese naval gun bombardment and insisted he build it 60 miles inland at Fontana on a site served by Santa Fe and SP. Construction began

ABOVE: In 1953 SD7s replaced carbody units in Geneva ore service, slogging back and forth between Iron Mountain and Geneva. On January 1. 1964, three of them lay over adjacent to the joint LA&SL/Utah Railway Provo coaling dock, its roof now a pigeon roost. *Ralph Gochnour*

in March 1942 and the mill's 1,200-ton blast furnace was blown-in on December 30, 1942. Steel plate began flowing to Kaiser's shipyards in August 1943, enabling them to build 1,490 vessels by 1945. Kaiser paid off the government loan, with interest, in 1950.

After the war Kaiser converted his mill to peacetime products and by 1959 quadrupled its size to meet the demand for steel. A second 1,200-ton blast furnace was blown in during 1949, a third in 1953, and a fourth in 1959, making Fontana the largest mill west of Chicago. Three basic oxygen furnaces began replacing its nine open-hearth furnaces in 1959.

At full output after 1959, Kaiser used about 10,000 tons of iron ore, 7,000 tons of coal, and 2,100 tons of limestone daily. During the war most of Fontana's iron ore, about 2,500 tons daily, came from Kaiser's Vulcan Mine nine miles southeast of Kelso. It was trucked to Kelso, loaded into UP hoppers, and interchanged to the Santa Fe at Barstow. In 1944 Kaiser purchased an iron ore reserve at Eagle Mountain, California from the SP. Mining began at Eagle Mountain in August 1948; the Vulcan Mine closed in 1949. The UP also carried up to 400,000 tons of Utah iron ore and 300,000 tons of Nevada limestone a year to Fontana during the 1950s.

From the mid-1960s to about 1974 the UP hauled up to 500,000 tons of iron ore a year from Cima to Berth 49 at the Port of Los Angeles for export to Japan. Most of this ore came from Standard Slag Co. at Beck Springs, California, and was trucked 49 miles to Cima, where a front-end loader filled 50-car unit trains. Four assigned SD45's (later four or five SD24's) hauled this train, symboled CUW/CUE (Cima Unit West/East), on a 72-hour turnaround.

In the late 1950s iron mining companies began building pellet plants for magnetic taconite ores in northern Minnesota's Mesabi Range. Steel mills discovered they could make better steel at lower cost with pellets, because pellets are uniform in size and composition, and are higher in iron content. Southern Utah's highly variable natural ores presented a particular problem for Geneva, because Geneva's product line was focused on sheet products, where uniformity is crucial. The southern Utah iron ore deposits are comparable to Mesabi Range natural ores in iron content, about 54 percent by weight, but are uneconomical to pelletize. Instead, in 1960 U.S. Steel began building a 1.5-million ton annual capacity pellet plant near Atlantic City, Wyoming to pelletize a 30-percent iron content ore body, and a 76.7-mile railroad to connect the plant with the UP at Winton Junction, Wyoming. Geneva received its first 40 cars from Atlantic City on August 17, 1962. UP's 94-car Atlantic City trains initially left Winton Junction every other day. By 1971 this had become 120-car unit train ACU (Atlantic City Unit). In total the UP had four unit iron ore moves on the South-Central District in the early 1970s: the ACU, 1.5 million tpy; the SUE/SUW, 500,000 tpy; the MNQA, 500,000 tpy; and the CUW/CUE, 500,000 tpy.

By the 1970s American steel makers, though the most productive in the world, were in deep trouble, beset by high costs for labor, pollution controls, and modernization programs on one side, and competition from imported steel and world-wide overcapacity on the other. CF&I shut down its basic steel making facilities in 1982, and Kaiser followed in 1983. California Steel Industries, Inc. used Kaiser's rolling mills until summer 1994 to make plate and sheet steel from Brazilian slabs; Fontana's blast furnaces, basic oxygen furnaces, and coke ovens have been razed. U.S. Steel's expensive-to-operate Atlantic City pellet plant shut down on October 1, 1983. After emptying the stockpiles in late October, its railroad shut down, after which Geneva's pellets came from U.S. Steel's Minntac plant at Mountain Iron, Minnesota, in 105-car unit trains via C&NW and UP. Symboled MIGW/MIGE (Minntac to Geneva West/East), they started up in November 1983. The pellets made up about 85 percent of the iron ore needs at Geneva, the remainder supplied by the Comstock Mine in one to two 80- to 150-car trains weekly. Geneva also received some imported ore via Los Angeles.

For many good reasons, U.S. Steel ceased investing in Geneva after the late 1950s, and by 1986 it was a museum of World War II technology. Looking at what it believed to be a $1 billion modernization bill

for Geneva, USX (U.S. Steel's successor) decided in January 1986 to enter into a joint venture with Pohang Iron & Steel of South Korea, under which Pohang would contribute $300 million to modernize the Pittsburg finishing mill, share in its ownership, and supply its hot-rolled coil steel. This would leave Geneva without a customer for 70 percent of its output. When Geneva's employees went on strike in summer 1986, Geneva looked to be dead. Instead, two Utah lawyers, believing the mill viable, purchased Geneva in July 1987 for $44.1 million, which included USX's and CF&I's southern Utah iron ore deposits. Geneva Steel, the new company, began producing steel a month later. Since 1987 Geneva has spent over $300 million to modernize its mill, installing two Q-BOP basic oxygen furnaces to replace the 10 open-hearth furnaces, a continuous caster, the world's largest coil box to roll coils, and extensive pollution controls. Geneva Steel is now the only basic steel plant in the West. Currently about 90 percent of its 1.5 million tons of steel a year becomes hot-rolled coils of up to 60,000 pounds each and steel plate. The rest of its output is steel pipe, plus coal chemicals. These products are distributed principally in the midwestern U.S. The structural mill is closed.

Initially the UP hauled all of Geneva's iron ore and most of its finished steel. In 1994 Geneva rebid these contracts. The UP was shocked to find that SP and Wisconsin Central won the Minntac pellet contract, and won about 70 percent of Geneva's finished steel output, the UP retaining only the Pacific

Northwest and portions of the Midwest. SP took over the Minntac trains in August 1994. SP also delivers all of Geneva's coal, along with occasional unit trains of imported coke from Richmond, California. In 1994, Geneva halved its use of southern Utah iron ore to about 215,000 tpy, or two 78-car trains monthly. Since 1983 the UP has considered abandoning the Cedar City and Iron Mountain Branches. This possibility now looms large.

BELOW LEFT: On June 28, 1989, the OCMGV (Ore Comstock to Geneva) descends into the Escalante Desert near milepost 6.1 of the Iron Mountain Branch. The waste heaps of the Comstock and Mountain Lion Mines terrace the pinyon-and-juniper forested slopes of Iron Mountain in the background. Gilbert Construction Co. of Cedar City operates these mines for Geneva Steel. Most of southern Utah's iron ore output now comes from Comstock. *Blair Kooistra*

BELOW RIGHT: During September 1970, a road freight backs onto a cut of empty hoppers bound for Provo and coke loads bound for Los Angeles after dropping off a string of empty coil steel cars. At left are Geneva's open hearths, at center are its three blast furnaces, and at far right are the stacks of its by-product coke and coal chemicals plant. *Keith Ardinger*

## The Orient Connection

*The arrival on May 21 of the steamer* Hercules *at the port of San Pedro, Cal., inaugurated the establishment of a steamship line to the Orient in connection with this road. A cargo consisting of merchandise from Chinese and Japanese ports was immediately transferred to cars of the Salt Lake road and started on to eastern destinations.*
—*Railway Age,* June 8, 1906

The adjacent and competitive Ports of Los Angeles and Long Beach have become the two most important ports on the West Coast despite their greater distance from the Orient than Seattle, Tacoma, Portland, and San Francisco, their lack of a big natural deep-water harbor, and their lack of portside heavy industry. Industrial development at the ports has not been large, consisting of a Ford assembly plant built in 1925 and now closed, and shipyards significant only during World War II, when they built over a thousand Liberty and Victory cargo ships, tankers, and small warships. In 1979 a Procter & Gamble soap factory at Long Beach, a borax-processing plant, a gypsum-wallboard plant, 20 oil refineries, two shipyards, and several fish canneries constituted the majority of port industry.

The ports' first big business was construction materials arriving by ship to build the city of Los Angeles. Lumber from the Pacific Northwest made them the largest lumber importing ports in the world. Cement came from Belgium, steel from the East Coast and Germany, and coal from Australia and England, all

by ship instead of rail because ocean rates historically have been much lower than rail rates. From about 1905 to the present, most of the ports' tonnage has been oil. At first the oil flowed out, to the East Coast and the Orient via tankers, because southern California's oil fields produced much more than the state could consume: in 1923, California produced one-fourth of the entire world supply of oil. Now, the oil flows in, because these fields have been nearly exhausted while at the same time Californians' appetite for gasoline continues to soar. The portside Wilmington Field, UP's greatest prize ever, was minuscule by world standards, producing 38,000 barrels a day at its peak in 1952. (For comparison, Alaska's Prudhoe Bay Field produces two million barrels a day.) By the late 1980s the Wilmington Field's production had dwindled to 6,500 barrels a day; reflecting the field's decline, the UP sold the Wilmington Refinery, the Calnev Pipeline Co., and a 50-percent share of subsidiary Champlin Refining in 1988 for $661 million, and 725 acres of land and 300 active oil wells on Terminal Island on May 17, 1993, to the Port of Long Beach for $405 million. Most of southern California's oil needs are now met by crude from Alaska, Indonesia, and the Mideast.

The principal commodities of interest to the UP now handled at the Ports of Los Angeles and Long Beach are imported manufactured goods, mostly in containers, and export coal. In 1979 4.8 million tons of iron, steel, machinery, motor vehicles, and other manufactured goods came into the U.S. at Los Angeles and Long Beach, dwarfing the 383,000 tons of out-

bound manufactured goods. At present the UP hauls Toyotas from Long Beach to North Platte and Denver on trains LANPV, LANPZ, and LADET. Cargo containerization began at the ports in 1958 but at first grew slowly, to 70,000 TEUs (20-foot equivalent units) in 1968. Then this business began to skyrocket. In 1994 2.6 million TEUs passed through the Port of Long Beach and 2.38 million TEUs through the Port of Los Angeles, making them respectively the number one and number two container ports in the U.S. The export of large tonnages of dry bulk commodities at the ports began in the 1950s with Utah iron ore to Japan. In 1974 the UP began moving unit trains of potash, soda ash, and fertilizer from Idaho and Wyoming to Metropolitan Stevedore's bulk ship-loading facility at Long Beach. In 1979 the UP hauled 286,000 tons of Wyoming soda ash to Long Beach, about one unit train every 10 days. Grain exports did not account for large tonnages until 1976, when the UP established 25- and 50-car grain rates to the West Coast. Grain increased from practically nothing in 1975 to 2,467,000 tons in 1979, about one unit train daily. Most of this grain, destined for Pacific Rim countries and the Soviet Union, had previously gone to Gulf Coast ports. In 1979, outbound grain and nonmetallic minerals totaled 3.96 million tons, almost all arriving by rail. Coal exports were not significant until April 1980 but remain important, totaling 2.1 million tons at Los Angeles and 1.2 million tons at Long Beach in 1994 (almost all of this arriving on the UP) whereas grain has not been exported in significant tonnages at the ports since 1986. The soda ash now goes to the Port of San Diego.

At present the growth in container traffic at the ports shows no sign of slowing, and coal exports are also growing. Both ports expect to double their capacity by 2020, at a cost of at least $2 billion. At Pier 300 at the Port of Los Angeles, American President Lines is building the nation's largest container terminal. The nation's largest-ever dredging project is underway to increase the channel depth at Pier 300 to 67–72 feet (the dredged material will create a new 230-acre Pier 400). A new $155-million coal port at Pier 300, capable of handling 10 million tons annually, will replace the existing coal terminal in 1997. The Long Beach coal terminal may also expand its capacity. After several years of acrimonious negotiations, in 1995 the UP, SP, and Santa Fe reached agreement with the ports on the $1.8-billion Alameda Corridor project, which will consolidate the three rail lines to the ports into one high-capacity line using SP's San Pedro Branch. The UP will sell its San Pedro Branch to the ports for $75 million.

Currently, the UP hauls coal and some metallic ores and concentrates to Kaiser International at the Port of Los Angeles, and coal and other minerals to Metropolitan Stevedore Co. at Pier G at the Port of Long Beach. Both coal terminals can accommodate both rotary -and bottom-dump cars. Metropolitan Stevedore loads ships at a rate of 5,000 tons per hour, and Kaiser at a rate of 2,400 tons per hour. Container vessels from American President Lines, Evergreen, Matson, Mitsui OSK, Showa, and YS Line call at the Port of Los Angeles; container vessels from COSCO (China Ocean Shipping Co.), Cho Yang, DSR-Senator Lines, Hanjin, Hyundai, "K" Line, Maersk, Mexican Line, Mitsui OSK, NYK Line, OOCL, Philippine Line, Sea-Land, and Zim at the Port of Long Beach. Because of vessel and train sharing arrangements, containers from the different lines may arrive and depart from either port.

ABOVE LEFT: In August 1983, UP Extra 3190 East assembles empty grain hoppers at Pier A Yard at the Port of Long Beach after doubling its grain loads into the short yard tracks. Metropolitan Stevedore's bulk facility at Berths 212–215 is behind the train; Koppel Bulk Terminal's grain terminal at Berth 211 is out of the picture at right. Koch Carbon now uses the former Koppel facility for petroleum coke. *Rob Leachman*

RIGHT, TWO PHOTOGRAPHS: For 1,700 miles westward from milepost 5 a Los Angeles-bound UP train need climb nothing steeper than 1.0 percent, up which three healthy SD40-2's should haul these 80 loads of grain at 11 to 12 mph. The 1,700 miles ends right here at Frost, where Santa Fe's North Track swings away from the South to climb to the flyover. Today, this train would have two SD40-2's or C30-7's tacked on the rear at Victorville, but on April 28, 1981, the UP was still entraining helpers at Yermo. On the South Track an eastbound empty covered hopper train waits at the Frost crossovers. The UP no longer hauls export grain to southern California, but it continues to haul grain to southern California for animal feed.

Originally, the LA&SL ran helpers out of San Bernardino and Victorville, using Santa Fe's San Bernardino roundhouse to service its helpers. During World War II the Santa Fe roundhouse could not turn the LA&SL's helpers quickly, so in early 1944 the LA&SL built its own two-stall engine house and servicing facilities nearby. Shortly after the war the LA&SL abolished its Victorville helper pool, and abolished the San Bernardino helper pool in 1959 when EMD supplied six-axle SD24's to the South-Central District. The UP rated an SD24 at 1,700 tons westbound and 1,250 tons eastbound (on the North Track) over Cajon Pass. After 1959 heavy westbound UP trains reduced tonnage at Yermo to avoid exceeding drawbar limits of about 5,500 tons from Victorville to Summit, or picked up a Santa Fe helper at Victorville.

With the influx of unit trains in the 1970s the UP had to reestablish helpers on Cajon Pass. At first, UP's unit trains picked up a cut-in helper at Yermo; in June 1981 the UP reestablished the Victorville helper, using a pair of GP38-2's which pushed on the rear to Summit. The Geeps were too light; by August UP replaced them with a pair of SD40-2's. A second two-unit set joined them in April 1988. The Victorville helpers generally help downhill for additional dynamic braking as well as uphill, cutting off at (or just east of) San Bernardino and returning light to Victorville. *Tim Zukas*

# CALIFORNIA FAST FREIGHT

*The highway is just to our right, but few are the motorists with the daring to match our headlong speed.*
—reporter Tom Baxter describes his ride on LA&SL fast freight CN-CUX, April 1947

Always at a disadvantage compared to the Santa Fe in fast merchandise service between the Midwest and Los Angeles (because of grades and distance), to the Santa Fe and the SP for perishables (because of its lack of a rail network in southern California), and to trucks in speed and door-to-door service in decentralized Los Angeles, the UP has had to work very hard to garner a share of California's fast freight. Even though the SP and UP jointly owned the Pacific Fruit Express Co., the SP hauled its perishables as far east as possible, generally giving to the LA&SL at Colton only those carloads destined for UP points. But at times, the LA&SL's perishable business was respectable. Fruit trains such as the CN (Colton Fruit) sometimes departed Colton in several sections beginning at noon, arriving Salt Lake City by 11 P.M. the third day. More often, the CN filled out with ordinary freight or empties. By the 1980s the CN was just a heavy scheduled freight that occasionally hauled perishables; the UP dropped the train in 1985.

Los Angeles developed an aggressive trucking industry at a very early date. The city's dispersed geography was a natural for truckers, not for railroads' downtown freight houses. By the 1930s

truckers had begun to venture into the desert and take away much of the LA&SL's less-than-carload business. In 1939 the UP responded with Challenger Merchandise Service, an expedited LCL service with free door-to-door pickup and delivery. By handling LCL on the head end of secondary passenger trains 5 and 6 (the *California Fast Mail*) between Los Angeles and Salt Lake City, and train 41 (the *Northwest Express*) from Salt Lake City to Boise, Idaho, the UP could offer first morning delivery to Las Vegas and second morning delivery to Salt Lake City and Boise, cutting up to 24 hours from its previous best freight schedules. By fall 1939 UP's Omaha Shops had turned out 100 special roller-bearing Challenger boxcars (30 more followed in 1940). Challenger service recaptured some of the lost traffic; in 1940 the UP reported a 50 to 100 percent increase in its merchandise tonnage out of Los Angeles and Salt Lake City.

With the outbreak of war in December 1941 there was more traffic than the UP could handle. Short of boxcars, the UP discontinued its Challenger Merchandise Service and lengthened its Chicago to West Coast freight schedules by 24 hours. Not until 1952 did the UP again seek to improve service, by speeding up its fastest trains. Westbound to Los Angeles, the CB (Council Bluffs Manifest) cut its schedule from 93 hours 45 minutes to 78 hours 30 minutes, the KC (Kansas City Manifest) from 98 hours 44 minutes to 78 hours 30 minutes, and the DP (Denver Pacific) from 76 hours 45 minutes to 59 hours. The CN (Colton Fruit) cut its time from Los Angeles to Omaha from 99 hours 20 minutes to 81 hours. The next year (in response to the

Santa Fe) the UP slashed its best perishable service from southern California to Chicago to 62 hours, matching the Santa Fe, albeit at a stiff surcharge–$1.20 per 100 pounds.

Between Los Angeles, Las Vegas, and Salt Lake City, truckers were killing the UP on fast freight by the late 1940s (long before parallel Interstate Highway 15 was started). By 1948 truckers were even eating into UP's steel shipments from Geneva to Los Angeles, because many steel users in California were off-track or did not want to buy in carload quantities. On May 4, 1953, the UP restarted its LCL service between Los Angeles and Las Vegas, with rates and transit times competitive to trucks. UP trucks provided free pickup and delivery in both cities Monday through Friday, and its new, fast MDSE SPL (Merchandise Special) hauled the high-speed roller-bearing boxcars. Shipments reaching UP's Los Angeles freight house by 7 P.M. were delivered to Las Vegas by 6 the next morning. Beginning with two boxcars daily, by June it took eight cars to handle the business. In July 1953 the UP expanded its fast LCL service to Salt Lake City, with second-morning delivery by truck from Payson on the south to Ogden on the north.

Recognizing the inefficiencies of transferring LCL from a truck to a boxcar and back to a truck, in August 1953 the UP began its first-ever piggyback service, between Los Angeles and Las Vegas, limiting its "Trailer Freight Service" to LCL to avoid diverting carload traffic. The UP loaded its piggyback trailers circus-style onto converted 42-foot and 52-foot flatcars, and blocked the flats into the Merchandise Special at East Los Angeles to permit a quick set-out at Las Vegas. The UP quickly expanded Trailer Freight Service to Salt Lake City, reaching by highway into Idaho, eastern Oregon, and western Wyoming, providing second morning delivery to over 100 Utah and Idaho communities. In July 1954 the UP expanded Trailer Freight Service to the Pacific Northwest, and in October to San Francisco, through interchange with the SP at Ogden and Wells, Nevada. By December Trailer Freight Service had 120 flatcars and 154 UP-owned trailers in service: flat beds with stakes and side boards for steel going west and lumber, roofing, pipe, and machinery going east; ordinary vans for groceries, tires, appliances, and automotive products; and insulated vans for dairy products going west and produce going east, re-icing with dry ice at Las Vegas.

By the mid-1960s UP's LCL business had dwindled to practically nothing. In 1965 the UP gave up on it, focusing instead on carload and trailerload traffic. Also in 1965, the UP added carload and piggyback freight to its 62-hour perishable schedule between Los Angeles and Chicago, with the new LAX running on a 21-hour 15-minute schedule from Los Angeles to Ogden to once again match Santa Fe's latest speed-up. With the advent of Santa Fe's Super C in 1968, the UP had to speed up its service to Los Angeles again. In 1972 the UP established the VAN, a hot all-piggyback train, on a 19-hour 55-minute schedule from Ogden to Los Angeles, 6 hours faster than UP's previous best schedule. In 1976, UP captured the Chicago-Los Angeles mail which had previously moved on the Super C with the SUPRV (Super Van), which ran on an 18-hour schedule from Ogden to Los Angeles (50 hours Chicago to Los Angeles). It also sped up the LAX to 18 hours and added eastbound LAC on a 19-hour 40-minute schedule. Along with the VAN, westbound LAF on a 22-hour 40-minute schedule, and eastbound LAD on a 22-hour 30-minute schedule, the UP now had six fast TOFC trains between Los Angeles and Ogden. (The CN had a leisurely 30-hour 50-minute schedule in 1975.)

Between 1971 and 1976 UP's intermodal business increased by 63 percent. At the same time containers began to displace trailers. As early as 1972 the UP began hauling single-level container trains to and from Los Angeles for ocean shippers such as "K" Line and APL. In April 1981 American President Lines (APL) expanded its "Liner Train" COFC service to the South-Central District, with weekly container train LACRT (Los Angeles-Conrail Trailers) between Los Angeles, Chicago, and South Kearny, New Jersey. APL had discovered it could save both time and money by using railroads to haul its containers across North America instead of slow ships through the Panama Canal (in 1977 the savings amounted to eight to 10 days and $117 per TEU).

In 1983 APL recognized it could slash its costs and get a big jump on its competitors by rapidly adopting the double-stack technology just developed by Sea-Land and SP. APL first went to the SP and offered to provide its own double-stack cars loaded with its containers in trainload quantities. Recognizing that APL's containers would cannibalize its piggyback business and drive rates downward, SP turned APL down. So did the Santa Fe, APL's second choice. So APL went to the UP and here it found a railroad eager to do business. After investing $31 million to add capacity for export coal trains on the South-Central District, that traffic had vanished, and the UP wanted trains. UP's APL double-stack service began in spring 1984 and soon increased to three weekly trains from the Port of Los Angeles to Chicago via the UP and C&NW. Double-stack trains from "K" Line and Mitsui OSK have also used the South-Central District. At present the UP runs one or two pure double-stack trains to and from Los Angeles each day for

FAR LEFT: On a clear July morning in 1975 the LAX climbs east through Sullivan's Curve on Cajon Pass. Railroad-supplied trailers made up much of the intermodal fleet prior to the 1980s; trailers visible here are from Seaboard Coast Line, Penn Central, and C&NW. *Joe Blackwell*

ABOVE: On September 25, 1984, the SUPRV has just begun its 18-hour run from Ogden to Los Angeles. By supplying lots of horsepower, limiting tonnage, and running very fast wherever it could to make up for its mileage handicap, the UP successfully fielded six intermodal trains on the South-Central District by the mid-1970s. UP's DDA40X's and 8000-series SD40-2's were geared 59:18 (good for 80 mph) and so were regularly given these trains. *Doug Harrop*

AT RIGHT: On December 4, 1993, carman Jaime Lopez inspects eastbound Mitsui OSK double-stack train LAMS7 as it pulls out of East Los Angeles en route to Chicago. The UP has since lost—or given up as unattractive—the Mitsui OSK contract. *Dave Crammer*

APL and other ocean shipping lines. The UP also frequently adds stacks to trains such as the CSLAZ (Canal Street-Chicago to Los Angeles Intermodal) and LASCZ (Los Angeles to Salt Lake City).

# FURTHER READINGS

Other than an additional 200 pages for more detail and more photographs, I wish I had the space in this book to include citations. Citations, whether they appear in footnotes or endnotes, give the author a means to check for mistakes or analyze discrepancies; they would help me retrace my steps. More importantly, citations allow you, the reader, to decide if this book is reliable, or if I am just making things up. Citations are also a valuable reference document for the reader; they will take you straight to the source you need.

When I began this project I anticipated I would include a comprehensive bibliography. I then discovered that the space required to list all of the documents, manuscripts, articles, and books I consulted would easily use up six or more pages, not an attractive idea when those pages must run through an expensive four-color press. I have instead listed some of my sources that you might also find useful. If you would like a copy of my bibliography, or citations on some aspect of this book that interests you, please write to me in care of the publisher.

The Union Pacific, as one of the nation's most important railroads, has attracted many historians. Its best general history to date (though mostly it's about UP's management rather than UP's railroad) is Maury Klein, *Union Pacific: The Birth of a Railroad, 1862-1893* (1987), and *Union Pacific: The Rebirth, 1894-1969* (1989). For a more dispassionate view see Nelson Trottman, *History of the Union Pacific: A Financial and Economic Survey* (1923). UP's passenger trains are detailed by Harold E. Ranks and William W. Kratville, *The Union Pacific Streamliners* (1974); its locomotives by Kratville and Ranks in *Motive Power of the Union Pacific* (1960); and its diesel locomotives by Don Strack, *Union Pacific 1992 Annual* (1992), and F. Hol Wagner, Jr., ed., *Union Pacific Motive Power Review, 1968-1977* (1978). The transition from steam to diesel and turbine power is discussed by Lloyd E. Stagner, *Union Pacific Motive Power in Transition, 1936-1960* (1993). Many articles in *The Streamliner*, the publication of the Union Pacific Historical Society, provide good detail on UP's locomotives and passenger trains. UP's freight operations have received less attention. UP's refrigerator-car business is discussed in part by Anthony W. Thompson, Robert J. Church, and Bruce H. Jones, *Pacific Fruit Express* (1992). For a sharp analysis of intermodal freight with some reference to the UP see David J. DeBoer, *Piggyback and Containers: A History of Rail Intermodal on America's Steel Highway* (1992).

The LA&SL has attracted relatively little attention from historians. The exception is David F. Myrick, *Railroads of Nevada and Eastern California* (2 vols., 1962-63). Future railroad historians would do well to emulate Myrick's descriptive, readable, and thoroughly-researched works. For the Oregon Short Line see Merrill D. Beal, *Intermountain Railroads* (1962). For many fascinating old photographs of the Los Angeles & Salt Lake see John Signor, *The Los Angeles & Salt Lake Railroad* (1988). William Andrews Clark is critically examined by Michael P. Malone in *The Battle for Butte: Mining and Politics on the Northern Frontier, 1864-1906* (1981). George Kennan looks uncritically at E. H. Harriman in his adulatory *E. H. Harriman: A Biography* (2 vols., 1922).

The history of Utah's railroads is only partially explored. A good treatment of UP's efforts to expand into Utah is found in Robert G. Athearn, *Union Pacific Country* (1971), and the history of early Utah railroads is covered by Clarence J. Reeder, *The History of Utah's Railroads, 1869-1883* (1981). The Mormon lines are analyzed by Leonard J. Arrington in *Great Basin Kingdom: An Economic History of the Latter-Day Saints, 1830-1900* (1958). Arrington's brilliant works contain many aspects of Utah history which I could only briefly explore. The Utah Northern is detailed by Mallory Hope Ferrell, "Utah & Northern: the Narrow Gauge that Opened a Frontier," and Cornelius W. Hauck, "OSL&UN: the Oregon Short Line Era," in *Colorado Rail Annual No. 15* (1981). Brief discussions of many abandoned UP lines are found in Stephen L. Carr and Robert W. Edwards, *Utah Ghost Rails* (1989). The careers of railroad builders John W. Young and David Eccles are found in Charles L. Keller, "Promoting Railroads and Statehood: John W. Young," *Utah Historical Quarterly* 45: 289-308 (Summer 1977); M. Guy Bishop, "Building Railroads for the Kingdom: The Career of John W. Young, 1867-91," *UHQ* 48: 66-80 (Winter 1980); and Leonard J. Arrington, *David Eccles: Pioneer Western Industrialist* (1975).

For the construction of railroads in southern California see James Marshall, *Santa Fe: The Railroad that Built an Empire* (1945); Edward L. Lyman, "Outmaneuvering the Octopus: Atchison, Topeka & Santa Fe," *California Historical Society Quarterly* 68: 94-107+ (June 1988); Franklin Hoyt, "The Los Angeles & San Pedro: First Railroad South of the Tehachapis," *CHSQ* 32: 327-348 (Dec. 1953), "San Diego's First Railroad: The California Southern," *Pacific Historical Review* 23: 133-146 (May 1954), "The Los Angeles and San Gabriel Valley Railroad," *PHR* 20: 227-239 (Aug. 1951), "Influence of the Railroads in the Development of Los Angeles Harbor," *Historical Society of Southern California Quarterly* 35: 195-212 (Sep. 1953); and "The Los Angeles & Independence Railroad," *HSSCQ* 32: 293-308 (Dec. 1950). Also, Frank B. Putnam, "Serape to Levi: Southern Pacific," *HSSCQ* 38: 211-224 (Sep. 1956), and Richard W. Barsness, "Los Angeles' Quest for Improved Transportation," *CHSQ* 46: 291-306 (Dec. 1967), "Railroads and Los Angeles: The Quest for a Deep-Water Port," *HSSCQ* 47: 379-394 (Dec. 1965), and "Iron Horses and an Inner Harbor at San Pedro Bay, 1867-1890," *PHR* 34: 289-303 (Aug. 1965). For a wonderful look at UP and Santa Fe operations and the changing scene on Cajon Pass see Chard Walker, *Chard Walker's Cajon: Rail Passage to the Pacific* (1985).

Surprisingly many rail historians make little use of industry periodicals, perhaps because they are poorly indexed. Indeed, these sources are horribly time-consuming; for example, my search for information on the steel industry in Utah and California required looking through over 100,000 pages of *Blast Furnace & Steel Plant* and *Iron Age*. There is a tremendous amount of information on the UP and its predecessors in *Railway Age* and *Railroad Gazette*. Other periodicals I found invaluable for this book included *Railway Signaling & Communications, Railway Engineering & Maintenance of Way, Railway Locomotives & Cars, Engineering News, Coal Age, Utah Economic & Business Review, Salt Lake Mining Review*, and *The Mining Congress Journal*. Beginning with *Trains* magazine and *Railroad* magazine, rail enthusiasts began to fill the gap when the railroad trade press started to decline in the 1960s. A search through *Trains* revealed many articles of use to this book. Also useful for recent information are *Pacific Rail News, CTC Board, Railfan & Railroad*, and *Extra 2200 South*.

Of great value are the publications of the Interstate Commerce Commission. See *Statistics of Railways in the United States* (issued annually), and "Valuation of the San Pedro, Los Angeles & Salt Lake Railroad Company," *Decisions of the Interstate Commerce Commission of the United States* (vol. 75, 1924). Annual reports of the Union Pacific Railroad and its predecessors are full of information, as are its profiles and engineering drawings, timetables, and train schedules.

I have left out the hundreds of books, articles, and documents I consulted which covered aspects of Idaho, Utah, Nevada, and California not specifically about railroads, such as their geology, environment, resources, prehistory, history, economics, cities, farms, mines, factories, and people. These were my most important sources, as they provided the answers to many of my questions, questions that most railroad books fail to ask or answer. Why is a railroad built? What does it haul? Who does it serve? Railroads are only one of man's many creations. They are ultimately inseparable from their natural, cultural, and historical context.

Under desert skies, first #203, the westbound *Utahn*, meets 4-10-2 helper 5091 at Summit, California, on December 17, 1950. *Chard Walker*